# FALLEN ICON

## SIR DAVID ATTENBOROUGH AND THE WALRUS DECEPTION

## S J CROCKFORD

Published in 2022 by Susan J. Crockford

Printed by KDP

ISBN 978-0-9917966-9-4

# Table of Contents

# Preface

The scene was unexpected and horrific: in an otherwise benign Netflix documentary, one after another, several giant walrus were shown falling off a high cliff, their bodies twisting and tumbling head over tail as they glanced off the cliff face to land heavily on jagged rocks below.

These agonising deaths, captured in slow motion, were followed by the gruesome specter of lifeless bodies by the hundreds scattered along the beach as the camera panned the shoreline.

Viewers were not told precisely where or when this had happened, only that it was Russia and that lack of sea ice was the cause, for which they were collectively to blame because of their selfish use of fossil fuels.

It was an extraordinary claim delivered with an unforgettable gut-punch by the grandfatherly voice of renowned and respected BBC broadcaster Sir David Attenborough.

Attenborough's narrative in the 2019 Netflix nature documentary *Our Planet* implied his statement about the walrus was supported by science.

I knew it wasn't – and knew I could prove it – but I was up against an icon. Attenborough was one of the most trusted and admired men in the world.

In addition, the involvement of the World Wildlife Fund with Netflix in this endeavour was unprecedented and perverse: it immediately raised a red flag.

I am a professional zoologist with a profound interest in evolution and Arctic biology. I had been investigating polar bears since the late 1990s and blogging about them and wider issues of conservation in the region since 2012 (see Appendix A for a list of publications).

In 2014, I had pushed back hard against activist American biologists and conservation organisations who had been falsely promoting Pacific walrus (n.b. both 'walrus' and 'walruses' are correct for the plural) as helpless victims of climate change. I simply documented the fact that their claims were unsupported by scientific evidence.

This meant that by April 2019, when *Our Planet* was released, I was uniquely positioned to expose the truth behind Attenborough's outlandish claims.

As I went through the scientific literature and prepared my case, I struggled to understand why a man like Attenborough – given his exalted position of trust – would do something so unprincipled.

The raw brutality of the images seemed uncharacteristic for one of his films: the harsh realities of nature were his style, not this tragedy sensationalised by slow-motion camera work that captured one death after another, and then blamed them on the viewer. However, I ploughed ahead because it was important to me that his inaccuracies not become accepted as scientific truth by the public.

Others assisted me in getting the word out, and within days, my challenge of Attenborough's message generated an international controversy.

A few people were outraged at my temerity: how dare I criticise Britain's national treasure, a universally-beloved public figure? I had the facts and a more plausible narrative on my side, but never mind: to them, Attenborough simply could do no wrong.

Six months later, however, we were all astonished when Attenborough himself corroborated my account: polar bears had indeed been involved.

A BBC television documentary also narrated by Attenborough revealed the extent and scope of the deception in that Netflix walrus death sequence. Regardless of the fact that virtually no mainstream reviewer of the BBC film seemed to notice or even to recall the Netflix walrus controversy, this was absolute proof that my assertions were spot-on.

Attenborough is more than a simple voice-over artist: producer and writer Mary Colwell, who worked with him years ago at the BBC, revealed in a 2019 interview, 'he won't say anything he doesn't want to say'.[1]

On top of that, his previous work as a high-level television executive and producer for the BBC means he has clout with the productions in which he is involved.

If he had objections to how things were being done in the *Our Planet* production, he would not have been ignored. So why had he agreed to participate in this walrus deception?

Why go along with constructing an elaborate ruse with the Netflix film when he knew it would be exposed within months – by his own work? At first glance, it seemed like an ill-conceived climate change PR stunt meant to garner public attention, something many had learned to expect from conservation organizations like the WWF but not from a man of integrity like Attenborough.

Surely an apology – or at least an acknowledgement of the inconsistencies – would be forthcoming from Sir David?

But we waited in vain: this scam generated no excuses or acts of contrition.

Over the next two and a half years, Attenborough went on to produce several more documentaries containing even more outrageous claims about harms the world faced if climate change was not addressed immediately, accompanied by public demands for political action.

Attenborough's crusade kicked off by the falling walrus fiasco has been an astonishing phenomenon to witness and I felt it warranted further investigation and analysis. I dove in to find what was below the surface.

I never paid much attention to politics before this happened. It was never of much interest to me: it's partly why science had such a strong appeal. To me, science was the antithesis of politics.

I was taught at home to be a critical thinker and this skill not only served me solidly during my professional career but it influenced my educational choices as well.

For example, it was apparent to me as a young undergraduate at university in the early 1970s that fields like conservation biology were not only biased by assumptions that might not be true, but also by a lack of detailed exposure to the critical companion fields of evolution and geology.

Biology students around me were being encouraged to specialise in the narrowly defined field of conservation from their second year at university, which seemed far too early to me.

I craved the exact opposite. I took many general zoology courses grounded in evolution (like anatomy, physiology, and embryonic development) as well as classes in geology, geography, and archaeology. I discovered that when it came time to earn a living, those historical perspectives were crucial. They eventually led to me to earning a PhD on the evolutionary topic of speciation.

I have never stopped looking back in time for potential answers to contemporary questions or questioning accepted dogma.

I knew from my Arctic research in the 2010s that advocacy for polar bear conservation had gone rogue and allowed the science behind it to be manipulated.

However, Attenborough's walrus deception and the climate change crusade it kick-started was different: here, manipulation of science intersected politics in a way I'd never imagined was possible. The entire phenomenon – taken as one blatant, start-to-finish example – opened my eyes to the way that science had been corrupted to achieve political objectives.

It changed me.

I now have to assume that the walrus deception is just one example of many.

However, understanding exactly how this drama unfolded was a revelation for me and I feel sure it will have the same effect on you.

# Chapter 1

# Major Players

## *Sir David Attenborough*

David Attenborough is a broadcaster famous internationally for producing and narrating documentaries for the British Broadcasting Company – the BBC. At 95 years old in 2021, he is the same age as Queen Elizabeth II and a year younger than my own mother would have been had she lived this long. The photo of him shown here was taken in 2015 (courtesy Wikipedia).

He is the middle child of three brothers. His older brother Richard Attenborough, who died in 2014, had a long and successful acting career: I remember him best from *The Great Escape* (1963) and *Jurassic Park* (1993).[2]

He has two children, a son and a daughter. His daughter Susan was born a few months after I was in 1954, which I suspected might be the case (and was able to confirm) because of her name: Susan was the most popular name for a baby girl born in England and Canada in 1954, when it emerged that the young Queen Elizabeth II, who had ascended the throne the summer before, had a beloved dog (a corgi) she called Susan.[3]

David Attenborough is a member of the elite upper class: those privileged few cocooned by social position and money. He came from a well-to-do family, went to Cambridge University, landed a secure job at the BBC at the tender age of 26, spent decades in front of cameras, and was knighted in 1985 for his services to the development of television. He is a close friend to the British royal family and said to be worth at least 35 million dollars.[4]

The elevated social position Attenborough has held for decades is nothing short of phenomenal: between his money and television fame, he easily consorts with royalty, film stars, and political leaders.[5] He has been described variously as 'the most trusted man in Britain', 'a universally beloved public figure', 'an icon', and 'a man of integrity'.

In 2016, his name was given to an ice-strengthened British Antarctic Survey research vessel, via public opinion poll, after the most popular suggestion of 'RRS Boaty McBoatface' was over-ruled.[6]

When Attenborough talks; people listen. He has become an icon because, above all else, people trust him. He knows how to tell a good story with confidence and authority.

His greatest skill is storytelling, honed over decades. In an interview with journalist Patrick Barkham in 2019, he was asked to list his failings as a person and Attenborough responded, 'I'm too convincing...when it comes to, as it were, conning your way through, I'm not bad at it'.[7]

Attenborough does not consider himself to be an expert on natural history, as many people assume – although he did study natural sciences at university as an undergraduate. He is not a scientist or a professional researcher, and never has been.[8]

Similarly, he doesn't go to every location shown in his documentary films: most of the time, he sees the action for the first time on film – and likely highly edited film at that. In addition, he apparently doesn't actually write any of the film scripts himself: his production team does that.

According to a BBC colleague Barkham interviewed, who formerly worked with him extensively, Sir David edits and adapts scripts to his own narrative style so that his storytelling skill can shine through. Although the same colleague said Attenborough 'checks for accuracy', it seems in practice he rarely questions the interpretation of natural phenomena presented to him in these scripts – no doubt because, as he told Barkham: 'I'm not the great all-seeing source of all information, knowledge and understanding'.[9]

In other words, Attenborough is not a fact-checker: he depends on his production team to do that.

It's ironic, really. Attenborough got into the exalted position of trust he has with the public because he entrusts others to do the careful checking of facts on which his reputation rests. Yet when Attenborough narrates a script, the words come out of his mouth and he must own them. That has been the arrangement since his early years in the business, and it's clear he has fully understood the implications.

According to colleagues, he takes responsibility for the scripts he reads, so he has always been careful about precisely how he says things. However, if the production team and their advisors get the facts flat-out wrong or not-quite right (because they have done inadequate research or have let their biases colour their interpretation of facts), problems can arise – as we shall see in the pages ahead.

Regarding the human-caused global warming movement, which began to get some serious media attention about 1988, Attenborough came rather late to the party.

By the turn of the 21st century, his reticence to speak out on this topic in his BBC films frustrated a number of people, who thought he should be using his powerful platform and position of trust to 'educate' the public about the risks of global warming – including British naturalist Richard Mabey, climate change author Leo Hickman, and radical environmental journalist George Monbiot.[10]

It wasn't until 2004 that Attenborough met a scientist who convinced him that dangerous warming was afoot and a grim future lay ahead – and he suddenly became willing to say so publicly.[11] Note he hadn't done any research himself on the topic: as he had always done, he simply accepted someone else's word as verified fact.

As a consequence of this late start, the idea that human-caused global warming posed a threat to human societies and the natural world was not addressed in Attenborough's BBC films until 2006, when the BBC broadcast a two-part special: *Are We Changing Planet Earth?* and *Can We Save Planet Earth?* (released as *The Truth About Climate Change* outside the UK).[12]

Once he was on board with the concept, however, Attenborough quickly became frustrated at the slow pace of action. This was evident in 2013, when he infamously called humans 'a plague on the Earth' because of the effects of climate change and – another issue close to his heart[13] – unchecked population growth:[14]

> We are a plague on the Earth. It's coming home to roost over the next 50 years or so.
>
> It's not just climate change.
>
> It's sheer space, places to grow food for this enormous horde.
>
> Either we limit our population growth or the natural world will do it for us, and the natural world is doing it for us right now.

As I will show, from his first foray into the climate change narrative it was clear that people with agendas – including activist scientists – could readily manipulate Attenborough into becoming a mouthpiece for them.

Nowhere was this more evident than his blind faith in the conservation organisation, the World Wildlife Fund.

## *World Wildlife Fund*

The World Wildlife Fund (WWF) was founded in 1961 by businessmen as a way to help raise money for the newly-formed International Union for the Conservation of Nature (IUCN), which was having financial trouble carrying out its mission to protect species at risk of extinction. WWF set up shop at IUCN headquarters in Switzerland and the two organisations quickly developed close financial ties.[15]

Because it aimed to attract wealthy benefactors – many of whom had a passion for African safaris – the WWF did not condemn hunting. It finally did impose restrictions on hunting in 1965 for those holding office at the WWF and specifically on land 'set aside for prosperity with WWF money'. Hunting in general or even trophy hunting specifically was never actively discouraged.[16]

Prince Bernhard, consort of Queen Juliana of The Netherlands was the first high-profile president of WWF International, while Prince Philip, consort of Queen Elizabeth II of the United Kingdom, became the president of WWF-UK. In European royal tradition, both were avid big game hunters and generated considerable controversy for doing so in the early 1960s while promoting the WWF. They both eventually stopped hunting overseas, although they continued to do so closer to home.[17]

The WWF had lofty goals from the beginning, but it took a while to amass the funds needed to really make a difference. Its first major grant was $38,000 to the Smithsonian Institution in 1973 to study the tiger population in Nepal.[18] Over the years, WWF became very effective at fund raising and lobbying for conservation causes.[19]

By 2010 it was an exceedingly wealthy and successful business: it had offices in 82 countries, more than 5000 staff, and total operating revenues of €525 million (equivalent to just under three-quarters of a billion US dollars at that time).[20]

The WWF's first venture into promoting the concept of human-caused global warming as a looming catastrophe appears to have come in 1999, when it established a 'Climate Savers' program, through which it partnered with corporations to help them reduce greenhouse gas emissions.[21]

In 2004, they developed a program to encourage members of the public – who they called 'climate witnesses' – to describe how they had personally experienced the effects of human-caused climate change. Although such stories were not verified and therefore could not be considered facts or evidence, a 'Climate Witness Scientific Advisory Panel' of experts was established, many of whom were contributors to the 2007 report of the Intergovernmental Panel on Climate Change (IPCC).[22]

Its job was to put a quasi-scientific stamp of approval on the tales of climate woe.[23] Were they, or were they not, *consistent with* expected effects of climate change? Approved anecdotes were later published as 'Climate Witness Fact Sheets' that could be downloaded from the WWF website.

These initial ventures into the climate change narrative seem to have been the impetus for the WWF to start positioning and promoting itself as a trusted scientific authority on topics related to conservation and environmental protection (as it did to the UK House of Commons in 2014), rather than merely a fund-raising organisation whose role was to help other organisations save species and habitats.[24]

For more than a decade, the WWF has been wealthy enough to employ people with degrees in conservation biology – who we are encouraged to think of as unbiased scientists rather than activists with university degrees – and to fund research projects – which we are encouraged to think of as unbiased scientific studies rather than exercises in circular reasoning.[25]

However, the very nature of the organisation means that all employees and associates have a skewed vision of the world and an agenda that must be served, which tends to distort any research before it can even begin.[26]

Starting in 1998, the WWF has been producing a 'Living Planet Report' on the state of the environment, based on studies developed, carried out, and interpreted through the peculiar lens of WWF advocacy. It wasn't mainstream science but it certainly presented itself as such.

After trying to position themselves as scientific researchers, the WWF then began campaigns to actively support 'victims' of climate change.

As part of this movement, in 2006 the WWF began assisting cash-poor small communities across the Arctic (including Russia, Greenland, Canada and Alaska) protect themselves from polar bear attacks. Polar bear problems across the Arctic had became increasingly common after the turn of the 21st century as polar bear numbers hit new highs in response to decades of international protection but the WWF insisted these issues should all be blamed on reduced sea ice caused by climate change.[27]

The amount of cash invested in these programs has been small when considered against the organisation's enormous wealth.

For example in 2020, WWF-Russia finally – after more than a decade of partnership – assisted in the purchase of an ATV and a snowmobile for the village of Ryrkaipiy in Chukotka (which plays a part in this story). In this and other remote Arctic communities, WWF trains and pays the small wages for a few polar bear 'guards' who are undoubtedly happy to have any amount of cash for a few months (living as they do in economies where opportunities to earn money are rare).[28]

At the same time, the WWF exploit these occasions to indoctrinate local residents and their children to the current WWF view of the world, which gives them loyal local contacts they can depend upon. However, most critically, these WWF programs are promoted heavily to the general public as 'good works': often, journalists are convinced to write about these helpful programs, giving the organisation important free publicity.[29]

On balance, the PR value of these Arctic programs – in terms of the increased donations to the WWF they generate – is likely much larger than the costs to run them. This is almost certainly one of the reasons the organisation has become so rich.

However, in the greater scheme of things the Arctic programs were small potatoes.

In 2015, the organization finally branched out into big-ticket climate change documentaries. Through this medium, its distorted interpretations of science could be turned into high-definition environmental activist infomercials sold as educational entertainment – which is where Attenborough and the story of Pacific walrus came into play.[30]

The unique deal it brokered with Netflix (see below) launched the WWF into whole new category of influence and it was no accident that David Attenborough played a huge part.

David Attenborough has had a long association with the WWF in Britain. WWF-UK was the first national organisation established after WWF-International was formed. As mentioned above, in 1961, Prince Philip (Duke of Edinburgh, husband to Queen Elizabeth II) served as its first president until 1982, a role his son Charles (Prince of Wales) took on in 2011.

Remarkably, Prince Philip withdrew his support for the organisation when the WWF began its aggressive campaign against global warming, even as his son Charles became a more fervent advocate.[31] Attenborough never had such an epiphany: he came on board the WWF-UK along with the royal family in the early 1960s and has served as an official WWF 'Ambassador' since at least June 2015.[32]

Attenborough has always held the WWF in high regard – even after it morphed from a conservation fund-raising organisation of the IUCN into a billion dollar conglomerate that required many millions of dollars in donations annually just to cover its operating expenses and lobbying activities.

Not being a scientist himself and therefore able to know better, he trusts the scientific authority of the WWF: if they say a Sixth Mass Extinction is imminent or that unsustainable human activity is pushing the planet's natural systems that support life on Earth to the edge, he not only believes them but enthusiastically passes along the message.[33]

It is therefore hardly surprising that Attenborough would see a business deal to make a documentary with the WWF as a wonderful opportunity.

## Silverback Films

Silverback Films was established in 2012 by Alastair Fothergill and Keith Scholey, two documentary producers who had worked in the BBC Natural History Unit in Bristol for many years. They of course knew Attenborough very well. Their experience with the BBC but financial independence from it ended up being key to the company's success although their head office remains in Bristol.

These company directors appeared to realize that high-quality, block-buster natural history documentaries for television and cinema were in demand and that they were uniquely positioned to provide them. They produced a few feature films after their start-up but soon moved on to the big stuff: *North America*, a seven-part series for the Discovery Channel in 2013, *Mystery of the Lost Island/Deadly Islands*, a six-part series for Discovery International in 2014, and *The Hunt*, a seven-part series for the BBC in 2015.[34]

However, the *Our Planet* deal with Netflix and the WWF in 2015 (see details below), just three years after its inception, was a serious game-changer for Silverback Films: it put them in a different league altogether.

## Netflix

Netflix was founded as a movie rental service by Marc Randolph and Reed Hastings in 1997 but eventually became an international powerhouse in subscription-based streaming services (aka 'video-on-demand').

By late 2015, it was considered to have become a legitimate television network by virtue of the original content it was producing.[35]

As part of that push for original content, on 15 April 2015 Netflix announced a surprising collaboration with the WWF in the UK and Silverback Films to produce an eight-part documentary series with a strong climate change message called *Our Planet*.

The collaboration with the WWF was unprecedented and so was the project itself.

This would be the largest and most expensive endeavour of its kind ever attempted: it would take four years to complete, employ more than 600 people, and involve travel to 50 countries around the world.[36] The eight one-hour episodes were entitled: 'One Planet', 'Frozen Worlds', 'Jungles', 'Coastal Seas', 'From Deserts to Grasslands', 'The High Seas', 'Fresh Water' and 'Forests'.

The WWF had a huge amount of control and influence over the production of *Our Planet*. Not only did it fund the considerable cost of four years of film-making, it provided exclusive access to its conservation projects underway in protected areas around world.

In addition, the WWF was also in charge of the scientific facts presented in *Our Planet*.[37]

According to a report by CBC News (Canada) in June 2019:[38]

A cornerstone of the series is research from the World Wildlife Fund's *Living Planet Report* on global biodiversity and the state of the planet.

In 2018, the WWF report concluded that 'unsustainable human activity is pushing the planet's natural systems that support life on Earth to the edge'.

Exactly when Attenborough became involved in the project is not clear, but in early January 2018, he alluded to an up-coming collaboration with Netflix, stating (as if he knew none of the details): [39]

Netflix want me to do something on conservation and have asked me to do it, and I've said I would.

There's certain things that the BBC can do and can't do, and I can see some reasons why to do a programme on Netflix rather than the BBC.

However, his association with *Our Planet* was not formally made public until 8 November 2018, only five months before the official release date, when his work editing and narrating the scripts was almost certainly complete, or nearly so. That's modern-day marketing for you: it's very strategic with respect to timing.

Attenborough's role as narrator for *Our Planet* was announced at a splashy WWF 'State of the Planet' address in London, the same day the first trailer of the film was released. [40]

The high-profile interviews he gave in the wake of the announcement were essentially free publicity: they created a buzz for the series that no amount of advertising money could have replicated.

Attenborough made it clear why he had broken away from the BBC to make the documentary: he wanted a bigger audience. He apparently had become more and more frustrated with the poor reach of BBC documentaries on climate change, as well as the lack of political action, which he thought came down to not enough people getting the message. [41]

While it was true that his BBC climate change documentaries got relatively high viewership in the UK and eventually were released into international markets, it was usually years before they were seen around the world.[42]

However, by 2018 at least, most of Attenborough's BBC documentaries were held in the Netflix catalogue, which made it one of the few places they were easily accessible to viewers worldwide.

Most importantly, Netflix could promise him hundreds of millions of potential viewers for *Our Planet*: at the beginning of 2018, it had almost 120 million subscribers, all of whom could access a newly-released film simultaneously. By the end of 2019, this number had grown to 167 million, and a year later it had reached almost 204 million.[43]

In contrast, the first episode of Attenborough's *Blue Planet II*, which aired in the fall of 2017 on the BBC, is said to have reached 14 million viewers – the best of any of his films to date – but discouragingly, this was almost two million less than the previous year's 26 October episode of BBC's *The Great British Bakeoff*.[44]

Another big draw to the *One Planet* project was that Attenborough had for many years worked with the two owners of Silverback Films – Alastair Fothergill and Keith Scholey – when the two produced documentaries for the BBC. He trusted the pair to apply the same standards to *Our Planet*.[45]

These background facts about the major players – David Attenborough, the WWF, Netflix, and the owners of Silverback Films – become important as this story unfolds from the release of the 'Frozen World' episode of *Our Planet*.

# Chapter 2

# The Falling Walrus Fiasco

The final storyline of the 'Frozen Worlds' episode of the Netflix/WWF documentary *Our Planet* is both astonishing and heartbreaking.[46]

After a brief introduction about the recent loss of Arctic summer sea ice and the 'inevitable' devastation this will cause for Arctic animals, it shifts to a series of amazing shots of tens of thousands of walrus, crowded cheek-by-jowl as far as the eye can see.

Only a drone-mounted camera could have caught the truly spectacular nature of the gathering – you simply need a birds-eye view to take in over a hundred thousand walrus on one long stretch of beach.

They were mostly mothers with calves, but there were also quite a few half-grown youngsters and some fully adult males weighing two tons or so. Bodies steaming in the chill air, the heaving mass huffs, barks, and grunts – with the occasional roar as conflicts arise between neighbours. Tusks are raised in threat but there's limited room for a serious fight.

The animals are not simply side by side; they are on top of each other as well. Any walrus that needs to get to the water must climb over the bodies underneath and beside them. Calves too young for their growing tusks to be visible are clearly at great risk of being trampled, especially if something startles the herd and it stampedes for the safety of the water.

Because the camera segues so smoothly, it appears to have simply moved to one end of the heaving mass on the beach and we suddenly see a rocky headland with a cliff said to be 80 metres high – 260 feet.

The camera pans to walrus in the water and on the narrow rocky beach below, then narrows in on an individual lumbering slowly up an unconsolidated dirt slope behind the beach, fighting to gain ground without sliding backwards.

The camera moves again to the top of the cliff, where one massive creature is perched perilously close to the edge. Then, with no warning, the one ton walrus is shown slipping off the cliff edge and falling onto the beach below – spinning head over tail in slow motion, bouncing off the rocky outcrops of the cliff wall as it falls.

And then the camera shows another one falling – and another, and another, and another. Slow motion catches every terrifying slide, wince-inducing bounce off jagged rocks, inconceivably awkward cartwheel, and deadly twisted landing.

It's the kind of horror you know you should look away from, but you cannot make yourself turn your head or close your eyes. You keep hoping for a clue that this is not what it seems, that these animals will waddle away in the end unharmed.

But then the camera pans across the faces of a few lifeless animals, and to a long line of carcasses spread out along the rocky beach, and the reality of it sinks in.

Here is my annotated transcript of Attenborough's narration of the walrus scene in *Our Planet* which I have now watched dozens of times:[47]

> [Shot of the Arctic sea ice as if from space].
>
> For thousands of years there's been a balance in the advance and retreat of the sea ice. But that is no longer the case. Today, during the summer months, there is 40% less sea ice cover than there was in 1980.
>
> [Aerial shot of a polar bear swimming towards a far-off ice floe]
>
> The Arctic is warming twice as fast as anywhere else on our planet. By 2040, the ocean here will be largely free of ice during the summer months. This loss of ice will inevitably have devastating consequences for all those that still depend on it.

[Shot of an enormous walrus herd on a beach that goes on and on, including some on top of a rock outcrop, then an aerial shot]

The far northeastern coast of Russia. This is the largest gathering of walrus on the planet. Over a hundred thousand have hauled out on one single beach. They do so out of desperation, not out of choice. Their natural home is out on the sea ice. But the ice has retreated away to the north, and this is the closest place to the feeding grounds where they can find rest.

[Close-up of mother and calf].

This calf must stay close to its mother. But every square inch is occupied.

[Shots of walrus fighting with their tusks, grunting, roaring]

Climbing over the tightly packed bodies is the only way across the crowd.

Those beneath can get crushed to death. [Close-up of calf]

A stampede can occur out of nowhere. [Walrus rushing on-mass into the water]

Under these conditions, walruses are a danger to themselves.

[Segue into shots of a high cliff with walrus on top and in the water below].

Some manage to find space away from the crowds. They struggle up the 80-metre cliffs, an extraordinary challenge for a one-ton animal used to sea ice.

[Shot of walrus waddling awkwardly up a rocky dirt slope; then shot of walrus at the top of the cliff, loose rocks falling below]

At least up here, there's space to rest. A walrus's eyesight out of water is poor. But they can sense the others down below.

As they get hungry, they need to return to the sea. [Shot of walrus in the water]

[Shot of a walrus falling from the cliff in slow motion from part way down the cliff, then five more falling, all in slow motion]

In their desperation to do so, hundreds fall from heights they should never have scaled.

[Shot of a dying walrus after its fall and a dead youngster awash in the surf, and then a panning shot of dead walrus along the rocky shore]

[Segue into new shot of a fat polar bear that approaches from the water and comes ashore to check out the dead]

These mass gatherings of walrus are now happening almost every year. So, the lives of walruses, like those of polar bears and seals, are changing. All are living at the frontier of climate change and all are suffering as a consequence.

[Shot of dead walrus at the water's edge, waves lapping against it] then [Segue into shot of a very fat polar bear walking in a blizzard]

For now, the Arctic winter returns and the sea ice reforms. Order is restored. Relief for the many creatures that depend on the ice. But for how much longer will their frozen worlds be a part of life on our planet?

THE END

[Attenborough's voice]: Please visit Ourplanet.com [as a 'with WWF' logo pops up] to discover what we need to do now to keep the polar wilderness.

The scenes were shocking enough, even if you watched with the sound off.

But Attenborough's iconic, grandfatherly voice got the full message across: less summer sea ice than 40 years ago has caused this; these enormous walrus land haulouts never happened before; the walrus crowd tightly together in huge numbers because there is nowhere else to go; some animals climb dangerously high cliffs in their quest to find more space and hundreds die falling from the top; now you have seen the proof with your own eyes that climate change causes hundreds of walrus to die a dreadful death.

These were extraordinary claims, delivered with an unforgettable gut-punch.

The gut-punch came from the slow-motion, falling walrus sequence, which was far more extreme than the usual death scene viewers were used to seeing in modern documentaries. A lion killing an impala, or a snake stalking a mouse, or even a whale trapped in sea ice by happenstance – these are the brutal aspects of nature most of us accept as part of life.

This falling walrus sequence was something else. It was film footage meant to elicit an intense emotional reaction: unforgettable, nightmare-inducing horror.

This much gruesomeness – the same dreadful action happening again and again, all in slow motion – had never been seen before in a natural history documentary. It would have been considered too shocking, even for adults.

It was the most grotesque kind of animal tragedy porn and was used to promote a political message about human-caused climate change.

And it's no wonder that it came at the end of the one-hour episode rather than at the beginning: this was the take-home message viewers were meant to absorb. There were no soothing shots afterwards to soften the impact: you were meant to remember the full awfulness of what you'd just seen.

The producers have said the falling walrus scene was the most powerful story they encountered during the four years of filming the series, and they used it to full effect,[48] as Silverback Films producer Keith Scholey explained in an interview with CBC News in Canada [my emphasis]:[49]

> We knew as soon as we saw that, that this was going to be the footage that would become most associated with the climate change horror that's happening to Arctic species...
>
> *What we desperately wanted to get across to people was that humanity cannot survive without nature.*

On the day of the series release, Netflix also issued a short 'Digital Exclusive' video about the walrus scene for news outlets to embed in their stories, which let non-Netflix viewers see the most lurid moments of the walrus-falling-to-their-deaths scene.

The promoters had this all planned. This two minute video exclusive lacked Attenborough's narration but instead had a tearful on-camera statement from Sophie Lanfear, director and producer of the 'Frozen Worlds' episode, about how surprised she was by the deaths, and then explained why climate change was to blame.[50]

The digital exclusive ratcheted up the news value because it meant every single reader would see at least one of the horrifying walrus falls, as well as the hundreds of dead on the beach, and would know what the story was about – and experience the horror of it – even if they weren't Netflix subscribers.

The official release date of the series was Friday, 5 April 2019, and both mainstream and online media went all out in their coverage in the days that followed.[51]

As Ed Yong at The Atlantic succinctly stated in his relatively balanced review:[52]

> *Our Planet* draws a straight line between climate change, sea-ice loss, bigger haul-outs, overcrowding, climbing walruses, and falling walruses.

A New York Times review repeated the take-home message bluntly, right in its title:[53]

> A Netflix nature series says to viewers: Don't like what you see? Do something about it.

Damien Whitworth at The Times (UK) on 5 April started his story with a statement Attenborough and the WWF probably hoped someone would deliver: [54]

> Two-tonne mountains of blubber and tusk may not be as iconic as polar bears, but the horrific deaths of hundreds of walruses could make these 'Arctic refugees' the grim new symbol of climate change.

A few days later, both Netflix and WWF International released a 'Behind the Scenes' video of the walrus shoot, featuring Russian science advisor Anatoly Kochnev repeating the same climate change message: walrus are dying and you are to blame for using fossil fuels.[55]

None of the other *Our Planet* episodes drew the media attention this one did.

There was an international explosion of dying walrus stories, many driven by the strong reaction of viewers who had taken to social media to express their anger as well as their anguish – and to warn others of what was in store.[56]

Even People magazine did a story, which focused on Sophie Lanfear as director/producer of the episode.

WWF received a huge benefit from all of this attention: according to one account, the organisation saw some of its biggest spikes ever on social media and a significant increase in traffic to its website, no doubt by many people wanting to donate money.[57]

*Our Planet* was marketed as educational entertainment but had left adults as well as children traumatised. A Canadian woman said her eight-year-old son sobbed inconsolably for an hour after watching the scene.[58]

Another comment, in a UK newspaper, rather sums up the responses:[59]

I was and will never be emotionally ready to watch a walrus fall to its death.

Five days later, on 10 April, Netflix issued a tweet that I found particularly condescending, with details of scenes from *Our Planet* that it thought 'animal lovers' might want to avoid:[60]

> As you make your way through *Our Planet*, here are some moments animal lovers may want to skip:
>
> One Planet: 16:04–16:43
>
> Frozen World: 16:29–17:47, 32:50–33:45, 48:45–51:00
>
> Fresh Water: 26:10–27:09
>
> Deserts and Grasslands: 28:45–29:10
>
> High Seas: 37:42–37:52

Rather than admit the walrus scene went too far, they lumped the time-code of the universally distressing falling walrus scene in with a few others that only devout vegans would find upsetting (a flamingo chick weighed down by salt on its legs; a polar bear killing a baby seal, a penguin being tossed around and then eaten by a killer whale, a jaguar wrestling with a caiman, cheetahs killing a wildebeest, and fish caught in nets).

By implying all of these scenes would be found equally disturbing – but only to a few overly-sensitive viewers – they belittled and ridiculed the intense emotional reaction virtually all viewers experienced watching half a dozen walrus fall to their deaths in slow motion.

However, social media complaints weren't the only problem Netflix had with this scene: they had me to contend with. Attenborough's narrative implied his statements were supported by science. I knew they weren't, and I wasn't afraid to say so.

# Chapter 3
# Walrus Biology and Life History

In April 2019, I knew quite a bit about Pacific walrus from a previous dive into the scientific literature and I'd learned even more since then. This meant I was uniquely positioned to make a quick but informed critique of the *Our Planet* claims.[61]

Here are the pertinent facts.

Figure 1. Walrus come to the surface during feeding to breath, poking their heads through broken ice in the Bering Sea (April 2004). Credit Joel Garlich-Miller USFWS.

Pacific walrus are gregarious animals that at times form large herds at sea and on land. Most Pacific walrus migrate seasonally between the Bering and Chukchi Seas although a small number of Pacific walrus remain year-round in the Laptev Sea because a large area of open water or thin ice called the Great Siberian polynya allows them to feed and mate over the winter.[62]

Migrating Pacific walrus of both sexes and all age classes spend the winter on the mobile pack ice of the Bering Sea, where the moving, broken ice allows them access to the clams, worms, snails, and other creatures that live on the sea floor (Fig. 1), which they find with their sensitive whiskers.

It simply isn't possible for walrus to feed where winter sea ice forms a solid mass, as it does further north in the Chukchi Sea: they must have access to at least some open water that is less than about 80 metres deep (Fig. 2).

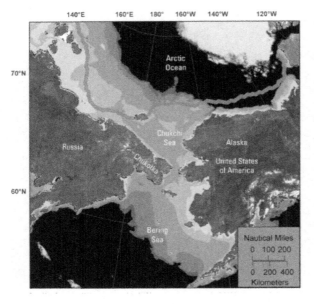

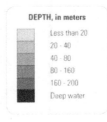

**EXPLANATION**

In summer, a major segment of the Pacific walrus population, especially females and their young, ranges in waters across the continental shelf of the Chukchi Sea (light blue shades). By September 2007, the sea ice (upper right) was far north of the continental shelf and over the deep Arctic Basin. Historically, the annual sea ice minimum edge (yellow line) occurred over the continental shelf.

**DEPTH, in meters**

| | |
|---|---|
| | Less than 20 |
| | 20 - 40 |
| | 40 - 80 |
| | 80 - 160 |
| | 160 - 200 |
| | Deep water |

Figure 2. The summer range of walrus females and calves over the continental shelf of the Chukchi Sea. Depth of water in meters; thick grey line indicates the minimum extent of sea ice (in September) for 1979-2000, which shows that the coasts of Russia and Alaska have often been ice-free. Walrus prefer water depths less than 80 metres for feeding, i.e., the three lightest shades of grey. Source: USGS Walrus Fact Sheet (2008).

The particularly open pack ice conditions usually present in the Bering Sea are important for another reason: mating takes place *in the water* (not on the ice) during the winter (January/February). Walrus need open water for mating as well as for feeding, and sea ice for resting between feeding bouts and for giving birth and nursing young.

Females impregnated the previous winter give birth on the ice from April to early June after a pregnancy of 15-16 months. This extraordinarily long gestation includes a period of 4-5 months when the newly fertilized egg stops developing but later resumes its growth into a foetus (a process called 'delayed implantation').[63]

Sexually mature adult males usually leave the ice around March after the mating season ends and head to ice-free beaches known as 'haulouts' or 'hauling grounds' in the ice-free southern Bering Sea, where they resume feeding, using the beaches as rest areas (Fig. 3).

The males aren't forced to leave the ice: they do so by choice, in a pattern that has been documented as far back as the 17th century.[64]

As the ice in the Bering Sea begins its retreat into the Chukchi Sea in April and May, females with newborn calves (often accompanied by newly-impregnated females, older youngsters and a few subadult males) travel north with the ice, feeding and nursing their young as they go (Fig. 4).[65]

After the ice clears the narrow Bering Strait around late May or June, the herds of mostly mothers and calves continue to feed from the edge of the melting ice that sits over very productive shallow areas in the southern Chukchi Sea (Fig. 5), some staying in the eastern portion north of Alaska and others moving west to around Wrangel Island where there is particularly shallow water.

The herds keep moving with the ice as it retreats north in response to warming over the summer. This movement is advantageous because continuous intensive feeding by thousands or tens of thousands of animals in one area can severely deplete the clams and other bottom-dwelling species they are feeding upon.[66]

Figure 3. Walrus males resting on an ice-free shore of Round Island in the southern Bering Sea in 2011. Credit USFWS.

By July through September, even if Chukchi Sea ice is still available over shallow water (< 80m), the northern herds may either stay with the ice as it retreats over deeper water where feeding is difficult or move to various land haulouts that have become ice-free along the coasts of the northern Bering Sea, Alaska or Chukotka in the Russian Far East (Fig. 6). In most cases, the herd moves frequently between available sites, often staying no more than a few weeks at each location.

Figure 4. Walrus cows nursing their calves on an ice floe in the Bering Sea, April 2006. The open water around the floe allows the cows to feed on the bottom between nursing bouts. Credit Brad Benter USFWS.

While obviously beaches can't be used by mothers and calves for resting between feeding bouts if they are packed with ice (as much of the Chukchi Sea coast was during the summer of 2021), historical data shows that as soon as some shorelines were ice-free during warm years in the past, they were used by feeding walrus as a resting platform – especially those on Wrangel Island and along the Chukotka coast.

For example, in 1972, herds chose to move 300 km from sea ice over shallow water to a preferred land haulout on Wrangel Island as soon as the beaches there became ice-free.[67]

Figure 5. A walrus female and her calf rest on ice in the Chukchi Sea (12 June 2010). What looks like open water under the pair is actually a 'melt pond' – a puddle of melted water with sea ice underneath. Credit Sarah Sonsthagen USGS.

In other words, these herds are flexible with regard to the resting areas they choose in the summer and fall, depending on ice conditions and locally available food.

In the fall, the herd moves south ahead of the advancing sea ice through the Bering Strait to rest and feed at land haulouts in the ice-free northern Bering Sea. The walrus are not forced to leave: they choose to do so.

It seems this has always been the case. In recent years, the large herds of mostly mothers and calves that spent September and October at various locations around the Chukchi Sea moved east to a staging ground at the enormous beach complex at Cape Serdtse-Kamen (which is about 20 kilometres long) and then left abruptly sometime in November to swim south together.

Adult males summering in the southern Bering Sea swim north to meet the mothers and calves. Together they wait for the winter ice to arrive in the northern Bering Sea and the mating season to begin again.[68]

Figure 6. Part of a herd of about 10,000 walrus that hauled out at Point Lay, Alaska on 18 September 2013 to rest between feeding bouts. The herd stayed for a few weeks and then moved on. Credit Ryan Kingsbery USGS.

Suitable land haulout sites for Pacific walrus are abundant, not rare.

There are at least 35 historically known land haulout sites for herds of both sexes and mixed ages in the Chukchi Sea and northern Bering Sea that have adjacent seas shallow enough for feeding (Fig. 7).

In the Chukchi Sea, massive haulouts of tens of thousands of predominately walrus mothers and calves are known historically at several beaches on Wrangel Island, especially in the 1930s and the 1960s-1970s; in 1990, an enormous haulout of more than 76,000 was documented.

At Cape Schmidt, just south of Wrangel Island, large haulouts were known from the late 1800s and early 1900s but disappeared after the village of Ryrkaipiy was built close by, only to reappear with a bang in 2007 when a herd of 40–50,000 appeared. Ryrkaipiy apparently means the 'limit of walrus moving' in the Chukchi language, suggesting that's about as far west as most migrating Pacific walrus travel in the summer.

Similarly, in the northern Bering Sea, a herd of about 60,000 mainly mothers and calves hauled out at one site in 1978 near St. Lawrence Island in the fall.[69]

Historically, the size of land haulouts seems to have been closely tied to overall population size – there weren't really massive herds seen on land after the population had been much reduced by overhunting in the late 1800s.

The huge population numbers of Pacific walrus known in the early 1800s were not seen again until after 1950: numbers declined precipitously due to severe predation by Yankee whalers from 1869-1880, then by American 'Arctic traders' in the early 1900s, and they by Soviet sealers from 1931-1950, when hunting restrictions were put in place.

The Pribilof Islands in the southern Bering Sea were a significant haulout location in the 17th and 18th centuries for adult males but after the whole-sale slaughter of walrus in the 19th century, walrus males stopped using this area. This is one example of 'suitable' walrus haulout sites that are currently available but simply not used today.[70]

Due to government protection, walrus numbers increased dramatically between the 1950s and the mid-1970s but declined significantly (apparently due to lack of food) in the 1980s. Numbers have increased again since then. This 'boom and bust' population cycle happens in other carnivorous species as well: numbers of predators grow until the animals start to run out of food and starve; when predator numbers are low (as they were for walrus in the 1980s), their prey species have a chance to increase in abundance and predator numbers can slowly increase – until food gets scarce again.[71]

However, by 2017, there had been no government reports or scientific papers showing starving walrus had become more common than they had been in the 1990s. There was no evidence that feeding from large, land-based haulouts in the 2000s rather than from sea ice had caused the population as a whole to run out of food or individuals to starve.

There was also no obvious decline in numbers; in fact, walrus abundance looked to be similar or higher than what it had been in 1980 before the population crashed.

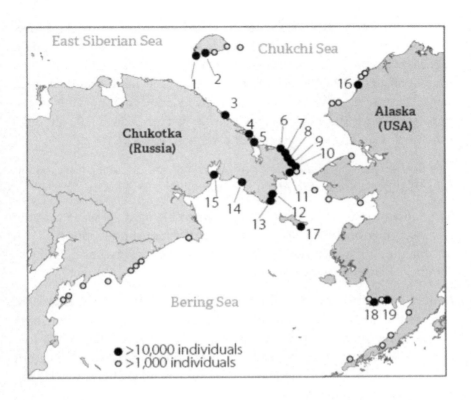

| Key |                        |    |                      |
|-----|------------------------|----|----------------------|
| 1   | Cape Blossom           | 11 | Cape Nunyamo         |
| 2   | Somnitel'naya Spit     | 12 | Nuneangam Islands    |
| 3   | Cape Schmidt           | 13 | Arakamchechen Island |
| 4   | Cape Vankarem          | 14 | Retkyn Spit          |
| 5   | Cape Onmyn             | 15 | Me'eskyn Spit        |
| 6   | Cape Serdtse-Kamen     | 16 | Point Lay            |
| 7   | Chegitun River         | 17 | Punuk Islands        |
| 8   | Cape Unikyn            | 18 | Cape Peirce          |
| 9   | Cape Inchoun           | 19 | Round Island         |
| 10  | Cape Pe'ek             |    |                      |

Figure 7. Pacific walrus coastal haulout locations reported in the past four decades (1980s– 2010s), with a maximum aggregation size of greater than or equal to 1,000 walrus. Redrawn from USGS 2016 by A. Montford.

The results of a 2013–2015 genetic mark-recapture project (a new method not used on walrus before) determined numbers were about 283,213 in 2014 (potential range 93,000–478,975) vs. 254,890 in 1980 (potential range 184,000–344,000). However, the huge potential error range of the estimate meant the researchers could not tell if the population size was really higher than it had been in 1980, although other indicators suggest it was not substantially lower.[72]

This presented a bit of a conundrum. Why had the population crashed in the 1980s due to lack of food but had not done so in the 2010s?

Some insight into explaining this came when biologists realized that the increased phytoplankton (e.g. single-celled algae) production they had documented in the Chukchi Sea and other Arctic regions was due to less summer sea ice between 2003 and 2020.

A much longer open-water period in summer means that more sunlight reaches the floating algae that, along with under-ice algae, form the base of the Arctic food chain. Since sunlight is their food, a longer ice-free period allows floating phytoplankton to reproduce prolifically. In recent years, some enormous blooms of the microscopic plants have been photographed by satellites.

More open-water phytoplankton means more food for all species in the food chain, including the bottom-dwelling creatures that walrus feed upon. Less summer sea ice since about 2003 has meant the so-called 'carrying capacity' of Pacific walrus habitat increased to accommodate a much larger population than was previously possible.[73]

This should have been anticipated by walrus biologists but apparently it was not. It almost certainly explains why Pacific walrus are still well fed despite high population numbers.

Of course, large numbers of walrus in the population means that very large herds will sometimes form.

However, whether in large herds or small ones a peculiar feature of walrus is that they like to huddle close together, even if there is lots of space for them to spread out (Fig. 8). They do this when they are on the sea ice as well as on land, and even males (in the non-breeding season) cuddle up to each other (Fig. 3, 4).

But walrus don't just lie close to each other: they pile on top of each other as well. Atlantic walrus do the same thing and historic records show they always have done so. In other words, forming tight aggregations of individuals is normal walrus behaviour.[74]

One down side to this huddling behaviour is that it makes it hard for individuals to move quickly. If the herd is startled and tries to run for the safety of the water in a blind panic, some animals can be trampled to death.

Figure 8. A haulout of about 1500 walrus at Point Lay, AK, at 23 September 2014 showing the preference walrus have to form a tight aggregation even when abundant space is available (Credit, Corey Accardo NOAA). This herd grew a few days later to about 35,000 animals (insert, top left) but still did not spread out along the available beach area (Credit, USFWS).

Anything can spook a walrus herd into a stampede, even the jostling of one animal moving around to get comfortable or a flock of birds flying overhead.

Apparently, this has always been so. Deaths by stampedes at large land haulouts of mostly females with calves were well known from the 1930s and 1970s before lack of sea ice became an issue. For example, adult females and even a few adult males died by trampling at a large haulout in 1978, although young calves suffered the highest mortality.[75]

In summary, what we know is female Pacific walrus use sea ice exclusively for only half the year and males for only a few months. Since mating takes place in the water, walrus only require sea ice for giving birth and the first few months of nursing newborns (i.e. from April to perhaps late June).

In other words, walrus utilise sea ice as a feeding platform when it is available over shallow water but they do not require it. Moreover, land haulouts in summer and fall are known historically from the late 1800s, well before climate change was an issue, and walrus are not starving due to their recent use of land haulouts.

As a consequence, on 4 October 2017, the US Fish and Wildlife Service issued a press release stating that Pacific walrus were not being harmed by recent declines in summer sea ice and were not likely to be in the future; therefore, they had decided not to list the species as 'vulnerable' on the US list of Endangered Species.[76]

These facts refute the claims that climate change is to blame for the deaths shown in *Our Planet*.

# Chapter 4

# My Investigation and Critique

Two days after the release of *Our Planet*, I wrote an essay for my blog, PolarBearScience, calling Attenborough's interpretation of falling walrus deaths 'contrived nonsense'.[77]

Based on a newspaper account of a similar event from 2017, I pointed out that polar bears stalking the walrus at the top of the cliff was the likely stimulus for the falls shown in the episode, and used evidence from the scientific literature to rebut the claim that the walrus would not have been on land if not for climate change.

At that point I was responding to media reports with quotes from the film and the director, as well as the 'Digital Exclusive' video clip, after being tipped off to the news by one of my supporters.[78]

Without that tip, I might well have missed the story: my book 'The Polar Bear Catastrophe That Never Happened' had been released only three weeks earlier, and I had been doing interviews almost non-stop. My mind was on polar bears, not walrus. In fact, the day before the *Our Planet* series was released, I had travelled all day to do an interview with US television news powerhouse Tucker Carlson.[79]

I hadn't yet seen Attenborough's film, being one of many without a Netflix subscription, but I knew that the basic claims being made about the incident – repeated in the many news stories that had appeared since the film's release – were simply not true.

Although the precise location of the cliffs from which the walrus had fallen was not given in any of the stories (described only as the 'Russian Arctic'), it only took a quick internet search to find an article describing an incident disturbingly similar to the one shown in *Our Planet*.

33

On 17 October 2017, the Siberian Times (a Russian, English-language news outlet) published a story called 'Village besieged by polar bears as hundreds of terrorised walrus fall 38 metres to their deaths'.[80] The event was said to have taken place on the Russian coast of the Chukchi Sea near a settlement called Ryrkaypiy.

The village of Ryrkaypiy is connected by a sand and gravel spit to a tear-dropped-shaped headland that rises gradually to a prominent rocky cliff known as Kozhevnikova Cape or Cape Schmidt (Fig.9).

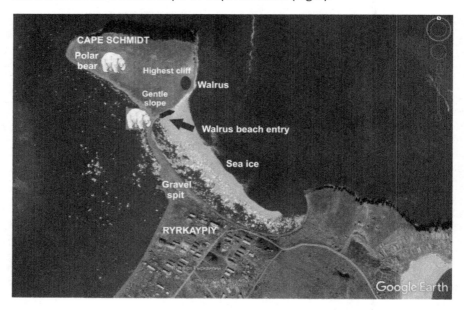

Figure 9. Aerial view of Cape Schmidt and the spit that connects it to the mainland and the village of Ryrkaypiy. This headland is essentially wedge-shaped in elevation: it rises from beach level at the narrow end near the spit and rises fairly gently at first and then more steeply to a plateau of sorts at the top; the highest cliffs (about 80m) are at the widest part. Walrus can access the headland from a fairly gentle sloping beach on the east (right side in image above) but apparently not from the west side, which is rocky and steep. Polar bears, however, can easily climb the slope on the west side and force any walrus that have climbed onto the headland over the cliff to their deaths. Modified from Google Earth image.

The story explained that earlier that autumn, a herd of about 5,000 walrus had hauled out on the beach at Cape Schmidt, which had attracted about 20 polar bears.

Several hundred walrus had accessed the headland at a low spot near the gravel spit where it intersected the beach and climbed up the dirt and grass slope to the top, where the only way down was back the way they had come – or over a high rocky cliff to the beach below. Surrounded and frightened by the polar bears stalking them, the walrus had fallen to their deaths from the cliff. The polar bears later fed off the carcasses that accumulated on the beach.

The person who took most of the photographs in the Siberian Times story, Maxim Deminov, was listed as a WWF affiliate. That sounded like an odd coincidence, given the collaboration of the WWF with Netflix for the *Our Planet* documentary.

In fact, this event not only sounded like the right location, but it appeared it may have been the very same incident as shown in the Netflix/WWF film. Although no precise date for the event was given in the Siberian Times story, it was clear that people representing the WWF were there when it occurred.

The only difference between the Netflix and the Siberian Times stories was the polar bears: except for a single individual shown on the beach in the final scene in the Netflix documentary, polar bears were not mentioned in the entire Netflix walrus sequence, yet they played a prominent part in the Siberian Times event.

If the two incidents were indeed one and the same, what had happened to the polar bears in the *Our Planet* story? Had there been two separate events?

Polar bears did not make an appearance in the Netflix 'Digital Exclusive' promotional video either, but the 'Behind the Scenes' video posted on the Netflix website a few days later showed that there had been bears on the slope above the beach during filming.

Were bears involved in the Netflix falling walrus sequence or not?

At this point I still didn't know for sure that the falling walrus incident at Cape Schmidt in 2017 reported by the Siberian Times was exactly the same event as the one show in *Our Planet* but it didn't take long to find out.

The internet community stepped up and Andrew Montford, deputy director of the Global Warming Policy Forum in London was particularly helpful. He was able to match up a profile photo of the cliff at Cape Schmidt that had been posted online by Russian naturalist Yevgeny Basov with the profile of the cliff from which the walrus fell in the Netflix documentary (Fig. 9).[81]

The Netflix filming location of the falling walrus had definitely been the cliff at Cape Schmidt.

Below is an excerpt from Basov's blog post about Cape Schmidt in 2017 and walrus falling from the cliff, which includes the odd notion that some of the animals were committing suicide. I've included it here because it seemed like it could be describing the same incident as the *Our Planet* event and therefore, Basov could have been a witness.

The somewhat stilted language comes from the Google translation of the original Russian. Note that Basov mentions no polar bears, except in a very general way, and that his estimate of the number of dead is much higher than alluded to in the *Our Planet* sequence:[82]

> In fact, walrus have chosen the east coast of the Kozhevnikov cliff. There are too few places there, and there are many walrus. When a new party of walruses comes out of the sea, it begins to crowd those who lie on the shore.
>
> The pressure is hard, so the first ones who have come out are forced to move higher. And above only the cliff itself, 60–70 meters high.
>
> It is not clear that they are being pushed upwards and not to the side, but they crawl on the rocks, like Abalakov, at the Peak of Communism. Climbing to the top, they cannot turn on the reverse.
>
> At least the first time. The walruses, although large, are very shy, frightening them [sic, frightened by?] all and everything: a loud sound, a bear, and even a low flying bird.

If they give in to panic, they move along the shortest path to the water, i.e. way down. A terrible and grand spectacle. Falling from the cliffs rare walrus breaks instantly to death.

Most often, he is injured incompatible with life and is in agony for one to three days. In addition to the 'fright' of walrus, congeners are also pushing towards suicide. More precisely, the sounds that make walruses lying on a rookery [*sic*, haulout]. The result is the same.

All this makes the rookery [*sic*, haulout] on the Kozhevnikov cliff unique (from the point of view of science, from the point of view of humanism – this term is blasphemy). Of the five or seven thousand walruses that went to the rookery [*sic*, haulout] this year, the death rate is about a thousand. Monstrously great figure.

The whole coast is littered with corpses. I saw this only on spawning rivers. But there is salmon, and then there are walruses.

Upon further investigation, I found out that the beaches and cliff at Cape Schmidt were famous for both walrus and polar bears (see Table 1, Appendix B).

The location was known historically as a walrus haulout but hadn't been used since at least the 1930s. That was until 2007, when seemingly out of the blue, a herd of at least 40,000 walrus descended on the area in September. By the time the herd left abruptly at the end of October, it was estimated that as many as 3,000 walrus carcasses were left behind: deaths that had been caused by stampedes and/or falls from the cliff.[83]

The walrus bodies attracted a large number of polar bears, which caused problems for the residents of nearby Ryrkaypiy into the winter. The bears seem to have arrived after the walrus deaths occurred (and after the herd had left) but it's possible that that a few bears might have precipitated some of the deaths and/or the abrupt departure of the herd without being seen. As a haulout of this size at this location was a new and unexpected event, some details might have been overlooked in the reporting.

However, a similar incident to the one described in the Siberian Times, involving polar bears and about the same number of walrus, occurred in 2011. In all, 123 walrus deaths by stampedes and falls from the cliff were noted, some of which appeared to have been caused by polar bears (at least 13 of which were seen).[84]

This means that as early as 2011, some bears had apparently learned that walrus on the headland could be forced over the cliff to their deaths: they didn't have to wait for this to happen naturally.

Then in 2015, a very large herd of walrus (about 30,000) again hauled out at Cape Schmidt from 14 August until 12 October, similar in scale to the initial 2007 event, and more than 100 animals died (mostly calves).[85] Polar bears were not mentioned as an associated cause of death as they had been in 2011.

As it turned out, all of the filmmakers involved in the *Our Planet* project really lucked out because as far as I can determine, no walrus hauled out at Cape Schmidt in 2016 or 2018: if the herd hadn't arrived in 2017, Lanfear and her crew would have missed their money shots.

However, the huge numbers of walrus documented ashore in 2007 and 2015 also indicate that the 5,000 individuals seen in 2017 and 2011 represented a relatively small example of a haulout at this location: clearly Cape Schmidt can accommodate tens of thousands of walrus for many weeks with varying levels of mortality.

Photos of from 2007 show 40,000 individuals packed all along the narrow gravel spit that connects the headland to Ryrkaypiy. This area appears not to have been occupied in 2017,[86] when newly-arriving walrus ignored the abundant available beach space on the spit, instead choosing to join their comrades on an already-crowded narrow beach below the base of the headland, forcing those at the back to move up the slope and towards the cliff top (Fig. 9).

Due the huge size of walrus – adult males can weigh almost 2 tons, females half that – even relatively low, sloping beaches can cause fatal falls if the animals head too quickly down the incline.

In fact, a video taken in 2009 at Ryrkaypiy shows some walrus barreling down the relatively gentle dirt slope at the base of the headland, with some falling head over tail in their panic: a closing shot shows several animals dead on the beach.[87]

And according to the Siberian Times article, most of the walrus that died in September 2017 after being stalked by polar bears must have been only part way up the headland, since they were said to have fallen only 38 metres to their deaths – not the 80 metres from the very top.

As for what polar bears were doing at Cape Schmidt, it turns out they have always spent the summer on that stretch of coastline.

The Chukchi Sea in this area has frequently been free of ice in September for a few weeks at least, even in the 1980s (See Chapter 3, Fig. 2). Some bears come ashore at this time although most stay on the ice.[88] As summer comes to an end, sea ice usually forms to the west of the cape and freeze-up proceeds eastwards, so bears that have spent the summer further east tend to make their way to the cape in the fall to meet the newly forming ice.

Western Hudson Bay polar bears in Canada do something similar: individuals spending the summer south of Cape Churchill make their way north in the fall because that's where the first ice tends to form. This migration happens every year in both places. When Ryrkaypiy was built in the 1930s, polar bear numbers were low but as numbers increased after international protection, the residents of Ryrkaypiy almost certainly experienced some of the same kinds of problems with polar bears in the fall that the residents of the town of Churchill endured since the 1960s.[89]

However, once walrus herds returned to Cape Schmidt, Ryrkaypiy's issues with polar bears exploded and since 2006, WWF-Russia has worked with residents to help protect them from polar bear attacks.[90]

It's not just Ryrkaypiy: polar bears are a problem for small villages all along this coast. Two hundred kilometres east of Ryrkaypiy, the beaches adjacent to the village of Vankarem had been attracting herds of walrus females and calves since the late 1990s – in some years 20,000 or more – and many died every year due to injuries suffered during stampedes. Walrus carcasses attract polar bears, which often wander into the village and threaten residents. WWF-Russia have also assisted this village in preventing polar bear attacks.

However, the proximity of Cape Schmidt to Ryrkaypiy heightens the polar bear problem when walrus carcasses are present. The village is only separated from the headland by 700 metres of sand and gravel, so when young bears or females get driven away from walrus carcasses by adult males (as often happens due to their social dominance hierarchy), they frequently wander into the nearby village.

In 2017, a bear broke a window of a house and entered the bedroom of a young boy. However, by 2020, the guards tasked with protecting the villagers had figured out how to successfully keep the bears out of town, even though they had at least 30 bears to contend with.[91]

Killing bears that cause problems is not an option here. Since 1956, Russian residents have not been permitted to kill polar bears due to their protected conservation status − even those that threaten human lives.[92]

However, historic and archaeological evidence indicates polar bears have been hunted locally at Cape Schmidt for a very long time.

A huge pile of more than 50 polar bear skulls at Cape Schmidt − a ritual feature made by hunters − was described by an ethnologist in the mid-1800s; there is also archaeological evidence of many polar bear skulls buried with humans which date to about 1,000 to 2,000 years ago.[93]

As for polar bears deliberately causing stampedes and subsequent deaths at walrus land haulouts, this is not a rare or unknown phenomenon.

Records from other walrus haulouts show that polar bears have learned to initiate stampedes, apparently because it is an effective hunting strategy that avoids confronting these dangerous animals head-on. The tusks that both male and female walrus possess are formidable weapons that polar bears ignore at their peril.

Ironically, *Our Planet* scientific advisor Anatoly Kochnev even wrote a paper about the practice of polar bears initiating walrus stampedes at haulouts. Having studied the deaths of 358 walrus in stampedes at two regularly used haulouts on Wrangel Island between 1989 and 1996, he concluded that most were caused by polar bears.[94]

Not only that: Kochnev and a colleague wrote a report on the haulout at Cape Schmidt in 2011 in which they noted that at least some of the stampede deaths that year were probably caused by the polar bears that hung out there.[95]

This means Kochnev knew that the presence of polar bears at Cape Schmidt was a huge risk factor for walrus stampedes over the cliff, but went along with the official *Our Planet* narrative that only lack of sea ice and poor eyesight were to blame for the carnage presented in the Netflix film.

There's one other issue that came up during my investigation that's worth keeping in mind regarding the climate change message conveyed in the *Our Planet* walrus sequence.

Although I knew in early 2019 that US wildlife authorities had decided not to add the Pacific walrus to the Endangered Species list in early October 2017, it was apparent that between 2015 and 2017 – when the Russian walrus scenes for *Our Planet* were being planned and filmed – the Center for Biological Diversity (CBD) and their conservation activist supporters (including the WWF) were anticipating the listing would go ahead.[96]

The Center for Biological Diversity is an America conservation organization run by lawyers that is famous for suing the US government to get plants and animals of their choice added to the Endangered Species List, which they had successfully done for the polar bear with a campaign that began in 2005 and ended in May 2008.[97]

Seeing the quick success they had achieved with polar bears, in early 2008 the CBD petitioned to get Pacific walrus declared 'threatened' as well, on the basis of the supposed risk posed by global warming.

While it had been a long wait, they were obviously expecting that by the final deadline for that legal process (October 2017) they would ultimately succeed with the walrus petition as well.

Therefore, the WWF and the Netflix crew no doubt expected that by the time the film was released in 2019, the falling walrus scene in the *Our Planet* episode would amplify the message that Pacific walrus were at risk of extinction in the future due to climate change.

Unfortunately for them, their message of doom was strongly contradicted by the official American report, which stated there was nothing to base a prediction of future harm due to reduced sea ice blamed on global warming.[98]

This had to have been a blow to the filmmakers but you wouldn't have known it by their response: they simply ignored the decision. None of them ever mentioned it.[99]

However, I certainly did. My blog post on the glaring inaccuracies in the *Our Planet* walrus episode, published 7 April 2017 (two days after the release of the Netflix series), included a citation of the 'not at risk' assessment by the US Fish and Wildlife Service.

When I wrote that piece, I had privately wondered what Attenborough's motive could have been for pushing this tragedy porn. To me, it seemed out of character for him to actively promote such disturbing footage.

Had he been a victim of the manipulation of science as much as viewers – believing what he was told by his producers and the WWF – or had he morphed into a full-blown fanatical activist? This wasn't the first time that Attenborough had claimed mass haulouts of Pacific walrus were due to global warming – there was a short clip in the BBC's 'Frozen Planet: On Thin Ice' (2011) on this topic – but the horrifying Netflix falling walrus sequence had taken this to a whole new level.

What was really going on behind the scenes? Throughout my investigation, that question was always in the back of my mind.

Unbeknownst to me at the time, Andrew Montford at the Global Warming Policy Forum (GWPF) had written an article about Attenborough's walrus subterfuge for submission to The Spectator, a major UK news magazine, quoting my comments and revealing his identification of the Netflix cliff location as Cape Schmidt.

The day after my blog post went up, Benny Peiser at the GWPF asked Montford and I to draft a press release to call attention to the issue.[100] However, we were too late.

Before we could get the press release finished, the UK Daily Telegraph beat us to it: science editor Sarah Knapton had read my blog post and on the afternoon of 8 April published an article highlighting my concerns that the Siberian Times event of walrus falling off the cliff near Ryrkaypiy was the same event shown in *Our Planet* – but with the stalking polar bears deliberately left out and blamed on climate change instead. The headline read: [101]

> Netflix walruses were driven to death by polar bears not climate change, claims zoologist.

Without any special effort on my part or due to actions of the GWPF, my humble blog post crying foul on Attenborough and his claims that global warming had caused the violent deaths of hundreds of walrus had reached the mainstream media and spawned an international controversy.

# Chapter 5

# International Controversy

My challenge was out there and by Monday morning 8 April, the internet was buzzing about the cliff-falling walrus and whether climate change or polar bears were to blame for their deaths.

Ironically, a long review article in The Atlantic magazine published online the same day provided some support for my criticisms about the Netflix walrus sequence. Journalist Ed Yong had interviewed *Our Planet* director Sophie Lanfear, who told him that blaming the falling walrus on climate change and lack of sea ice was a no-brainer:[102]

> It is not a normal event. It's such a tangible, obvious thing to show people. It's clear as day.

But Yong also talked to marine mammal biologist Lori Quakenbush, who worked at the Alaska Department of Fish and Game. She challenged Attenborough's notion that the walrus were climbing the cliffs to 'find space away from the crowds', telling Yong:

> Walruses thrive on crowds and haul out in tight groups, even when space is available.

Quakenbush and others also expressed doubt that the climbs and falls were related to climate change, because similar events had been documented before sea-ice declines had been an issue.

Yong quoted Lori Polasek from the University of Alaska Fairbanks:

> Walruses have shown similar behaviour on the US coastline when space and ice were not an issue, and the reason is unknown.

In my blog post, I had pointed out that journalists who reviewed the film and written about it should have asked the producers or the director where and when this footage was shot. None of them had. Yong apparently didn't either.

But Lanfear confirmed that the mass haulout of over 100,000 walrus and the one where the falls from the cliff had taken place were not at the same location, as they appeared to be in the film. She gave no reason for why the film had segued between sites in this way.

She explained to Yong what had happened at the cliff, claiming that polar bear weren't harassing the walrus, and that camera crews were filming from a distance so as not to startle them:

> ...walruses started climbing only once the area beneath the cliffs had completely filled up; gregarious or not, they had no room.

> Once at the top, they rested for a few days, and walked off only after the beaches below had emptied.

> Indeed, as the narration suggests, the sounds of their departing comrades may have lured the cliff-top walruses off the edge.

> 'They seemed to all want to return to the sea to feed as a group', Lanfear says.

Yong's balanced piece was refreshing, but didn't resolve any of the questions I had about the incident.

Even before my blog post had been published, Lanfear had insisted no polar bears were involved. But was she telling the whole truth?

Sarah Knapton at the Daily Telegraph had not received any response from Lanfear or the Netflix producers in time for publication of her story, but later that day, the Daily Mail (UK) also picked up the story, and they were more successful in getting a statement (more on that shortly).[103]

The next day, The Australian and Fox News also covered the story, largely quoting bits from the Daily Telegraph article; others followed, including a piece by GWPF director Benny Peiser.[104]

As this hullabaloo percolated within the mainstream media and internet communities, Andrew Montford and I were able to find out more critical details.

Once we knew we had the right place, it was relatively easy to confirm the timing. According to tweets sent by Silverback Films cameraman Jamie McPherson, the crew of *Our Planet* arrived in Chukotka to film walrus on 14 September 2017 and left on 26 October 2017.[105]

By examining the digital data from promotional photos of falling walrus released by Netflix (the 'EXIF photo metadata'), Montford determined they were taken on 19 September 2017.[106]

It also turned out that photos taken of walrus at Cape Schmidt by Yevgeny Basov and posted online, which I discussed in Chapter 4, were dated between 16 September and 22 September, 2017, and among these was one of Netflix science advisor Anatoly Kochnev taken on 16 September.[107]

Another Basov photo shows dead and dying walrus were already present at the base of the cliff on 17 September – two days before the Netflix film was shot.

That sealed the timing of the Netflix filming at 19 September 2017 and suggested the Siberian Times incident, involving the 20 polar bears, probably happened two or three days earlier – and that Kochnev was present for both. Moreover, Basov had indeed been a witness.

Another question was the location of the haulout with the 100,000 or so walrus shown the opening scene of the *Our Planet* walrus sequence, which was presented in the film as if it was right next to the Cape Schmidt haulout.

This was similarly easy to determine, since there are very few locations where such enormous haulouts are even possible. According to a US Geological Survey database of historical Pacific walrus haulouts throughout their range published in 2016, Cape Serdtse-Kamen further east along the Chukotka coast is the only location where such large herds have been documented.[108]

The Cape Serdtse-Kamen haulout beaches extend for about 20 kilometres along the coast without a cliff in sight. It is also at least 400 km (250 miles) east of Cape Schmidt.

In other words, the Cape Serdtse-Kamen haulout is nowhere near Cape Schmidt – they are not even in the same neighbourhood. Yet both the *Our Planet* sequence and the 'Behind the Scenes' short video present Cape Schmidt as a nearby 'over-flow' haulout to Cape Serdtse-Kamen – as if the huge expanse of beaches could not accommodate an extra 5,000 animals.

Scientific advisor Anatoly Kochnev – who is featured in the short PR video – of course knew this very well, as he had worked at Cape Serdtse-Kamen counting walrus since 2009.[109]

According to the records, this enormous stretch of beach was a known haulout location prior to 1927 and had been used regularly in the fall (with no more than 12,000 in any one year) during ice-free years of the 20th century, including 1937, 1960, 1960, 1964, 1975, 1980, 1985 and 1990.

According to the USGS database, local residents noticed the size of the haulouts increased during the 1990s and 2000s until an annual monitoring program began in 2009.[110] It appears that most years, walrus that spend the summer in the Chukchi Sea gather together at Cape Serdtse-Kamen late in the fall before starting their migration east and south into the Bering Sea.[111]

As a consequence, in recent years this area has been used by large numbers of walrus only from mid-October to early November, with estimates of about 100,000 or more counted there in 2009, 2010, 2011, 2015, and of course, 2017.

Over 100 deaths of mostly young calves and adult females have been recorded each year on this beach due to trampling during stampedes, which occur when the animals resting on the beach are frightened and flee suddenly towards the water. Some of these lethal stampedes have been caused by noisy crows or flocks of seagulls flying overhead but in many cases the cause could not be determined.[112]

Simply put, the literature showed that walrus are easily spooked at the best of times when they are on land and females with calves especially so – and if the animals are at the top of a cliff these stampedes can be even more deadly.

And as Lori Polasek had alluded to in Ed Yong's interview, falls from cliffs are nothing new – which Andrew Montford pointed out in his own critique of falling walrus sequence that was published in The Spectator magazine on 11 April.[113]

In the 1990s, male walrus at their summer haulouts in the southern Bering Sea at Cape Peirce in the Togiak National Wildlife Refuge in Bristol Bay were so numerous that some climbed to the top of a 200 foot cliff and fell to their deaths. An American TV news channel reported on this phenomenon in 1994, when 42 walrus died, and the New York Times reported 60 deaths in a single incident in 1996.

One US Fish and Wildlife Service scientist interviewed at the time suggested that the most likely explanation for these falling deaths at Cape Peirce was overcrowding – too many walrus! – although in reality this could only have been a contributing factor.

Ultimately, they really didn't know the cause and couldn't explain the phenomenon. Recall that these male walrus leave the sea ice by choice in the early spring to use these ice-free beach haulouts, so lack of sea ice cannot be blamed for some of them climbing cliffs and falling to their deaths.[114]

British blogger Paul Homewood looked at my critique and Montford's assessment and pointed out something both Andrew and I had missed: that the many aerial shots in the Netflix sequence must have been taken by a drone-mounted camera.[115] Of course!

Since even a bird flying overhead has been known to cause a walrus herd to stampede, there is no reason to expect that a drone buzzing around wouldn't elicit the same reaction, or at least cause the herd to be agitated so that some other very small disturbance would set them off.

In fact, for that very reason drones are prohibited in US National Refuge areas in Alaska and are actively discouraged near walrus haulouts on the American side of the Chukchi Sea.[116] I suspect Netflix would not have been permitted to film any of the very large walrus haulouts in the US using drones, which gave them all the more reason to go to Russia.

About a week after all this began, on 15 April, Montford made another confounding realisation: that the position of the Netflix film crew on the beach may have discouraged the walrus on the cliff at Cape Schmidt from coming back down the way they had gone up (as shown Chapter 4, Fig. 9).

He asked a critical question I hadn't thought of. Where was the camera? This is how he explained his reasoning: [117]

> If we now consider the geography of the site, it starts to get interesting. The walrus up on the cliffs could see, hear or smell other walrus in the water below them and on the rocks at the water's edge below.
>
> Obviously, they want to rejoin their fellows. But there is a problem.
>
> Northwards, there are only cliffs. To the west and south, there are beaches, but these are around 500 m away and it is more than likely that the polar bears were in that direction (why would they leave an area where there were so many dead walrus on which to feast?).
>
> Add in the fact that the camera crew was also flying drones over the cliffs, and you have a recipe for panic.
>
> But – and this is the crux of the matter – The best safe route back to the water would be to redescend to the water's edge...to the exactly the point where the camera crew seem to have been located.

It was clear from Basov's 2017 photo essay that the walrus knew how to get down to the beach safely: he included a shot showing them descending the gentle slope where the cliff meets the spit connecting the headland to the mainland.[118] They appear to be able to manage this as long as they don't go too fast.

It was near the bottom of this gently slope where the camera crew seemed to have set up for some of their shots. In one of her interviews, Lanfear commented that the crew cheered when they saw some of the walrus making their way down safely, but if they filmed that accomplishment it certainly wasn't shown in the 'Frozen Worlds' episode.

In other words, the camera crew – either due to their use of drones or their placement on the shore in order to get the best film shots of walrus at the edge of the cliff – may have exacerbated the agitation of the walrus that were perched near the top of the cliff, causing them to fall to their deaths.

What we had at this point was the following: the place was Cape Schmidt and the date of the filming was 19 September 2017; it looked like the Siberian Times incident involving the 20 polar bears had happened two or three days before – and that Kochnev and the entire Netflix film crew had been present for those three days.

Lanfear insisted that no polar bears were involved in the shots of falling walrus she filmed for the *Our Planet* episode, which amounted to only a half dozen that appeared in the documentary. That may have been true.

However, there were also hundreds of carcasses of dead walrus on the beach that were said to have died the same way (without polar bears being involved), which seemed utterly implausible.

There was circumstantial evidence that the film crew themselves may have been partly responsible for startling some of the walrus at the top of the cliff, setting in motion the falls that killed them.

Also, it was apparent from the scientific literature that large land haulouts in summer and fall, with walrus packed in closely together, are nothing new and neither are deaths by falls or stampedes – including stampedes initiated by polar bears.

The claim that lack of sea ice due to global warming was to blame for the deaths shown in *Our Planet* fell completely apart.

I wrote an opinion piece on the issue with Patrick Moore, one of the founders of Greenpeace, which appeared in the online magazine Townhall. Paul Homewood wrote one for The Conservative Woman and Andrew Montford's piece at Reason Magazine was published.[119] Even more mainstream and online media stories followed, including one in the American online aggregator commentary website, Twitchy, and the Washington Times.[120]

The story simply wasn't going away.

In my own 24 April op-ed in Canada's National Post, I pointed out that this incident seemed remarkably similar to the starving polar bear video that National Geographic famously claimed in late 2017 was 'what climate change looked like' only to be forced by public backlash to make a high-profile apology months later (see Chapter 8).[121]

On the surface, the walrus-falling-from-a-cliff movie sequence looked like the same ill-advised, overzealous activism that so often characterised the climate change movement.

I didn't know then how wrong I was. This was something altogether different.

# Chapter 6

# Pushback

Of course pushback was bound to come. But when it did, it came early and was surprisingly weak. As far as I can determine, only two direct responses to my critique came from the Netflix team.

One of the first stories about my blog post appeared in the Daily Mail (UK) on 8 April and it included a statement from producer/director Sophie Lanfear refuting my claim that polar bears were involved in the falling walrus incident [my emphasis]:[122]

> Sophie Lanfear, director of the Frozen Worlds series that features the Our Planet episode, defended the footage, saying two crew members watched the animals fall and claimed they were not being chased by polar bears.
>
> She said: 'We filmed Pacific walrus falling from high cliffs.
>
> *They were not being driven off the cliffs by the polar bears and we know this because we had two team members watching the cliffs from afar who could see the polar bears and were in radio communications with us to warn us about any bears approaching the crew closer to the walrus and the cliffs.*
>
> 'Once the walrus had rested at the top for a few days they wanted to return to sea when all the others below started to leave.
>
> 'We would watch them for hours teetering back and forth on the edge before finally, falling off.

'Fundamentally, the reason walrus used this haul out location is because of a lack of sea ice in the region, meaning they are coming ashore more frequently than they did in the past.

Note that Lanfear admitted that there were polar bears present, which was not revealed in the film (except for the one polar bear shown at the end, on the beach) or in any of her other interviews.

She only said that the half dozen walrus they filmed falling for the *Our Planet* sequence had not been 'chased' by any bears.

She also implied that the crew had been watching the walrus for 'a few days' (i.e., three or four), something she stated outright in her People magazine interview.[123] I had not noticed this before I began writing this all down but perhaps others did at the time.

Since we knew the falling walrus sequence presented in *Our Planet* was filmed on the 19th of September, this means Lanfear and her film crew had been watching the cliff since at least the 17th.

As discussed previously, we know from the photos posted online by Russian photographer Yevgeny Basov that there were already dead walrus on the beach on the 17th and that *Our Planet* science advisor Anatoly Kochnev was there on the 16th.

Now we know for sure the entire Netflix film crew was at Cape Schmidt from at least the 16th to the 19th.

This was a critical point because it suggested the event described by the Siberian Times involving 20 polar bears stalking walrus on the cliffs and 'hundreds' of them falling to their deaths happened while the Netflix crew was watching.

Bears were clearly still in the area on the 19th. Lanfear's admission that they had been watching for three or four days (while keeping an eye out for bears) meant this had been a drawn-out, multi-day event, which began on the 16th or 17th with polar bears stalking walrus on the cliff and ended with the herd leaving the haulout on the 19th, when perhaps a dozen or so walrus appeared to simply walk off the top of the cliff, which was when the Netflix footage was shot.

In other words, most of the walrus had died because polar bears had frightened them over the cliff – well before the falling walrus footage for *Our Planet* was filmed – and the entire camera crew knew this.

But by including shots in the documentary that panned the beach filled with hundreds of dead walrus and having Attenborough state that they had all died the same way, Lanfear and cameraman Jamie McPherson made it appear that hundreds had died on the 19th, when they knew it wasn't true. They then continued to insist the footage presented in *Our Planet* had not involved polar bears stalking walrus at the top of the cliff.

They both deliberately misrepresented what had actually happened to support their chosen narrative.

The only other 'statement' I could find that contradicted my suggestion that polar bears had probably been responsible for the hundreds of walrus carcasses on the beach was a Twitter exchange from 8 April 2019, in which Lanfear stated simply that 'the bears were not driving them off the cliffs'.

However, a brief article on 9 April from online entertainment news outlet TMZ about my blog criticisms stated, without any actual quotes from a specific person:[124]

> Netflix is standing firm behind what they say is a documented fact – that walruses are being forced to gather on land because there's less ice available...which leaves them in unfamiliar, dangerous territory.

> Additionally, Netflix tells us the *Our Planet* team worked with a seasoned Russian biologist who's worked on that stretch of coastline – and with those walruses – for 35 years.

A large number of other online entertainment outlets and even newspapers repeated this same statement over the following few days, including the 'Netflix told us' line.[125]

But even that statement wasn't actually true: as I've already pointed out, the walrus haulout at Cape Schmidt was not 'unfamiliar' territory: it was a traditional beach that had been used for decades, if not centuries.

And the walrus were not forced to gather in that particular spot during the ice-free season: there were many other less 'dangerous' beaches available (including several not far away on Wrangel Island) but they chose Cape Schmidt instead.

Lastly, the fact that the production team worked with a 'seasoned Russian biologist' familiar with the area is no guarantee of veracity, as I explain in Chapter 9.

Fatefully, this turned out to be the last response from Netflix. After Lanfear had responded directly to the allegations in the Daily Mail, it looked as if Netflix decided only to respond in general terms to the TMZ request for comment – and thereafter did not respond at all.

Throughout the entire media circus, David Attenborough didn't say a thing.

If anyone asked him what he thought of my criticisms, they never said. Neither of the producers at Silverback Films made a statement, nor did the WWF.

The only other condemnation of my comment about the *Our Planet* walrus sequence came from a predictable source. Bob Ward, a communications specialist, used his blog at the Grantham Institute in the London School of Economics on 10 April to complain that my criticisms were a 'daft conspiracy'.[126]

This was a common activity for Ward, who seems to spend an inordinate amount of time making formal complaints to the UK body that handles press disputes ('IPSO') every time he sees or reads something in the media that challenges any aspect of his interpretation of man-made climate change. He does this so often he makes quite a nuisance of himself.[127]

He claimed that my critique was a 'ridiculous climate-denying propaganda campaign' seeking to 'discredit Sir David'. Ward insisted that 'the public's trust lies with Attenborough, not the deniers'.

He went on to insist the program's explanation for the events were 'based on solid scientific evidence' and then pointed to references that Montford and I had also cited – as if we hadn't mentioned them.[128]

He stated categorically that even though there had been no scientific analysis on the behaviour of walrus along the Chukotka coast, it was 'indisputable' that the huge haulout of walrus shown in *Our Planet* had been 'due to the loss of Arctic sea ice that has resulted from climate change'.

In other words, someone who was not a biologist and had not examined the available scientific literature on walrus felt he was capable of accurately assessing the accuracy of the film.

Regarding my blog post in particular, Ward stated that I had never published any research on walrus, as if this meant that anything I had to say about them must be wrong.

I have never claimed to have studied walrus (or polar bears) in the field, but I am a professional zoologist with more than 40 years of pertinent experience. I have a PhD (which Ward does not) and more than a dozen peer-reviewed journal articles and book chapters on a range of topics, including Arctic ecology and evolution (see Appendix A). In 2014, I wrote and published a review of the literature on walrus haulouts.[129]

I make no apologies for using my knowledge of biology and the peer-reviewed scientific literature as the basis for writing scientific commentary: it is what I was trained to do.

While acknowledging my PhD and that I had 'published papers on the impact of prehistoric climate changes on animal species', Ward then stated that the only reference I had cited in support of my critique was the Siberian Times article – without acknowledging that I had linked to several previous fully-referenced walrus posts as well as my published walrus review paper and the US Fish and Wildlife assessment that concluded Pacific walrus were not being harmed by lack of summer sea ice. Links are meant to be consulted, not ignored.

Then he added what he obviously considered his most damning evidence:

> ... [Crockford] is fêted by climate change deniers for her outspoken views about the impact of current man-made global warming on polar bears.

Ah! Not only was I outspoken but some people found my arguments convincing.

Frankly, however, once anyone gets into the name-calling business, the childishness of the game becomes apparent. Ward's use of this 'denier' nonsense against me and others (and there is a lot of it in his piece) – and linking to a slanderous paper that does this even more – tells every reader that adult rational discourse and scientific rigor have been left behind.[130]

His entire tirade amounted to whining that my criticisms of Attenborough's film were getting too much attention.

Moreover, he was completely wrong in blaming all this attention on the GWPF ('the press release fooled journalists at The Daily Telegraph and the Mail Online'): the GWPF press release appeared on the 9th of April, the day after the two newspapers broke the story on the 8th.

Without those mainstream media stories, my critique would not have been seen by millions of people. I can see why Ward was annoyed, but his wrath was misplaced.

Oddly, however, Ward insisted that my claims had been 'conclusively disproven' by the statement provided by director/producer Sophie Lanfear to the Daily Mail – when in fact she denied only that polar bears had chased the particular walrus that she had filmed falling.

She provided no dates, no facts, no photographs: only her word.

Ward further insisted that the 'programme-makers' had treated my 'unfounded allegations with scorn' even though, aside from that one statement by Lanfear, 'the programme-makers' had in fact been extraordinarily reticent and non-specific.

They never denied that the filming had taken place at Cape Schmidt and Cape Serdtse-Kamen, as Montford and I had surmised, or that polar bears were in the area – or even that the footage had been shot on 19 September 2017.

They did not deny that they knew about the incident involving hundreds of walrus that died falling off the same cliff after being stalked by polar bears, as described in the Siberian Times. In fact, it seemed rather odd that their pushback was so feeble.

After Ward's tirade was published, a couple of other nameless commentators piled on, but no one was willing to admit to being the author.[131]

However, spring was turning into summer and other news items took precedence. In early August there was the usual handwringing in the US media about walrus haulouts in the Chukchi Sea, with lack of sea ice being blamed, but this had been happening every year since 2008.

The Netflix issue was firmly on the back burner, but not for long.

At the middle of August, the *Our Planet* documentary was nominated for an unprecedented ten Emmy television awards, including one specifically for the 'Frozen Worlds' episode in the 'Outstanding Documentary or Nonfiction Series'. Another nomination was for Attenborough for his 'Outstanding Narration', while the other categories were for cinematography and writing for other episodes, music composition, theme music, and sound mixing/editing.

At the time, I missed the news that one of these prestigious television awards might go to Lanfear and her team for their part in the falling walrus fiasco: I was recovering from hip replacement surgery that summer. However, I'm sure others took note.

Even to be nominated was an important coup for Attenborough and the entire production crew.[132]

Ultimately, 'Frozen Worlds' won and so did Attenborough: *Our Planet* had racked up two Emmy awards. Attenborough had previously won an Emmy (in 2018) for his narration of *Blue Planet II*.[133]

The *Our Planet* wins were perhaps not entirely surprising considering how unusually ambitious the project had been, how pressured the entertainment industry has been to take a stronger stance on climate change, and how positively the most influential media outlets (including the New York Times) had responded to the hard-hitting walrus sequence.[134]

Sophie Lanfear got to dress up and attend the Los Angeles awards ceremony in October and be treated like a movie star.

More importantly, the wins kept Attenborough in the limelight, and no doubt boosted Netflix subscriptions, Silverback Films business prospects, and WWF donations.[135]

In one of the many interviews he gave in the wake of the awards, producer Keith Scholey said a few words about the climate change issue that was the focus of the series:[136]

> We tried to get the balance right, but we took some risks.
>
> In natural-history filmmaking, the old rule was, 'Oh, you'd better have a happy ending'. But our 'Frozen Worlds' episode, about life on the poles, doesn't have a happy ending, because there isn't one there.
>
> *Our policy was to speak for wildlife, for the natural world, and to be honest with the audience.'*

Keep that last sentence in mind: 'Our policy was...to be honest with the audience.'

# Chapter 7

# Vindication

What happened next was so unexpected I could hardly believe it was true. I was gobsmacked. But this time, I saw it with my own eyes from the beginning.

On 4 November 2019, BBC Television aired its latest documentary series, produced and narrated by David Attenborough, called *Seven Worlds, One Planet* (hereafter, *Seven Worlds*).

In Episode 2 ('Asia'), it showed fat polar bears stalking hundreds of walrus at the top of the cliff at Cape Schmidt before falling to their deaths, with some of the same film footage shown in *Our Planet*.

This seemed to be precisely the event described by the Siberian Times in 2017, which the Netflix producer/director insisted had not happened while they were filming *Our Planet*.

I was in Europe on a lecture tour and thus had immediate access to the original BBC footage; I might have missed it if I'd been home in Canada.

Before I go any further, have a look at my annotated transcript of Attenborough's narration of the walrus scene in *Seven Worlds* ('Asia') to see what was actually said and shown:

> [Aerial shot of an enormous walrus herd hauled up on a long beach]
>
> This is one of the biggest gatherings of mammals to be found anywhere on Earth. These are Pacific walrus. For most of the year, they feed out of the Arctic Ocean, emerging to rest on the sea ice.

But now, climate change has melted the ice here, and the only place within reach of their feeding grounds where they can rest are a few beaches, such as this one. A hundred thousand of them, almost the entire world population are here. They are gigantic. A male can weigh over a ton and many die at the scrum.

On a beach 250 miles to the west, there's a further danger.

[Shot of a young walrus in the water as a polar bear surfaces within a few feet]

Polar bears! They too have been forced to spend more time ashore by the dwindling ice.

[Shot of two polar bears swimming].

And now they're very hungry.

[Ominous music and shot of bear catching a young walrus's rear flipper as it reaches the shore — but it turns and defends itself from the bear with its tusks]

But adult walrus are tough, well armed, and agile in water, and could fatally injure the bear.

[Shot of bear retreating]

He's failed.

[Aerial view of the top of a cliff]

The narrow beaches here are backed by cliffs and some walrus scramble up them, escaping the crowd. At the top, they are 80 metres above the beach. But this is not a place where a walrus should be. Nor are they the only ones to have found it.

[Shot of three polar bears behind the walrus herd at the top of the cliff]

The bears have got up here too.

[Ominous music as one of the bears approaches the group and gets very close]

The walrus' instinct is to find safety in the water. They can still smell the sea and they can hear it. Just the polar bear's presence is enough to spook the walrus.

[The first walrus falls, in slow motion]

Many walrus that climb the cliff never make it back to the ocean.

[Shot of dead walrus on the beach]

Even once the polar bears have moved on, the walrus need to return to the sea and some take the nearest way to do so.

[Shot of another walrus, already part way down the cliff, falling in slow motion: this is the same shot as the one showing the first walrus falling in Our Planet]

As one crashes on the rocks, those on the beach stampede and more lives are lost.

[Another shot of a walrus falling in slow motion – then walrus in the water – then a group shot of 6–8 or more falling together, all in slow motion so you see every bounce]

In the course of just a few days, over 200 walrus die.

[More shots of falling walrus]

[Shot of the narrow beach at the base of the cliff, where a polar bear picks its way over the rocks at the shoreline, within reach of a dozen or so live walrus – then another shot of two polar bears, a female and nearly-grown cub, on the less steep, less rocky slope, also within a few feet of twenty or thirty walrus]

Now the polar bear can feed on the carcasses.

[Polar bear walking away from a pile of carcasses]

These events only occur once every few years but as the world warms and the ice retreats still further, they may become more frequent.

Although this series was billed as a production of the BBC Natural History Unit, it is clear that Netflix walrus footage from the *Our Planet* series had been shared.

Mike Hale, reviewer at the New York Times, not only noticed this but said so [my emphasis]:[137]

> ...you might entertain a question or two as you watch *Seven Worlds, One Planet*, such as, do we really need this many nature documentaries?
>
> That thought might suggest itself most acutely during the fourth episode, set in Asia, when a sequence about walruses tumbling off a cliff on the Arctic coast is highly reminiscent of a much talked-about scene in last year's *Our Planet*.
>
> *Why does it seem so familiar?*
>
> *Because the two shows shared film from the same shoot, and some of the most dramatic images in the 'Seven Worlds' scene are the very same shots that were in* Our Planet.

Hale mentioned no other overlap of scenes that he noticed between the two series, which means the walrus segment was unique in that respect.

Joe Kasper at The Sun (UK), who had also seen a preview, also noticed the shared footage and obviously asked the BBC about it. He wrote [my emphasis]:[138]

> Sunday's episode of *Seven Worlds, One Planet* will show walruses falling down a cliff in Asia.
>
> But it is the same footage that shocked viewers of *Our Planet* on streaming giant Netflix in April.

It shows the mammals plummeting to their death in the Russian Arctic having been chased by polar bears.

They are seen gingerly moving towards the edge before falling and eventually landing at the foot of the cliff with other lifeless walruses.

The Beeb and Netflix versions, both narrated by Sir David, 93, blame global warming for melting ice caps that would have kept them safe.

Ahead of the BBC series' first episode, Sir David and the show's producers had boasted about 'new' footage.

*A BBC spokeswoman said: 'It was a shoot share, which isn't uncommon.*

'The BBC sequence reveals a different phenomenon of the natural world that has not been shown on TV before.

'It shows the presence of polar bears spooking the walrus and causing them to fall over the edge of the cliffs.

*'It is not uncommon to share filming shoots in natural history and there are only five shared shots out of a total of 60, which can hardly be described as the same footage.'*

No, it wasn't exactly the same footage. The polar bears stalking the walrus sequence was omitted from the Netflix *Our Planet* episode to make it appear there were no polar bears causing hundreds of walrus to fall to their deaths.

As I had surmised in the last chapter, Netflix producer and director Sophie Lanfear and her team were at Cape Schmidt for three or four days in the middle of September and shot the entire polar bear stalking/walrus falling to their deaths event – start to finish – and this was the proof.

The biggest difference between the two films is the presence of polar bears shown stalking walrus at the top of the cliff shown in one and missing in the other.

In addition, the walrus sequence was the last in the episode of *Our Planet* but the very first one in *Seven Worlds*.

In *Our Planet* – even though only a half a dozen walrus were actually shown falling – it was stated explicitly that the cause of hundreds of walrus deaths was the motivation to return to the sea: '…in their desperation to [return to the sea], hundreds fall from heights they should never have scaled'.

However, in *Seven Worlds* many more walrus were shown falling (several dozen) and it was apparent that hundreds died from falls due to the polar bears stalking them, as well as from stampedes at the beach haulout caused by bodies falling from above.

In addition, a time frame is given for the event in the BBC film that is not provided in the Netflix episode: 'in the course of just a few days, over 200 walrus die'.

In short, the BBC film looks like a video representation of the event described in the Siberian Times (which never mentioned that there was a film crew present) and the Netflix film looks like a snapshot taken at the very end of that event.

Predictably, the 'Asia' episode of *Seven Worlds* traumatised a whole new pool of viewers who were totally unprepared to see the walrus carnage.

But the backlash wasn't nearly as strong as it had been for the *Our Planet* sequence, probably because the presence of the polar bears made the event make sense. Predators stalk: prey panic and run. Seeing walrus falling off a cliff in that situation is disturbing but at least it's a logical consequence of events.

It's also understandable why the producers wanted to include the sequence in the series: it was a very dramatic piece of natural history involving two iconic species that had never been captured on film before, made possible only by the use of drone-mounted cameras.

Surprisingly however, most of the reviews of the series went through the walrus-falling-off-a-cliff story as if learning of the phenomenon for the first time.[139]

Only the two reviewers mentioned above admitted that this was the second time viewers had been through this falling walrus distress, except neither of them bothered to mention that the first time had been without polar bears, while the second time around had been all about the bears.

Most astonishing was the fact that even the two reviewers who noticed the overlap in film footage failed to bring up the previous controversy that was all over the news back in April. Neither of them acknowledged that this meant Attenborough had totally misrepresented the facts in *Our Planet* – or pointed out that statements made by 'Frozen Worlds' producer/director Sophie Lanfear in April had been just short of outright lies.

Lanfear had filmed the entire event and knew that polar bears were what had driven the vast majority of the walrus over the cliff even if a half dozen or so had indeed simply walked off the cliff-top a few days later as the herd left the haulout. Yet that's not what she told Chris Dyer and Cheyenne Macdonald at the Daily Mail back in April.

And come to think of it, where was Sarah Knapton over at the Daily Telegraph now that I had been vindicated, since she had been the first to publicise my claims and opened the gates to the controversy? Silent: neither she nor the newspaper that employed her said a thing.

Lots of people were willing to print allegations of misrepresenting the facts, but not the proof that dishonesty had actually happened.

One entertainment outlet in New Zealand did mention the earlier controversy, but failed to connect the dots.

Brittney Deguara not only brought up the overlap in walrus film sequences between *Our Planet* and *Seven Worlds*, but pointed out that issues had been raised about the role of polar bears in the falling walrus sequence presented in *Our Planet*. She provided links to the April coverage of the falling walrus controversy, but neglected to remark that the BBC footage provided incontrovertible evidence that polar bears had indeed provoked hundreds of walrus to fall to their deaths at this location.[140]

It took a bit more digging to discover how this whole mess came about.

There had to have been collaboration between the BBC and Netflix, and yet nothing of the kind was mentioned in the official BBC production credits, either in the website version or the credits that rolled at the end of the episode.[141]

While the BBC admitted to journalist Joe Kasper that there had been a 'shoot share', this information was missing from the film credits.

The history between Attenborough and the two former BBC producers from Silverback Films almost certainly made possible a deal between Netflix and the BBC regarding this walrus footage.

Here's how we know we can discard the possibility that BBC paid Netflix after-the-fact to use the Russian walrus footage.

Richard Evans, part of the BBC production team, was the person given credit for directing the walrus sequence for *Seven Worlds* and was clearly present in Russia for the filming.

So I went back and looked at the credits at the end of the *Our Planet* 'Frozen Worlds' episode, which I had not done before. Lo and behold, Richard Evans was also mentioned in the Netflix credits, under the catch-all 'thanks to' category – along with Russian scientific advisor Anatoly Kochnev.

Jamie McPherson was given primary credit for 'photography' for the Netflix episode, with credit for 'additional photography' given to Hector Skevington-Postles and Barrie Britton – all three of whom also showed up on the list of credits for the BBC production under 'Camera and sound'.[142]

In other words, the shared filming was arranged well ahead of time – perhaps years before. There had been no purchase of footage after the fact: what had been shared was camera crew. Both the BBC and Silverback Films had sent people to Russia for that 2017 shoot.

A few other tidbits of information came out of my examination of the *Our Planet* film credits, which I admit I had not thought to look at before writing this book.

Interestingly, Yevgeny Basov – the friend of Anatoly Kochnev who posted photos of the walrus at Cape Schmidt taken at the time of the Netflix filming – is listed on the film credits under 'field assistants'. This means Basov had an official attachment to the production, which may explain why there were no polar bears in the photos he posted in November 2017 – the presence of the bears was still a secret then.

In addition, under 'thanks to' in the film credits are the names of two communities: Ryrkaypiy and Enurmino. Ryrkaypiy is the village next to Cape Schmidt and Enurmino is the village nearest Cape Serdtse-Kamen.

That means Andrew Montford and I could have easily confirmed the locations of the walrus shoots by reading the film credits! Who would have thought?

However, this information was missing from the BBC list of credits, which strongly suggests the Netflix team took the lead on the walrus shoot and the BBC boys were allowed to come along for the ride.

Between the BBC and Netflix film credits and a BBC 'Behind the Scenes' feature called 'Walrus on the Edge',[143] we can confirm that there was a mixed crew of at least seven people involved in the walrus film expedition: Sophie Lanfear from Silverback Films, Patrick Evans from the BBC, Russians Anatoly Kochnev, and Maxim Tchakilev, and photographers Jamie McPherson from Silverback Films and Hector Skevington-Postles and Barrie Britton from the BBC. Yevgeny Basov was likely hired only for the Cape Schmidt shoot.

Note that the BBC behind the scenes walrus feature on their website confusingly lists Patrick Evans as the director of this episode, when elsewhere Emma Napper is listed as the producer and director. However, it is apparent from the biography provided for the film credits that Napper did not travel to Russia for the walrus shoot, but Evans did.

Therefore, although Evans is said to have 'directed' that particular part of the episode, he got no official credit except in the web feature – his name does not appear as a director on the credits that roll at the end of the film nor does it appear on the official webpage for the documentary, except in the list of the 'production team'. Napper produced and directed the overall 'Asia' episode, which means she had to have known about the shared filming deal well ahead of time.[144]

Finally, the BBC online walrus feature also made it clear that drones were an integral part of the walrus shoot at Cape Schmidt, as Paul Homewood had correctly surmised. The film could not have been shot without them: the aerial views showed the polar bears advancing on the walrus at the top of the headland, apparently without their notice.

Reportedly, *Seven Worlds* was broadcast, or set to be broadcast, in more than 235 territories around the world by the end of November 2019 and hit North American markets in January 2020.[145]

This was an extraordinarily fast distribution timetable for a BBC documentary, but the skids had no doubt been greased by the success of the Netflix series and the promotion of both films by Attenborough, who in 2020 won another Emmy for his narration of the 'Antarctica' episode of *Seven Worlds*.[146]

By November 2019, all the evidence suggested that this had been a well-planned and well-executed operation.

The question was why.

But before I get into that issue, I will take a slight diversion into a similar controversy that played out in public just after the walrus sequence was filmed in the fall of 2017: National Geographic's starving polar bear video.

# Chapter 8

# National Geographic's Starving Polar Bear

For some perspective on Attenborough's falling walrus deception, it's worth comparing it to another incident that was similarly horrifying, garnered similar levels of media attention, and also generated a controversy that exposed it as fraudulent.

In early December 2017, National Geographic promoted a now-infamous video of an emaciated and mangy-looking polar bear, close to death, stumbling around a tundra landscape devoid of snow and picking some kind of garbage out of a rusty oil barrel. The first caption plastered across the heartbreaking image of the starving bear said, 'This is what climate change looks like'.

To say the video went viral on the Internet is a bit of an understatement: within days after its release, it had garnered millions of views. By the end of December, only three weeks after its release, it was, by a large margin, the most shared climate change story of the entire year on social media and, according to National Geographic, by early August 2018 it had been viewed about 2.5 *billion* times.[147]

Paul Nicklen, who took the video, and Christina Mittermeier, who took the still photographs, were partners in an organisation called SeaLegacy, whose mission was to generate climate change propaganda: photographic footage that they could sell to other organisations eager to bolster the 'climate change emergency' message.

In August 2017, Nicklen went to the Somerset Island area in the central Canadian Arctic (Fig. 10) specifically looking for a starving polar bear or some other iconic 'climate change' image he could sell.[148]

He was, in effect, scouting for animal tragedy porn. He may or may not have received a tip from a local about the starving bear (no one has said), although it seems unlikely he just stumbled across this gold mine without any prior knowledge.

Regardless, when he came across the bear, in a near-death state at a remote abandoned fishing camp, he called his so-called 'SeaSwat' team – probably on a satellite phone – to come in with all the camera gear for a photo shoot.

Figure 10. Somerset Island (Nunavut) in the Central Canadian Arctic.

The fact that the organisation had a name for this on-demand field team (described quaintly as 'a deployable unit of storytellers') indicates this was a standard method of operation: Nicklen flew in to some remote location and walked, boated or flew around until he found something horrifying enough to use as the basis of a moving climate change story, and then the SeaSwat team hustled in on command with all the equipment, probably by chartered helicopter.

The fact that chartered planes, helicopters-on-demand, satellite phones, and all the camera gear that SeaLegacy needed in order to operate would not be possible without the fossil fuels blamed for climate change was obviously an irony lost on its owners.

More likely, they didn't really care: good animal tragedy porn photos – and especially video – are commodities in high demand. It was then possible (and likely still is) to make an obscene amount of money with a great shot. It's one of the ways to make money at the conservation game: Nicklen left his undergraduate studies in marine biology early to pursue this career.[149]

However, wildlife photography is an exceedingly competitive business and in order to succeed you need some kind of edge.

While SeaLegacy may legally be a non-profit organisation it is obviously not a shoe-string outfit: it must require large influxes of cash from selling product to do all that remote field work, purchase fancy photographic equipment, and be able to pay its owners and staff wages.

At any rate, Nicklen and Mittermeier got the footage they were after at that abandoned fishing camp.

Whatever the bear plucked out of the oil drum (shown briefly in the video and several of the still shots) was clearly attractive to the bear – although it's possible someone 'baited' it with a chunk of meat or blubber, there is no conclusive evidence they did – and it kept him interested enough to stay around the camp and keep moving for the cameras.

Mittermeier later claimed in an interview that this was a piece of burnt snowmobile seat, even though it looked surprisingly like an over-cooked joint of meat. That said, polar bears are indeed strongly attracted to vinyl because it's made from oil so Mittermeier could have been correct.[150]

Baited barrel or not, they got the shots. But before the team left to edit and market their photo-booty, they watched the emaciated bear slowly swim away from the little cove. As far as we know, no one ever saw it again.

The bear likely died a slow painful death somewhere nearby, luckily without attacking some innocent Inuit family out for a summer camping trip. Bears in this emaciated state are exceedingly dangerous because they are desperate for food and still strong enough to kill.

As evidence of this, in the summer of 2018, a bear in similar condition ambushed an armed guard on a remote island north of Svalbard in the Barents Sea and seriously wounded him before a companion was able to shoot it.[151]

According to his biography, Nicklen had spent several years of his childhood living on Baffin Island with his family, and had spent a lot of time in the Arctic as an adult, so he should have known this.

It is apparent the team took precautions to keep themselves safe while taking their photos, but they seem to have ignored the safety of local Inuit, who might have encountered the bear in the days before the SeaSwat team arrived or after the bear swam away – Nicklen and his team seem to have told no one about the bear.

Of course they didn't: that would have risked seeing their exclusive footage lose all its value. As was apparent with the Netflix falling walrus sequence, secrecy was critical.

It was also crucial to release this powerful tragedy porn at exactly the right time – and for Nicklen and Mittermeier, a few weeks before Christmas seemed like the moment to achieve maximum shock.

We don't know if Nicklen had made an exclusive deal with National Geographic prior to December, but regardless, the strategy he used worked.

He posted the short video on Instagram on December 5th, saying 'This is what starvation looks like', along with a sob story about predictions of doom for the species and a suggestion that perhaps every single polar bear in the global population would soon die in this manner.[152]

Social media ate it up: almost instantly, it got millions of views. Two days later, National Geographic had acquired the rights to the film and the photos. The fact that money changed hands over this deal wasn't stated explicitly, but anyone who thinks Nicklen simply gave them away is being naïve.

At the bottom of Nicklen's original Instagram post was this note: 'This video is exclusively managed by Caters News', and gave contact details to obtain licensing rights.

Perhaps National Geographic made a substantial donation to SeaLegacy or simply paid a hefty licence fee, which would have been perfectly legal for the non-profit organisation to receive.

We don't know who else may have been bidding for the video, but we do know that by early December 2017 the WWF had its own priceless tragedy porn 'in the can' (since their Russian expedition to film walrus for Netflix had returned home by 26 October), so they probably were not in the market.

National Geographic added captions to the video to make it their own, and posted it on their website on 7 December, accompanied by an essay written by Sarah Gibbens.[153]

Media outlets picked up the story as Mittermeier and Nicklen made themselves available for interviews.

The Daily Mail (UK), CBC News (Canada), Victoria Times-Colonist (because Nicklen once went to the University of Victoria in British Columbia, where I now live, and thus qualified as a 'local'), and the online site LiveScience all uncritically pushed the climate change narrative and predictions of polar bear catastrophe.

Only a few mentioned that some Instagram followers had been angry that Nicklen had not fed the bear or tried to save it (or even put it out of its misery). Most outlets repeated the original error in the National Geographic story that the bear had been found on Baffin Island (it soon emerged that it had been Somerset Island, which is further west).[154]

As soon as I became aware of the video, I wrote a scathing blog post ('One starving bear is not evidence of climate change despite gruesome photos'), published just after midnight on 9 December, in which I said:[155]

> This may be how you get gullible people to donate money to a cause, but it isn't science: there is no evidence that this starving bear was a 'victim' of sea-ice loss caused by global warming...

In August, this bear would have been only recently off the sea ice: since most bears are at their fattest at this time of year, something unusual had to have affected his ability to hunt or feed on the kills he made when other bears around him did not starve and die.

It could have been something as simple as being out-competed for food in the spring by older animals.

A few days later, several polar bear specialists said it was a male bear and that the lack of scars on its head and neck suggested it was relatively young: sexually mature adult males fight viciously during the mating season and almost always have visible scars from those battles.

It is possible the bear was sick or injured, and had been unable to hunt successfully during the spring, which is the critical period for bear survival because this is when prey is abundant.

But I pointed out that if sea ice loss due to man-made global warming had been the culprit, it would not have been the only one starving: the landscape would have been littered with dead and dying bears. The fact that this was the only starving bear Nicklen found was proof in itself that climate change was not to blame.

I also noted that back in 1974, when polar bears had in fact been dying in droves due to thick spring ice in the Southern Beaufort Sea, there had been no attempt to mobilise public assistance through conservation organisations or the media. At that time, not a single polar bear specialist thought to contact the media when they saw one dying bear after another.

I quoted a passage from a 1997 paper co-authored by polar bear biologists Ian Stirling and Nick Lunn in which they described that mortality event:

> ...in the spring of 1974, when ringed seal pups first became scarce, we capture two very thin lone adult female polar

bears that had nursed recently, from which we deduced they had already lost their litters.

A third emaciated female was accompanied by two cubs which were so thin that one could barely walk. We have not seen females with cubs in this condition in the Beaufort Sea, or elsewhere in the Arctic, before or since.

I concluded:

One starving bear is not scientific evidence that man-made global warming has already negatively affected polar bears, but it is evidence that some activists will use any ploy to advance their agenda and increase donations.

Similar to my judicious remarks over the Netflix falling walrus sequence, my blog post about the starving polar bear seemed to open the floodgates of criticism about the National Geographic video – but this time, it was even more pronounced.

This was surprising, because only the month before I had been publicly branded a 'climate change denier' in the mainstream media for my inconvenient views on the unexpectedly healthy state of polar bear populations, and journalists had been told in no uncertain terms that they should not listen to me.[156]

That negative publicity was the result of a paper (with 14 co-authors, only two of whom were polar bear biologists) in Bioscience, a scientific journal aimed primarily at high school biology teachers and students. It was called 'Internet blogs, polar bears, and climate-change denial by proxy.' In it, readers were encouraged to ignore anything I said on polar bears. Over the next few weeks, my reputation and scientific integrity were further disparaged by several of the paper's authors during media interviews.[157]

However, that didn't seem to matter when I spoke an obvious truth the following month: several mainstream media outlets quoted my blog comments and, all of a sudden, everyone was critical of the starving polar bear video. The truth resonated around the world.[158]

Once I said it, it became obvious to virtually everyone that there was no evidence whatsoever that the pitiful condition of the starving bear could be blamed on climate change.

The opening caption ('This is what climate change looks like') generated most of the flak for National Geographic, as well as some condemnation for using such graphic images as a marketing strategy in the first place. Nicklen and Mittermeier also took a good amount of criticism for their part in the scheme.

Even one of the co-authors of the BioScience 'climate change denial by proxy' paper agreed: Steven Amstrup, an outspoken employee of activist conservation organisation Polar Bears International and a former US Geological Survey lead scientist, stated in a web essay, 'we cannot say, from the footage captured here, that this bear's malnutrition was caused by global warming and its associated sea ice loss'.

He still insisted that polar bears faced certain catastrophe unless rising emissions of greenhouse gas were 'halted' and of course suggested that people should 'join us' (i.e. make a donation) to help the polar bears.[159]

However, Arctic biologist Jeff Higdon was more forceful in his criticisms.

He took to Twitter on the afternoon of 9 December to express his disapproval. He said he thought it possible that the bear had an aggressive form of cancer (which is known in bears).

He also suggested that not having an Inuit hunter with him (none was ever mentioned) was a huge mistake on Nicklen's part: firstly because any local hunter would almost certainly have shot the bear (which would have been the right thing to do), but also because not having an Inuit representative with him in the field was considered highly disrespectful.

Hiring a local guide is a requirement for non-resident hunters and is considered an important courtesy for other travellers. Not only does this provide much needed employment to cash-strapped Inuit residents but provides visitors a measure of security that comes from the guide's local knowledge.

Higdon concluded:[160]

> What the Sea Legacy crew should have done was contact the [Government of Nunavut] Conservation Officer in the nearest community and had this bear put down.

> And necropsied. The narrative of the story might have turned out quite different if they had.

However, Higdon was missing the point: Nicklen and Mittermeier could not have done any of those ethical things because changing the narrative would have cost them a sure shot at celebrity as well as a boat-load of money.

The narrative of the story as it played out was *exactly* what they had planned, and all available evidence suggests they were not prepared to let anything stand in their way. Fame and fortune appeared to be more important to them both than being decent human beings.

The New York Times came late to the story on 11 December, but took the approach of earlier outlets in emphasising climate change and the catastrophe that modellers predicted for polar bears, without mentioning any criticisms.

In addition, it appears Nicklen told the newspaper that he had taken a still photo of the bear as soon as he had seen it in August and immediately posted it on Instagram – and that he'd only decided to go back with his crew and all their photographic equipment two days later, after he'd seen the strong response from his followers.

It may be that the reporter misunderstood what was he was told. However, that version of events is quite at odds with Mittermeier's version of events (which I quote at length below), and as far as I am aware, there is no evidence of a photo of this bear posted on Instagram in August.[161]

Some of the criticisms in the media were even more emphatic than mine.

In a broad review of all the negative feedback written by Tristin Hopper for Canada's *National Post* near the end of December, biologist Marco Festa-Bianchet from the University of Sherbrooke was quoted as stating snidely via Twitter that 'arguing (climate change) is real because of a video of one sick bear is like claiming that it is a hoax because yesterday it snowed in southern Texas', and one Inuit representative called the video and photos a 'stunt' and a 'complete disservice to climate change science'.[162]

On CBC Radio in Canada, there was a heated back and forth on the topic (over a few days) after an interview with Mittermeier had aired.

Apparently, after being criticised by several Inuit residents, Mittermeier sent an email to the news outlet, stating:[163]

> Inuit people make a lot of money from polar bear trophy hunting.
>
> Of course it is in their best interest to say that polar bears are happy and healthy and that climate change is a joke, because otherwise their quota might be reduced.

In fact, no one had said climate change was a joke.

In addition, it was simply a fact that most polar bears were fat and healthy, and that population numbers had not declined, as other news outlets had pointed out.

This email only served to reveal that Mittermeier was rabidly anti-hunting and probably racist towards the Inuit because of that conviction, which didn't sit well with Inuit who depended on hunting for their day-to-day existence.

Margaret Redfern, who was then Mayor of Iqaluit (the capital of Nunavut) called Mittermeier's remark 'very racist and factually untrue' and insisted 'we are not climate deniers'.

Mittermeier later felt obliged to walk back her comments, saying she had never intended 'to speak against the Inuit or their traditions' and that 'my only purpose was to awaken the world to the effects of climate change.' Luckily for Mittermeier, this exchange didn't get reported widely.

Through all this, it became apparent that Nicklen was also in over his head when it came to facts about polar bears.

During some interviews, he just made stuff up. For example, he told one reporter:[164]

> Bears are designed to go as much as two months without ice, but they are not designed to go four or five months without ice.
>
> Well, this [the video] is what it actually looks like when polar bears are stranded on land.

This is totally untrue. It is a documented fact that polar bears in Western Hudson Bay, for example, have routinely gone at least four months without ice. Four months was normal in the 1980s but extended to almost five months for most years between 1998 and 2015. [165]

Moreover, pregnant Western Hudson Bay females traditionally spend at least eight months on land without food, a period that became closer to nine months in recent low-ice years: after mating, females come ashore fat from spring feeding, build a maternity den to give birth in December and nurse their cubs until they are about three months old, then emerge in March to resume feeding on the ice.

Only if they do not get fat enough the previous spring is this successful reproductive strategy disrupted — if, for example, they have bad luck hunting or if young seals are difficult to find, as happens in some years.

Furthermore, there is no evidence that Hudson Bay bears are unique in having a capacity to go four or five months without food: bears across the Arctic spend various amounts of time on land during the summer, a fact that has been documented in historical records and scientific reports.

Nicklen wasn't alone, however, in passing along misinformation.

Dr Donald Moore, the director of the Oregon Zoo and senior science adviser to the Smithsonian National Zoo (and supposedly an 'expert' on polar bears), claimed in an interview about the starving bear video that 'the population of about 25,000 polar bears in the wild has declined about 20 percent over the last decade or so'.[166]

Well, you could have searched the Internet high and low, but you'd never have found that statistic anywhere, or got such a statement from any polar bear biologist: it simply was not true.

Of course, anyone can make a mistake, but this happens far too often in similar contexts. The facts are these: in 2005, the IUCN had estimated the global population at 20–25,000 (with no average suggested), but by 2015 that number had changed to an average of 26,000 with a range of 22–31,000 and the trend over time was determined to be 'unknown' (i.e. *not* 'declining'). Population surveys since then would almost certainly put the average about 30,000, which is positively not evidence of a decline.[167]

But speaking of facts: what about the self-appointed media 'fact-checkers on the Internet? What did Climate Feedback for example, have to say about this starving polar bear falsely blamed on climate change?

Not surprisingly, they were exceedingly lenient.

As I mentioned earlier, their review of climate change stories of 2017 found the starving polar bear video was the most popular on social media by a wide margin, even though it came onto the scene only three weeks before the end of the year. But in addition to popularity, the fact-checkers also assessed the scientific credibility of these stories, and found that the top five articles were 'at least somewhat misleading'.

Filling #1 spot on the hit parade, the Sarah Gibbens article for National Geographic on the starving polar bear video received a disappointing '0.3' – 'Neutral: Accurate, Misleading' – on Climate Feedback's 'scientific credibility' scale of -2 to +2.[168]

The fact checkers asked Steven Amstrup from Polar Bears International, whose affiliation here was listed as 'Adjunct Professor, University of Wyoming Laramie', to comment [my emphasis]:

> This reveals what declining survival looks like for polar bears, a trend we will see increase as the world warms. But the article neglected to point out this bear's problems may or may not have had much to do with declining sea ice in the Baffin area – an error of omission that can become a target of global warming deniers.
>
> The important lesson from the observations shown is that ever-more polar bears will be suffering this kind of fate as we allow the world to continue to warm.
>
> Largely by omission, this article suggests we know what led to this bear's demise, and we don't. Starvation is the main cause of death among wild polar bears. After all, they have few natural predators.
>
> Starvation rates will increase (decreased survival rates) as sea ice continues to decline.
>
> But we must be careful in presenting an observation like this as the fingerprint of climate warming.
>
> *Without proper context, observations and stories like this can distract from the critical message we need to get out.*

So, the fact-checkers considered that saying climate change was to blame for the bear's emaciated condition – even when the consensus among experts was that there was absolutely no evidence that this was true – did not qualify as being 'inaccurate' but was only 'misleading'. No bias there!

However, Amstrup stated what many others would not say out loud: that the video's 'misleading' caption had sidetracked the critical message he and other activist scientists were trying to get across to the public. In other words, it was an own-goal.[169]

The video continued to circulate through the first six months of 2018, although the air had gone out of the story.

However, by late July it became apparent that the public criticisms aimed at National Geographic and Nicklen that had dominated the media in December were not the only messages of disapproval.

It seemed that National Geographic subscribers – and perhaps shareholders too – had expressed their displeasure directly, because an 'editors' note' in the August issue of the magazine stated bluntly:[170]

> *National Geographic* went too far in drawing a definitive connection between climate change and a particular starving polar bear in the opening caption of our video about the animal.
>
> We said, 'This is what climate change looks like.'
>
> While science has established that there is a strong connection between melting sea ice and polar bears dying off, there is no way to know for certain why this bear was on the verge of death.

They also changed the offending caption in the video posted on their website: from, 'This is what climate change looks like' to 'This is what a starving polar bear looks like' (however, the original is still available on Youtube).[171]

This apology was issued alongside an essay by Mittermeier detailing her account of what had happened and what she felt had gone wrong.

Here is an excerpt from Mittermeier's description of what she and Nicklen had done in that remote bit of the Canadian wilderness. In it, she perversely excused their part in the fiasco by claiming they had simply 'lost control of the narrative':[172]

> Photographer Paul Nicklen and I are on a mission to capture images that communicate the urgency of climate change. Documenting its effects on wildlife hasn't been easy. With

this image, we thought we had found a way to help people imagine what the future of climate change might look like.

We were, perhaps, naïve. The picture went viral – and people took it literally.

Paul spotted the polar bear a year ago on a scouting trip to an isolated cove on Somerset Island in the Canadian Arctic.

He immediately asked me to assemble our SeaLegacy SeaSwat team. SeaLegacy, the organization we founded in 2014, uses photography to spread the message of ocean conservation; the SeaSwat team is a deployable unit of storytellers who cover urgent issues.

The day after his call our team flew to an Inuit village on Resolute Bay. There was no certainty that we would find the bear again or that it would still be alive.

...Only when it lifted its head were we able to spot it lying on the ground, like an abandoned rug, nearly lifeless. From the shape of its body, it seemed to be a large male.

We needed to get closer; we boarded a Zodiac boat and motored to land. Strong winds covered our noise and smell. From the shelter of one of the empty buildings, we watched the bear.

He didn't move for almost an hour. When he finally stood up, I had to catch my breath. Paul had warned me about the polar bear's condition, but nothing could have prepared me for what I saw.

The bear's once white coat was molted and dirty. His once robust frame was skin and bones. Every step that he took was pained and slow.

We could tell he was sick or injured and that he was starving. We could see that he was probably in his last days.

I took photographs, and Paul recorded video.

When Paul posted the video on *Instagram*, he wrote, 'This is what starvation looks like.'

He pointed out that scientists suspect polar bears will be driven to extinction in the next century. He wondered whether the global population of 25,000 polar bears would die the way this bear was dying...

*National Geographic* picked up the video and added subtitles. It became the most viewed video on National Geographic's website – ever.

...The mission was a success, but there was a problem: We had lost control of the narrative.

The first line of the *National Geographic* video said, 'This is what climate change looks like' – with 'climate change' highlighted in the brand's distinctive yellow.

In retrospect, *National Geographic* went too far with the caption.

Perhaps we made a mistake not telling the full story – that we were looking for a picture that foretold the future.

We had sent a 'gut-wrenching' image out into the world.

We probably shouldn't have been surprised that people didn't pick up on the nuances we tried to send with it.

Yet we were shocked by the response.

Most of the media outlets that covered this remarkable reversal fixated on the apology and what a black-eye it was for National Geographic: they accepted Mittermeier's account that she and Nicklen had simply 'lost control of the narrative'.

Mark Hodge at The Sun (UK) passed off the blatant *National Geographic* falsehood as harmless by dubbing it a 'white lie'.[173] Others were less accommodating.[174]

I was aghast at the tone of the essay. She implied that being on a 'mission to capture images that communicate the urgency of climate change' relieved her and Nicklen of any other responsibilities.

She absurdly put the blame for the controversy that ensued after the release of the video on the public (because they had taken the images 'literally') rather than take any responsibility herself.

Her account also made it clear that Nicklen had made a conscious decision to put his own need for a valuable piece of video footage over the suffering of a defenceless animal.

Her final comment on the filming was this:

> After finding nothing of value in the fuel drums, the polar bear waddled into the water and swam away. Paul worried that he would waste energy and die, but the bear seemed to have an easier time in the water.
>
> He disappeared around a bend in the shoreline.
>
> We never saw him again, but we hope that our images of this dying bear moved the conversation about climate change to the forefront, where it must remain until we solve this planetary problem.
>
> Until then, when we come across a scene like this one, we will again share it with the world – and take pains to be sure that our intentions are clear and the narrative remains our own.

In a blog post on 26 July 2018, I wrote:[175]

> Not only did Nicklen and Mittermeier cold-bloodedly exploit a defenceless, suffering animal without a thought to ending its pain, they still think that what they did was noble and self-sacrificing (they were 'on a mission').

They apparently think that their advocacy for climate change relieved them of the responsibility of being humane.

They still don't understand that many people were as sickened by their lack of compassion as by the film footage itself. People were also angry that Nicklen and Mittermeier misrepresented the situation: by their own admission, they knew the bear was sick, yet peddled their images as climate change tragedy porn anyway.

Their response to the public backlash ('National Geographic went too far') is laughable.

They just don't get it: they did real damage to their cause by filming that dying bear.

And in an opinion piece published in Canada's *National Post* in late August, I concluded:[176]

Mittermeier claims the public should never have taken the video literally.

However, it's apparent people took it literally because it was presented as a simple message: Blame climate change for this bear's suffering.

Mittermeier and Nicklen still don't understand why their efforts backfired but it's simple.

They tried to dupe people with obvious lies and allowed an animal to suffer for days in order to satisfy their agenda.

Mittermeier says she'd do it again. Sadly, I believe her.

I wasn't the only one upset by Mittermeier's tone.

It turned out that Iqaluit Mayor Madeleine Redfern was still angry on behalf of Inuit and Mittermeier's explanation of events appeared to have made things worse.

In an interview later in August with Emily Blake at the CBC, she said that 'something' was still missing from Mittermeier's article – 'any mention of northerners or Inuit':[177]

> Clearly the green movement has a diversity problem and [the] conservation movement has a racism problem.'

> I understand the Arctic is important to global citizens but at the same time we need to ensure that Southern voices, or the 'white saviour complex' based on misinformation, are not the views that dominate national and international stories.

> The imbalances and hypocrisies are endless and those must be challenged.

# Chapter 9

# Insights into Motivation

The entire starving polar bear controversy played out in public from December 2017 through to September 2018, while Silverback Films continued filming for the *Our Planet* series, editing the fateful falling walrus sequence, and writing the script for Attenborough's narration.

In retrospect, it appears none of the public fury over the starving bear video had any impact on what the WWF, Netflix, or Attenborough had planned for their Russian walrus footage. It may even have spurred them on.

It was apparent to me and others that Attenborough must have known that the walrus claims made in the Netflix *Our Planet* film were false. The question was when.

If he wasn't in on the plan to split the Russian walrus footage from the beginning, he certainly should have noticed, when presented with the BBC script and film footage for *Seven Worlds*, that the narrative he had been provided for *Our Planet* – that the falls of hundreds of walrus were motivated by their desire to return to the sea – was inconsistent with the BBC version that attributed those hundreds of deaths to the stalking activities of polar bears.

The two series involved multiple hour-long episodes each (eight for one, seven for the other) and *Seven Worlds* aired only six months after *Our Planet*. Every one of these episodes required Attenborough's attention and time must have been tight.

Since the walrus scenes were the only ones common to both series, it seems likely he would have recorded the narrations for them one after the other. The discrepancies in the narratives would have been obvious.

It seems almost certain that he knew about the walrus deception, at the latest, in November 2018, when he was finalising his narration for the *Our Planet* sequence (which Anatoly Kochnev bragged that he had helped him with), and thus before *Our Planet* aired in April 2019 and before the special preview edition of the film was shown to WEF audiences in late January.

It's also possible (although I think it unlikely) that he was given some superficially plausible explanation for the discrepancy by the producers and naïvely accepted both versions as true. Since he hadn't travelled to Russia for the filming, he could only go on what he was told about the events that appeared on-screen.

However, all of the others involved cannot be let off the hook so easily: they all knew years earlier.

Director Sophie Lanfear knew the claim that the hundreds of deaths at Cape Schmidt had been due to walrus simply walking off the cliff were false, because she had filmed the polar bear stalking action from start to finish.

Her public statements that polar bears were not involved in the falling walrus event were more than 'misleading'. Photographer Jamie McPherson and science advisor Anatoly Kochnev also went along with this false narrative in the making of their 'Digital Exclusive' and 'Behind the Scenes' videos, even though they had both watched polar bears stalk the walrus several days before until hundreds had fallen to their deaths.

Why the subterfuge when they all knew the truth would come out within months? As soon as the BBC series was released, their deception would be exposed.

Why didn't they care? It seems they rightly determined that the shock value of presenting the last few hours of the Cape Schmidt polar bear stalking event, taken entirely out of context, would be worth any small embarrassment that might ensue when the truth came out – if anyone even noticed.

They got their Emmy for the 'Frozen Worlds' episode (and for Attenborough's narration) before the damning BBC polar bear footage was released, which must have been a happy surprise.

They seem to have been fairly well prepared for the backlash from the public over the raw brutality of the scenes, but not for the immediate accusations that polar bears had been involved. They almost certainly hadn't expected someone like me to challenge their implausible story so early and so strongly – or that the media would give my counter-narrative legs.

In the end, while the embarrassment was more than they expected, they all appeared to have simply ignored it and moved on. Certainly, no one had felt it necessary to apologise, as National Geographic had done.

However, presuming that Attenborough had indeed known about the plan as late as November 2018, why had he taken that risk?

An off-hand remark he made early in 2018 about a possible new documentary deal with Netflix takes on new meaning in the context of the dishonesty that was involved in putting together the 'Frozen Worlds' walrus scene (my emphasis):[178]

> Netflix want me to do something on conservation and have asked me to do it, and I've said I would.
>
> *There's certain things that the BBC can do and can't do, and I can see some reasons why to do a programme on Netflix rather than the BBC.*

Although Attenborough had been making bold statements about climate change and over-population since 2004 (see Chapter 1), by late 2018 it looked as if he considered climate change a legacy issue: that after he died, he wanted to be remembered for motivating people to implement policies on climate change.

I'll get back to that shortly, but before I do it's also pertinent to ask about the other people involved in this deception. Are there any clues as to *their* motivation? We can't know for certain what was in their minds, of course, but we can make some reasonable guesses based on history, actions, and public statements.

WWF has been all about tragedy porn for years as a way to increase donations. They have used distressing images of polar bears (a polar bear falling through thin ice, a bear alone on a small ice floe, a thin bear) in TV ads, email messages, and website donation campaigns.[179]

It also appeared they were aiming to make the walrus their next distressed climate change victim. For example, the WWF magazine article authored by *Our Planet* science advisor Anatoly Kochnev in 2017 was part of an entire issue devoted to the plight of the walrus, called 'Walruses: Going with the Floes?'.

In 2015, they also posted online a video of a walrus calf falling off a rocky point that was one of many examples of their promotion of walrus as victims of climate change.[180]

WWF has never forgotten its primary mandate as a money-making enterprise: just because there is a 'cause' involved does not negate the fact that virtually everything they do is first and foremost about making money for the organisation.

It seems virtually certain to me that WWF suggested the falling walrus footage in the first place, and entirely possible they were the ones to initiate the Netflix/WWF *Our Planet* collaboration.

They would have been aware of the previous polar-bears-stalking-walrus-off-the-cliff events at Cape Schmidt in 2011 and 2015 (described in Chapter 3), and they would have been in no doubt that exclusive high-definition film footage of such events would be dynamite for their climate change campaign: they just needed the right partners to make it happen.

They likely approached Silverback Films first and then formulated a joint approached to Netflix with a concept for the *Our Planet* project.

The project was not a simple one, but they had loyal people on the ground there to facilitate it: they had for years been paying Anatoly Kochnev and numerous 'polar bear guards' in the two communities nearest the walrus haulouts of interest.

These contacts could also help with the logistics of getting the film crew in place.

Travel to the Russian Arctic is horrendous at the best of times because of political and geographical issues, which explains why western filmmakers rarely gain access.

But it has also true that the Russian Far East is less tightly controlled and less well-serviced by the Russian government than the Western Arctic: being a long way away from the centres of political control is likely how the WWF got such a strong foothold in Chukotka to begin with.

Silverback Films appeared to have been eager collaborators. Producers Keith Scholey and Alastair Fothergill have stated outright that they were eager to 'make a difference' in the climate change industry. Here is what Keith Scholey said about their thoughts in planning the *Our Planet* series:[181]

> We wanted to make a difference.
>
> We, and especially Alastair, have made some of the biggest landmarks in natural-history filmmaking, but we looked at each other and said, 'Yeah, the audience really loved them, but have we changed things? Have we changed the mood toward conservation?'
>
> So we set out to try and do that, to communicate to the audience that the world is in difficulty.'

What about the minor players in this drama?

For example, Sophie Lanfear: the 'Frozen Worlds' episode director and producer. As mentioned in Chapter 5, it is apparent that the Netflix/WWF crew was in charge of the walrus filming expedition, while the BBC crew went along for the ride.

Statements that Lanfear made to journalists after the release provide considerable insight into what went on behind the scenes and when the planning for the walrus shoot had begun.

For example, in an interview with Megan McLachlan at Awards Daily in September 2019, after being nominated for an Emmy for directing and producing the 'Frozen Worlds' episode, Sophie Lanfear revealed that this had been her first producing job, that no one else wanted the 'Frozen Worlds' episode, and that she was the youngest producer on the project.

She told McLachlan that as producer, it was her job to 'decide the narrative'. However, it seemed to me from these and other comments, described in more detail below, that the most important part of the 'Frozen Worlds' story – the walrus sequence – had been carefully laid out for her in the planning stages of the episode and that part of her job was to pretend, after the fact, that no polar bears had been involved in the walrus deaths.[182]

In April, she also told PBS television journalist Christiane Amanpour that having David Attenborough do the narration for the film gave it a 'stamp of authority':[183]

> I think David, I mean like no one else in the industry he's a trusted voice with no agenda actually, and I think that's what makes him more powerful – and his genuine passion...

> So, having him kind of voice the series is a stamp of authority on it, it's great.

Given what we know she and her colleagues planned to pull off, this would have been crucial.

In the same PBS interview, she went on to tell Amanpour that she'd expected to film walrus falling 'down some shallow verges' and polar bears interacting with walrus:

> We went to that location expecting to maybe film a bit of tumbling down some shallow verges and maybe some polar bears interacting.

> I never – I mean, I was totally shocked.

> I didn't realize they could climb 80 metre cliffs, and then we watched them many hours on the top and we're just pretty shell-shocked when we saw the first ones deciding to back to the sea and walking off.

However, in her interview with Megan McLachlan at Awards Daily in September, she described this rather differently.

She didn't say how she came to know about Russian scientific advisor Anatoly Kochnev, but from her description of the time it took to set up the walrus shoot (which was done, if you recall, in late September 2017), she must have been given his name – and the assignment – virtually the minute she got the job.

Two and a half years from September 2017 takes us back to March 2015 – a month before the *Our Planet* series was announced to the public (see Chapter 1).

In this interview, she went on to claim that Kochnev had told her about walrus falling off a high cliff but hadn't mentioned that this had caused any deaths (and apparently, she had believed this)[my emphasis]:[184]

> We went to film at these mass haul-out events that had been happening more and more regularly and getting bigger and bigger, as the climate warmed and the ice disappeared.
>
> *It took two and a half years to set that shoot up.*
>
> And I'd been talking with Russian biologist Anatoly Kochnev, who studied the walruses for 36 years.
>
> *He hadn't really described it to us. He'd seen it happen, animals falling off of high cliffs, but he hadn't described what went on there.*
>
> I just thought maybe it was tumbling down and they'd get to the bottom and survive.
>
> Then when we got there, and we saw the height of the cliff, and what they did to get up there – that was a shock – and then watching what happens.

Finally, in an interview with Jennifer Vineyard at the New York Times in April, Lanfear was quoted as saying that she had seen 'old news footage' of walrus falling down a cliff and that she was hoping to be able to catch something like that on film:[185]

The walrus scenes were the hardest things I've ever had to witness or film in my career.

When I was planning the story, I knew about the mega haul-outs happening in the region, and we chose the Russian site because it was the largest aggregation in the world, bigger than the ones happening in Alaska and Canada.

But there was a bit lost in translation with Anatoly Kochnev, the Russian scientist studying these sites.

There's an old piece of news footage that I had in mind, and it was kind of like sausage rolls falling down.

I was expecting that perhaps the walruses would tumble down, but at the end, they'd be OK.

I really wasn't prepared for the scale of death.

When Lanfear said, 'There's an old piece of news footage that I had in mind', she was likely referring to the 1996 news footage from Cape Peirce that I mentioned in Chapter 3, and which has been available on the Internet since at least 2013 (Andrew Montford and I had found it too).[186]

But dozens of walrus died in those falls, so was she simply lying when she said she expected no serious injuries, or was she really that naïve?

Helpfully, the Times linked her phrase 'like sausage rolls falling down' to the video posted by the WWF in 2015 mentioned above, where a young walrus calf climbs up a steep rock outcrop – perhaps 3 metres high – to reach its mother and falls unharmed into the water in the process.

The footage is amusing rather than disturbing and could hardly be described as 'an old piece of news footage'. Ironically, what it does show is how good even a walrus less than a year old is at climbing and how comfortable the calf's one-ton mother and several older youngsters seem to be resting on the top of the rocky point.[187]

Lanfear's role in this project was critical to its success and her comments tell us a lot about her motivation for being involved and then doing the job expected of her to the very end. Ironically, they also provide some insight into why she was chosen for such a pivotal role in the first place.

Sophie was young, inexperienced, and female; she may consequently have been seen as even more eager to please and therefore more easily manipulated (or bullied, if need be) by the powerful men orchestrating this plan, compared to any young male director they might otherwise have chosen.

That may seem unnecessarily cynical – and it's certainly speculative – but I believe it needs to be stated outright that the men in charge of creating this film (producers Scholey and Fothergill from Silverback Films, executive director Colin Butfield from WWF, and 'new product development director' Paul Harvey, also from WWF)[188] had a specific agenda with regard to the walrus sequence and were likely to have been looking for a director who wouldn't push back at the deception they were planning.

It seems to me highly likely they deliberately selected an inexperienced and idealistic young woman for the job. And because Sophie had so much to prove it's highly likely she was willing to go along with just about anything her bosses demanded. Most women in her position, given the circumstances, would probably have done the same.

Although she was in theory responsible for creating the story the film told, her statements and other evidence suggest the walrus sequence was a predetermined part of the series and perhaps long before she got the job, all arranged by the WWF (including setting Kochnev up as scientific advisor).

Still, it also sounds as if Lanfear knew full well to expect polar bears driving walrus over the edge of the cliff at Cape Schmidt and that she was likely to get dramatic footage of walrus falling to their deaths.

Her disingenuous comments aside about being ill-prepared, surprised, and horrified (perhaps all part of the necessary theatre), why else would she have been sent to Cape Schmidt with part of her crew supplied by the BBC?

As mentioned above, a very similar event involving polar bears and walrus had occurred in 2011: WWF may even have had video footage of that event that has never been released and which they used to secure the *Our Planet* deal.

What about the other minor player, Russian scientific advisor Anatoly Kochnev? Who was he, and how did he end up playing such a prominent role in the production of this film?

He appears to be in his late 60s (about the same age as me) and has a PhD and a long-standing interest in walrus. He is affiliated with the Russian Academy of Sciences, and has in the past been affiliated with the Russia Beringia National Park and the Wrangel Island Nature Reserve.[189]

He had been paid to monitor the walrus haulout at Cape Serdtse-Kamen since 2009, with funding provided by the WWF in 2015 (and perhaps other years as well), and had also been involved in monitoring the haulout at Cape Schmidt (at least in 2009–2011) and therefore knew about polar bears hunting walrus at the cliff.[190]

That means he had a strong and perhaps long-standing financial tie to the WWF well before this project began. It's not hard to see why the WWF would choose to bring him on board the Netflix project: he knew the Cape Schmidt and Cape Serdtse-Kamen haulouts well, and had good reason to be loyal to the WWF.

In addition, his early reports about walrus suggest he had long believed that anything more than a few weeks of open water in summer were very detrimental for walrus, perhaps because his limited access to the English scientific literature — his English was poor and he would have required a translator to interact with the Netflix film crew — meant he may have been unaware of the known propensity of the species — both Atlantic and Pacific forms — to seek out land haulouts even when there is nearby ice available.[191]

In other words, he was fully on-board with the WWF climate change narrative and believed that lack of sea ice was a huge problem for Pacific walrus.

I got the impression from reading English translations of some of his papers that he sometimes conflates facts with personal opinion and has a tendency to be sloppy with scientific details.

For example, in early 2017, in an article in the magazine of the WWF Arctic program,[192] he included a photo of an emaciated female walrus, claiming she was 'exhausted' and that 'many of the animals are in poor physical condition'.

However, one can always find a few animals in poor condition among tens of thousands – they might be ill, injured, or very old – but the scientific record for walrus simply does not support his conclusion that many walrus were starving at that time. Neither do the other photos he provides, which are all of healthy animals.[193] I have not seen any other published photos of emaciated walrus taken in the last few decades.

Secondly, he also stated that a population estimate of 275-386,000 in the early 1980s was 'optimal' but these are numbers I have not seen cited anywhere. He then stated that an estimate of 201,000-296,000 in 1990 therefore represented a 25% decline in walrus numbers over ten years. However, the only estimate I have seen for 1990 was 201,039 and that was considered unreliable.[194]

Walrus are usually counted by aerial survey, but this poses problems because in summer or fall when these counts are undertaken, walrus have a very wide distribution and move around often: there will be walrus on land, in the sea, and on sea ice all at the same time over a wide geographic area – and in addition, large numbers may move suddenly without warning. These and other factors make the walrus one of the most difficult animals to count.

For example, the North Atlantic Marine Mammal Commission Report on Atlantic walrus of 2016 (updated in 2021) added that the tendency of animals to pile on top of each other at haulouts makes it hard to see every individual, even if you are counting them in a photograph. Large numbers of animals in the water are similarly difficult to count, especially if they are close together and actively diving and swimming.

As a consequence, officials determined that all recent counts of Atlantic walrus were probably an underestimate of the true population abundance.[195]

Kochnev mentioned nothing in his WWF magazine article of these known problems with counting walrus in Russia, including the fact that efforts by both the US and Russia to survey walrus populations every five years were suspended after 1990 because biologists acknowledged they were producing estimates that were essentially useless.[196]

In his article, Kochnev also quoted a figure from a 2006 survey that was known at the time to be a gross underestimate because bad weather had prevented much of the walrus habitat from being surveyed. However, he simply omitted this critical information and stated categorically that the estimate of 129,000 in 2006 represented a further serious decline (something no other biologist has suggested) which he blamed on climate change.[197]

These missing caveats to the established science reveal his inability to be honest in his walrus assessments. He comes across more as an activist than a serious scientist, although there is no doubt he is dedicated.

That said, some important details about life on Russian walrus haulouts are discernible from some of Kochnev's publications. Most of these are conference paper reports on his walrus monitoring activities in Chukotka (at least one of which was paid for by the WWF) that have been translated into English.

For example, in several he mentioned how often birds (seagulls and crows in particular) precipitated walrus stampedes.[198] In one paper, he mentioned harassment of the walrus herds by local dogs (both domestic and feral) in the 1990s at several locations, including Vankarem and Cape Serdtse-Kamen, which seems to have been dealt with by shooting the loose dogs.[199]

Yet another issue he has addressed is subsistence hunting and the potential toll this takes on the population: both by initiating stampedes and the actually killing. In one account, he described how, in late October 2013, village hunters from Enurmino surrounded about 20,000 walrus on the Cape Serdtse-Kamen haulout and killed and butchered about half of them. About a week later, he said hunters from the village of Neshkan, 100 kilometers further west, rounded up another 10,000 walrus at the same haulout and apparently killed them all.[200]

It appears the hunters try to time their killing to a period just before the herds leave for the winter, when they are hauled out in the greatest numbers – usually late October/early November in recent years.

Obviously, it is in the hunters' best interests to preserve the species for the future and not to scare the beasts off too early in the season in case they fail to return – or to kill too many. But it is also true that while they probably only kill what they can use, only in this one instance was it revealed how many animals were slaughtered by local hunters.

While it is entirely possible the numbers provided are exaggerations or mistakes made on the part of the translator, it is also barely conceivable that 20,000 or more walrus are taken every year by hunters at various locations across Chukotka. In a haulout situation, very large numbers of animals can be killed relatively quickly and easily – that's how the species ended up threatened with extinction in the first place.

My point in raising this issue is not to condemn the aboriginal hunts, but to point out that if the numbers provided in these accounts are anywhere close to being true, Kochnev and his WWF colleagues repeatedly express concern about the several hundred to a few thousand walrus that die every year due to trampling and falls from cliffs, but say nothing about the legal hunting activities in Russia that result in much higher mortalities.

The important point is that neither cause of mortality seems to be having a negative effect on the walrus population, which is one of the reasons why the US Fish and Wildlife Service decided not to list them as 'threatened' in 2017.

On a lighter note, an amusing point in this investigation was the discovery that the Netflix crew got more than scientific advice from Anatoly Kochnev: they got some photography tips as well.

In 2014, Kochnev won a prize for a photo he took in 2009 at the walrus haulout at Cape Serdtse-Kamen.[201] The photo is taken from the inside of a dilapidated, earthen-floor shed without a door, which is attached to the side of a small cabin.[202]

In the photo, Kochnev stands very nonchalantly to the left of the open doorway of the shed gazing out – while a curious young walrus with small tusks looks in at him over the back of another sleeping beast sprawled end-to-end across the opening. A dented old rusted oil drum has been pushed to the right side of the opening across from Kochnev and dozens of walrus can be seen behind the young animal gazing in and even more beyond that, swimming in the water.

Here is Kochnev's official description of the photo event: [203]

> In October 2009, 90,000 walruses hauled out to relax on the Keniskin Bay beach near Cape Serdtse-Kamen in the Chukchi Sea.
>
> They closely surrounded my field cabin, and during several days I lived in a 'walrus siege'.
>
> The roar of the walruses did not allow me to sleep, and I was afraid that my cabin would fall apart, and I would be flattened by their giant bodies.
>
> This image is dedicated to the memory of Alexey Nutewgi the Chukchi hunter who helped me create this image.

The BBC team members who came to Russia for the *Seven Worlds* episode used the same cabin, with the door-less shed attached, as their base in 2017.

The 'behind the scenes' BBC feature 'Walrus on the Edge', included a detailed description of the experience by crew member Patrick Evans:[204]

> I woke up one morning and went to open the door. Right at my feet was a giant walrus. Behind it there were dozens more. Beyond them, tens of thousands.
>
> Our crew of seven were literally walled in to our hut, which was not much bigger than a garden shed.
>
> Attached to the side of our hut was a small wooden lean-to, through which the snow would blow, which served as an indoor toilet.
>
> But sometimes the walrus even found their way into there. Going to the loo was a bit of a challenge, to put it mildly.

In the media blitz that ensued after *Our Planet* was released, it amused me to see that Netflix photographer Jamie McPherson had recreated Kochnev's photo almost exactly during their trip to the Cape Serdtse-Kamen haulout in 2017 – except he took risks that Kochnev shied away from.

For example, McPherson positioned the same rusty oil drum across the open doorway of the shed and put director Sophie Lanfear behind it looking out towards the sea.

An adult female with full-grown tusks that came to investigate stuck her head into the doorway, with nothing but the oil drum stopping her from coming further inside.

The photo is taken from the side, and across the oil drum the two faces in profile are only about 12 inches apart – with Sophie trying rather unsuccessfully to look as nonchalant as Kochnev did in his photo.

It is, without a doubt, a compelling image. But what if the stunt had gone awry? What would Sophie have done if the one-ton animal had pushed forward and entered the cabin? It wasn't even a necessary part of making the documentary: it was all for the promotion.

These are the kinds of chances such filmmakers take as a matter of course to get the impressive shots they know will sell. People Magazine bought the photo and published it on 9 April 2019 in their story about the uproar over the Netflix walrus sequence.[205]

I also discovered that in 2018 – after the filming took place but before the Netflix film was released – Kochnev had written an online report describing in detail polar bears stalking walrus at Cape Schmidt in September 2017 until they fell off the cliff and died, without ever mentioning the film crew that was there.[206]

In conclusion, the roles these major and minor players had in pulling off the walrus deception weren't insignificant (since the plan could not have proceeded without them) but understanding their motivation for being involved is relatively straightforward.

Determining Attenborough's motive, of course, is another story and requires some speculation. However, because actions almost always speak louder than words, I felt I could roughly deduce from events leading up to the release of the *Our Planet* falling walrus episode – and from what happened afterwards – where Attenborough's mind was at.

And I have to say that what I discovered was unsettling.

# Chapter 10

# The Radicalisation of Attenborough

Convincing people that a climate emergency exists – and that revolutionary changes are necessary to address that emergency – is a huge undertaking when nothing in their lives has visibly changed.[207]

However, over the last decade or so, Sir David Attenborough has taken on this enormous challenge with increasing enthusiasm.

As ecologist and former Greenpeace founder Patrick Moore has pointed out, the concept of a climate emergency primarily involves a series of claimed catastrophic events that are literally invisible (like carbon dioxide – the $CO_2$ gas molecule – and ocean acidification) or so remote for the vast majority of people that they are essentially invisible (like polar bears and coral reefs).

These 'invisible catastrophes' are impossible for people to verify, which leaves them at the mercy of high-profile experts: they must either believe everything they are told by the loudest voices or seek out the facts themselves and the opinions of lower-profile experts.

For example, people outside the Arctic cannot see polar bears starving to death, or not, due to lack of sea ice and people who are not SCUBA divers living in eastern Australia cannot confirm for themselves that the Great Barrier Reef is dying, or not.[208]

In order to keep these invisible catastrophes alive as talking points, climate activists need to continually keep these issues in the public eye and in that regard Attenborough has been an ally for almost two decades.

Since his moment of enlightenment in 2004 (see Chapter 1), Sir David has used his position of influence to frighten viewers (and especially children) by showing alleged animal victims of climate change.

There is a strong Arctic component to this terrorisation, which began for many youngsters in 2006 with Attenborough's two-part BBC documentary *Are We Changing Planet Earth?* and Can *We Save Planet Earth?* (released as *The Truth About Climate Change* outside the UK) that included a sequence that misleadingly claimed polar bears were already dying because of climate change – and continued up to 2019, with walrus falling to their deaths.

Over the years since 2006, many kids have gotten their climate change information from watching Attenborough documentaries at home and in school because these films have been considered trusted sources of information. However, on the topic of so-called Arctic victims of climate change, that trust has been betrayed.

Through Attenborough's productions, children and young adults worldwide have been presented with such emotionally-charged and deceptive or misleading information about the Arctic that many have lost hope for the future.[209]

These despondent kids, as well as their parents and teachers, need reminding that while summer sea ice has indeed declined markedly over the last few decades, polar bears, walrus, and other Arctic species are thriving.[210]

In early 2020, I produced a video that highlighted the most egregious Attenborough Arctic moments and provided a list of verifiable facts (with references) in a standalone file. As I pointed out in a press release issued by the GWPF:[211]

> It is the responsibility of teachers and parents to reassure these worried youngsters that polar bears and walrus are not suffering because of sea-ice loss blamed on climate change.
>
> Children need to be told the truth: that whatever scary stories some biologists come up with about what might

happen in the future, Arctic species have demonstrated that they are much more resilient to changes in sea ice than Attenborough's films suggest.

Below is my timeline of these Attenborough misrepresentations of facts used to scare children about climate change, which culminated in the infamous falling walrus sequences in *Our Planet* and *Seven Worlds*.

In Part 1 of a BBC TV special released in 2006, *The Truth About Climate Change*, Canadian polar bear researcher Nick Lunn appeared on-screen and suggested misleadingly that bears were being harmed by lack of sea ice in Western Hudson Bay.

He told broadcaster David Attenborough that females had been starving and their cubs dying because of reduced summer sea ice, in spite of documented evidence that a similar phenomenon happened in the 1980s and early 1990s – before ice loss was an issue. The show was later made available to teachers throughout Europe on DVD, which many school libraries probably purchased.

As I explained in my book, 'The Polar Bear Catastrophe That Never Happened', the only way that Lunn got away with this sleight-of-hand was by deliberately excluding data collected in the 1960s and '70s.

Those figures are available in the published scientific literature, and show that bear weights and cub survival rates fell inexplicably in the 1980s and early '90s compared to the 1960s and '70s (when weights of bears and cub survival were very high).[212]

In 1992, biologists Andrew Derocher and Ian Stirling suggested that polar bear numbers in Western Hudson Bay may have exceeded the ability of the habitat to support them – that there were simply not enough seals to eat because there were too many bears feeding on them.

They couldn't be absolutely sure about this because they didn't know what conditions had been like for the bears during the spring, which, as I discussed in Chapter 8, is the main feeding period and is therefore critical for bear survival. Deep snow over the ice in spring, for example, can limit the access of polar bears to the young ringed seals they usually consume because the bears are unable to find the snow cave birthing lairs that pregnant adults construct for their young.

As research efforts continued, results showed the weights of female bears and cub survival dropped again in the late 1990s and early 2000s, but this time the declines were blamed on early breakup of sea ice caused by climate change.

The biologists were only able to come to this conclusion by excluding the weight and cub survival data from the 1960s and 1970s and not mentioning that this was the second time that such declines had been documented in this population.

This misrepresentation of facts by biologists working with Western Hudson Bay was one of the 'compelling' pieces of information used to support the listing of polar bears as 'threatened' on the United States' Endangered Species List in 2008.[213] Attenborough, of course, accepted it without question.

After the listing 'success' of polar bears in the US – international news in 2008 – the misrepresentations continued. Conservation organisations like the WWF interpreted a 2009 report by the IUCN Polar Bear Specialist Group (PBSG) as saying that many regions of the Arctic now showed subpopulations in decline.

In reality, the report showed that only two subpopulations surveyed had shown a documented decline, while four were either stable or increasing; several other subpopulations were only *assumed* to have declined because September ice extent had also declined, or because it was feared there had been overhunting (neither of which turned out to be true). However, the global population size estimate had not changed.[214]

In 2011, Attenborough picked up WWF's misleading statements and ran with them: in the climate change episode of his BBC *Frozen Planet* series, which was entitled 'On Thin Ice', he repeated the WWF claim that polar bear numbers had been falling 'in many regions' and told viewers that polar bear mothers and cubs were starving, even while sitting beside a fat and healthy (but fully tranquillized) bear – and admitting it was fat and healthy!

Apparently, the biologists Attenborough was working with were unable to find any starving bears to tranquillize to illustrate his point.

Summer sea ice declined even further in the Arctic by 2015, to about 42% less than was present in 1979. However, the official estimate of global polar bear numbers rose slightly, from around 24,500 in 2005 to around 26,000. Despite the decline in summer sea ice, there had been no catastrophic decline in polar bear numbers as predicted.[215]

Nevertheless, the BBC Earth episode entitled *The Hunt* featured Attenborough describing a skinny Svalbard polar bear unsuccessfully hunting a bearded seal, as if this was a regular occurrence.[216]

Two years later, in 2017, the BBC's *Blue Planet II* documentary, narrated by Attenborough, showed 'frantic' Pacific walrus cows on melting ice floes trying to protect their newborn calves from predation attempts by so-called 'desperate' polar bears.[217] This was the year the US Fish & Wildlife Service in the US determined that walrus were not threatened by climate change and two years after an IUCN assessment had determined global polar bear numbers had still not declined.[218]

This record of Attenborough-narrated documentaries misleading people (and children in particular) about Arctic wildlife reached a peak in 2019.

That year was not only important for the false stories about the falling walrus in *Our Planet*. In addition, the 'North America' episode of *Seven Worlds* released a few months later showed polar bears hunting beluga whales from intertidal rocks at the mouth of the Seal River in Western Hudson Bay, which was filmed in 2017.

In Attenborough's narration, it was falsely claimed that this had never happened before, with suggestions the bears were doing it now because they were desperately hungry due to lack of sea ice, blamed on climate change.[219]

However, my quick search of the internet found a paper describing a polar bear, in the summer of 1985, hunting beluga whales in virtually identical fashion: leaping on the backs of young whales in shallow water north of Baffin Island in the central Canadian Arctic. The only difference was that the bear in 1985 had used a grounded piece of ice rather than a near-shore rock, as in the film.[220]

From other reports made by people watching this behaviour, it appears likely that one bear in Western Hudson Bay had figured out how to hunt young beluga whales from a rock near shore in 2010 or so, and over the next ten years others had learned by watching, until at least a dozen bears were doing it every summer.[221]

There is no doubt that this is a very cool phenomenon – a rare learned behaviour, made possible by the bears' incredible curiosity and intelligence – and by their known tendency to learn hunting skills from their mothers. However, it has nothing to do with climate change.

Polar bears are always looking for food: part of their Arctic survival strategy is to eat whenever there is food available. In contrast to Attenborough and the BBC, a Canadian Broadcasting Company (CBC) documentary included footage of these same bears hunting beluga calves (also filmed in 2017) without attributing the phenomenon to climate change: as a result, it's an honest and educational film, and well worth watching.[222]

It is apparent that these misleading or outright false climate change narratives in Attenborough's films had a lasting effect on young viewers.

Among the many children who have been taken in by his tales is the young Swedish activist Greta Thunberg – the most famous child affected by this campaign – who was about 8 years old in 2011.

Thunberg has said in various interviews that this was about the time she began to be shown films of starving polar bears and other environmental calamities at school. These films caused her such distress that by early 2014 (at age 11) she had stopped eating and going to school.[223]

We cannot be certain exactly what films Greta was shown by her teachers (and it's unlikely she knows herself). However, we know at least some of them were Attenborough's because in 2019, she was invited to be guest editor of a BBC Radio 4 broadcast, which featured her in discussion with Attenborough, acknowledging his role in educating her about climate change:[224]

> ...thank you for that, because that was what made me decide to do something about it.

From the release date, the film that is most likely to have brought about her 'education' was the 'On Thin Ice' episode, from the *Frozen Planet* series, although it could also have been the 2006 BBC special.

Greta's recollection of having seen films about starving polar bears is slightly odd, given that Attenborough's films didn't show any such images or footage, and because there were few examples from elsewhere in the media at the time.

That's counter-intuitive, because starvation is polar bears' leading cause of death. They have no natural predators, and so they starve when they get old, sick or injured. Starvation is also a problem among bears that are young and inexperienced at hunting, or when thick spring ice, or too much snow over sea ice, makes seals hard to find.[225]

However, lack of sea-ice has so far not been proven to have caused polar bear starvation, although there are a few instances where researchers have inferred this to be the case: that lack of ice is *correlated* with starvation.[226]

Still, stories about starving bears only appear in the media intermittently.

In recent years, there was the 2009 story of a lean (but not starving) male bear that killed and ate a young cub, the 2013 story of the carcass of an emaciated bear found in Svalbard by polar bear biologist Ian Stirling, the 2015 photo of an injured and emaciated bear spotted on the ice near Svalbard went viral, and the 2017 National Geographic video (see Chapter 8).[227]

Only one of these four widely publicised incidents of 'starving' polar bears fell within the period of Greta's conversion in 2011–2013.

In other words, I doubt she saw images of starving polar bears in 2011 or 2012, but she certainly heard about them in Attenborough's films – which the 2013 incident of a carcass of an emaciated bear found in Svalbard would have reinforced if she'd seen it.

By her own admission, this inaccurate view of polar bear conservation was instrumental in the formation of her view of the world, and seeded the rage that she unleashed on world leaders between 2019 and 2021.[228]

However, almost two decades of intensive media focus on polar bears had a down-side. By 2019, it was poised for a shift: the polar bear catastrophe narrative so often featured in Attenborough's films was faltering across the board.

By that time, a good deal of the misinformation fed to Attenborough by biologists and the WWF had been exposed as inaccurate, and most rational people realised that polar bears were doing fine despite declining summer sea ice and predictions of catastrophes on the horizon.[229]

Hollow tales about a bleak future for polar bears had lost their power to impress the public and the use of starving bears to emotionally manipulate viewers backfired once people discovered that starvation is the leading natural cause of death for this species.

As a consequence, a number of climate change activists and their promoters declared the polar bear immaterial to their cause. The false starving polar bear meme had come back to bite them and it was time to move on.

On 5 May 2019, a New York Times title proclaimed that 'These days, it's not about the polar bears', the story below featuring a picture of the fat bears that had invaded Belushya Guba in the Barents Sea, which had been international news in early 2019.[230]

And by October, The Guardian (UK) announced a formal policy decision to eschew polar bear images when promoting their climate change emergency narrative.[231]

Activist biologists and their supporters were still frantically trying to keep the polar bear relevant, but were rapidly losing ground: the experts had oversold their case and had lost.

This was a blow to the political climate change agenda. The frustration was palpable in those trying to keep the polar bear issue in the public's eye and some of that may have rubbed off on David Attenborough.

The hints that he was also getting frustrated came from the shift in Attenborough's public demeanour around the same time. Prior to 2018, he had not been reticent about the topic of climate change, but he was not especially forceful either. As late as August 2017, what came across more than anything was his optimism: his over-riding hope that things would work out OK.[232]

But as I will show in the following pages, by late 2018, he, like activist Greta Thunberg and others, seemed to be exasperated at the lack of action on climate change. We might even speculate that he was looking for a legacy less ephemeral than a long catalogue of nature documentaries.

A different approach was needed and the *Our Planet* series fit the bill – or more specifically, the falling walrus scene that would capture the world's attention.

We now know that footage of walrus falling to their deaths at Cape Schmidt was scheduled to be part of the *Our Planet* series from the very beginning: it had to have been, if it had taken two and a half years of planning to film during the fall of 2017, as director Sophie Lanfear had claimed.

But as soon as Attenborough and other members of the production team saw the raw falling walrus footage they would have realised that it was going to be PR dynamite – better than National Geographic's starving polar bear. The involvement of polar bears was unfortunate, of course, but, as we have seen, a veil could be drawn over that.

The *Our Planet* falling walrus footage was critical to the climate change agenda. It was essential that this otherwise invisible but emotionally traumatising event be interpreted as a consequence of climate change and subsequently viewed by millions of citizens and wealthy influencers around the world – even when it was known to be a sleight-of-hand manipulation of film footage and which anyone with an ability to read and access the internet could discover was not supported by scientific evidence.

It was presented as a 'see this with your own eyes' moment but turned out to be as fraudulent as the NG images of the polar bear supposedly starving because of climate change.

Attenborough's deceit about walrus dying from climate change jump-started a strategic plan to encourage 'action' on climate change but also fed into a utopian vision he had for the future that many people don't share.[233]

However, in order to have the effect that was intended, the falling walrus sequence had to be kept under wraps until precisely the right moment.

This particular film footage was *the* most important segment of the entire series to everyone involved in the production: we know this, in part because the producers said so themselves, but also because that sequence was successfully kept secret until the official release date, even while the series was being heavily promoted.

For example, none of the three *Our Planet* trailers released in late 2018 and early 2019 contained walrus images or walrus footage. There was not a hint that walrus would be covered in the series.

In a long interview with The Times (UK) in March 2019, Attenborough mentioned many of the scenes in the upcoming series but not the walrus one.[234]

That was odd, especially since in a similar interview in November 2019 (after the release of the BBC *Seven Worlds* documentary), he claimed that of all the horrifying things he had seen over his many years making nature films, he had been 'very affected' by the falling walrus sequence and had found the footage 'devastating'.[235]

The walrus scene also escaped notice at the gala premiere of *Our Planet*. This was attended by Attenborough, Prince Charles, Prince William and Prince Harry, David Beckham and his son, and Mark Carney from the Bank of England.

No one at the premiere seems to have said anything to the media about the horrifying walrus scene, and no one was photographed leaving the venue in tears, so it seems likely that particular episode was not shown.[236]

In other words, the Netflix falling walrus scene may have been one of the best-kept secrets of the documentary world, up to the moment of the series' release on 5 April 2019.

It seems obvious why this would have been necessary: the impact of the walrus footage depended on it being a sudden shock to the public. The effect would have been diluted if it was seen by small audiences over months rather than by everyone all at once.

However, it wasn't only the public that the producers wanted to shock out of complacency with this film: they wanted to be sure that truly influential policymakers felt the same gut-punch.

The *Our Planet* marketing plan included speaking directly to government policymakers and industry leaders, as producer Keith Scholey revealed in a pivotal CBC interview in June 2019.[237]

According to that CBC article, the week after the gala premiere, there was another screening of the series at the Smithsonian Museum of Natural History in Washington DC, introduced by Attenborough, and attended by ambassadors and members of Congress.[238]

To arrive in time, Attenborough would have had to leave London almost immediately after the premiere event, an impressive schedule for a 93-year-old man, but necessary to exploit the full impact of the falling walrus footage.

However, in order that the falling walrus scene had the biggest political impact, it became essential to risk exposing the secret in order to access the largest group of influencers on the planet: the attendees of the World Economic Forum (WEF) in Davos, Switzerland, which takes place every year in late January.

We now know that several screenings of a special version of *Our Planet* that included the falling walrus scene was shown at Davos in January 2019 – three months before the film's official release date.

Nowhere was there a more concentrated grouping of government policymakers and industry leaders than those that meet at Davos.

The WEF is an international organisation bent on 'Public-Private Cooperation', and its annual meeting brings together the richest and most powerful people in the world, including political leaders and business tycoons.

It aims to encourage 'the foremost political, business, cultural, and other leaders of society to shape global, regional, and industrial agendas', and claims to be 'independent, impartial and not tied to any special interests' – except, of course, to the premise that climate change is an existential threat to humanity.[239]

According to its mission statement:[240]

Our activities are shaped by a unique institutional culture founded on the stakeholder theory, which asserts that an organization is accountable to all parts of society.

The institution carefully blends and balances the best of many kinds of organizations, from both the public and private sectors, international organizations and academic institutions.

We believe that progress happens by bringing together people from all walks of life who have the drive and the influence to make positive change.

Attendees at WEF meetings have power, money, and unparalleled influence over politics, communication, and medicine.

They include heads of state such as Justin Trudeau of Canada, Boris Johnson of the UK and Joe Biden of the USA; wealthy influencers such as billionaire Bill Gates, youth activist Greta Thunberg, and Britain's heir to the throne, Prince Charles and his son, William – and climate change activist and filmmaker/narrator Sir David Attenborough. Organizations listed as WEF 'Strategic Partners' (at 13 May 2021) included, among many others: AstraZeneca, Pfizer, Johnson & Johnson, Dow, Novartis, JP Morgan Chase & Co., Procter & Gamble, Bill and Melinda Gates Foundation, PayPay, Facebook, Google, Microsoft, PepsiCo, Goldman Sachs, Bank of America, Barclays, Deutsche Bank, Mastercard, Visa, Wellcome Trust, Western Union.[241]

The WEF meeting in January 2019 was a perfect forum for promoting the message contained in the soon-to-be-released *Our Planet* series. Attenborough was already scheduled to speak at the meeting, as he was being given an award on the first day.

During a video-taped, on-stage 'conversation' that had been arranged with the Duke of Cambridge (Prince William) the following day, Attenborough talked about the *Our Planet* project and showed a brief excerpt from the film:[242]

'My next series – *Our Planet* – will go instantly to hundreds of millions of people in almost every country on Earth via Netflix.

If people can truly understand what is at stake, I believe they will give permission to business and governments to get on with the practical solutions.'

But the short film clip from *Our Planet* he showed to the audience gathered for that event did not contain the hard-hitting falling walrus sequence, as might have been expected.

However, what if there had had been another preview of the film that *did* include the walrus sequence that no one was (officially) allowed to talk about?

I came to this conclusion when I discovered that Russian science advisor Kochnev was told at the end of January 2019 that a preliminary version of the *Our Planet* series, that included the walrus footage shot in Chukotka, had been given a private screening at the WEF meeting.

In a blog post dated 7 April 2019, Kochnev revealed he had signed a non-disclosure agreement about his part in the walrus filming, and therefore couldn't say anything about it until the release date.

It appears he had published a short blog post detailing his involvement with the Netflix project in January after he had been told about the film screening at the Davos meeting, thinking this meant the embargo had been lifted and he was free to speak.

However, he was soon told to remove the post until the official film release date in April.

Here are his exact words, muddled a bit by Google Translate from the original Russian, which is his original post from January prefaced by an introductory paragraph written in April when the post was republished [my emphasis]:[243]

[Preface paragraph, presented originally in bold, dated April 7 2019]

I wrote this post at the end of January, when the film about which I am writing below was presented by Sir David Attenborough and Prince William at the World Economic Forum in Davos.

However, the show was closed, and one of the producers of the series *Our Planet* asked to hold the information and pictures until the official premiere. And the premiere took place. Yesterday. On the Netflix channel.

Now I have every right to remove the castle [sic — hold?] from the post and publish it again.

[Original post from the end of January 2019, which was pulled soon after]

Well, perhaps it was slowly and it was time to reveal some of the secrets of the 2017 field season. Perhaps one of my regular friends and readers noticed that during the winter of 2017-2018[sic — I?] wrote only about observations on the island of Matveyev in the Barents Sea. And about Chukotka was silent. And there is an important reason — I signed a non-disclosure paper. No, no, no military and strategic secrets)))

Just in the fall of 2017, I worked as an expert and field guide with a British team of filmmakers who shot walruses and polar bears for two programs of the BBC and the Living Planet [sic] company.

This year, films should appear on television and computer screens, and before that I was convincingly asked not to stammer [sic — gossip?] about the results and details of the shooting. And even made a piece of paper to sign)))

*But a few hours ago, a message came from one of the producers,* because of which I decided to take off the penance of silence.

*A couple of days ago, at the World Economic Forum in Davos, Sir David Attenborough and Prince William presented a preliminary version of the film, in which one of the key stories was presented with shots taken then, in 2017, in Chukotk*a...Two months ago, I, by the way, I had a little help in editing the offscreen text that Attenborough reads.

And the film raises a very sensitive problem for me. The death of walruses on coastal rookeries, where now due to the lack of ice, they have to stay for a long time, in huge quantities and almost without feeding.

The most vivid and dramatic shots captured the fall of walrus from the cliffs, where they climb because of the lack of space on the beach and to avoid unpleasant smells from the nearby village.

That year, only on one of the rookeries where we were shooting, about 800 walruses died, of which almost a third broke when falling from rocks.

*It is said that some of the important economic and political bosses could not keep tears when watching a film in Davos.* I would like to hope that our surveys will contribute to the restructuring of the mass consciousness in relation to the Arctic, its wildlife and climate change issues.

Although, as an old pessimist, I think that they will cry, but they will forget...

Well, then at least some of the participants in the economic forum would have thrown up some money for the field season, but now I'll have to go at my own expense ...)))

[Kochnev included a link to a Netflix 'Behind the Scenes' video posted on their website in which he was featured: this is essentially the same video as released a few days later by the WWF with their logo][244]

Confirming Kochnev's story about a confidential showing of *Our Planet* at Davos was challenging.

However, I have determined that there was indeed a private screening of the series preview, which may or may not have been introduced by Attenborough and Prince William. It was certainly *not* presented during the aforementioned and much-publicised 'conversation' between the pair, as Kochnev assumed.[245]

Moreover, according to the CBC interview with Keith Scholey mentioned above, there was not just one screening of the *Our Planet* preview at the 2019 WEF meeting but several:[246]

> ...the filmmakers weren't sure anyone would show up for screenings they scheduled at the World Economic Forum in Davos, Switzerland, said Scholey.
>
> But demand was so high, they added extra showings.

It is also apparent that this preview version of the series was one that no one else saw. Creating a special preview version of the series for this event would have been a strategic step (and one which was taken again in 2021, for another film series, for another critical event – more on this later).

Kochnev was told specifically that the walrus sequences were included in this version. Of course it was: the falling walrus sequence was the most compelling footage in the entire series and it was what Attenborough wanted these people to see.

However, no one else except Kochnev mentioned the specific contents of the Davos screening and no one else except Scholey even mentioned it had taken place at all (and even then, he did not reveal this fact until months after the film's official release).

I found nothing on the WEF meeting website about the screenings and no one who might have seen it at the meeting mentioned it publicly afterwards. But how were they able to keep it secret?

The standard method of secrecy in the film industry is the 'non-disclosure agreement.' We know that Kochnev was required to sign such an agreement because he said so in his blog post, which means it is highly likely the same condition applied to his friend Yevgeny Basov, who we know from the 'Frozen Worlds' credit roll had been hired as a field assistant for the project.

This explains why Basov, who had posted photos of the Cape Schmidt walrus incident in November of 2017, included no polar bears in his photos but described in detail walrus falling from the cliff (Chapter 4). He too was silenced about any involvement of polar bears in the events presented in the Netflix episode.

But were WEF audience members shown the special screening asked to sign non-disclosure agreements too?

It's impossible to know for sure but it's highly likely they were. The potential value of the screenings to this group was probably considered worth the risk of a leak but as far as I have been able to determine, no one let on what had been in the special screening except Kochnev, who was repeating what he'd been told.

Attenborough knew the power that lay behind the falling walrus sequence: it was dynamite footage and although it was important to keep it secret until the official release date, it was also important to use it to political advantage.

The heads of state, wealthy elites, and business tycoons present at Davos in 2019 would have been too influential not to exploit.[247]

The special screenings at the WEF meeting sent the *Our Planet* falling walrus message directly to government policymakers and industry leaders – well before it went to anyone else.

Although this was a money-making venture for Netflix, the other partners – and especially Attenborough – appeared to be serious about making a significant political impact with the series, and they knew the falling walrus sequence was the most influential footage they had.

The very fact that screenings of a special preview version of *Our Planet,* which included the falling walrus sequence, were shown at Davos highlights the political nature of the message it was meant to convey.

Calls for action on climate change would go nowhere unless politicians and business leaders with political clout were onboard. The Netflix partners knew this all too well, which is why they had a marketing plan ahead of time to target these influencers directly.

There is no doubt that his involvement with *Our Planet* marked a change in Attenborough's demeanour: he moved from a being a gentle but persistent advocate for environmental protection to being a strident activist for mitigation of climate change and political action to bring this about.[248]

It appears to me that the falling walrus footage was the impetus for that shift in approach – even before the film had been officially released.

Did he see it as the basis of the kind of climate change campaign that would guarantee his legacy? Either way, thereafter his voice on climate change had bite and he used it often.

For example, seemingly out of the blue, at the United Nations sponsored 'Conference of the Parties' on climate change (COP24) in Katowice, Poland, in early December 2018, Attenborough was astonishingly forceful in his insistence that action had to be taken on climate change because, he said, the collapse of civilisation and 'the extinction of much of the natural world' was on the horizon. He claimed that climate change was 'our greatest threat in thousands of years' and told the leaders of the world, '...you must lead'.[249]

The following month, at the WEF in Davos – on the first day of the meeting, before the special preview screenings of *Our Planet* – on receiving an award for his leadership in environmental stewardship, he told the world's most influential political and business leaders that, 'the Garden of Eden is no more.'[250]

I am not the only one to have noticed this abrupt shift in attitude. One film reviewer at The Guardian (UK) described the change in Attenborough quite succinctly [my emphasis]:[251]

> Once, a night in with David Attenborough promised *the TV equivalent of a warm blanket*.
>
> It was a chance to watch spectacular creatures revelling in the beauty of their natural habitats, as the man with a voice

as soothing as ice-cream described what we could see, from the violent to the serene.

*Those days are gone.*

Attenborough's recent move to Netflix, for *Our Planet*, was deceptive: *a seemingly gorgeous nature documentary that doubled up as animal kingdom snuff movies* in which the beauty of those natural habitats was revealed as a crumbling paradise, ruined by people and particularly by greed.

*One of the main points of praise for Our Planet, which was well received, suggested that Attenborough was no longer tiptoeing around the issue of climate change, the implication being that he had done so before.*

The following year, Attenborough made it clear that he had high hopes for dramatic changes to the way we live.

Critically, in a lengthy BBC podcast with presenter Liz Bonnin on 7 October 2020, he outlined the revolutionary future he envisions after the world has agreed to seriously address rising CO2 emissions:[252]

There should be no dominant nation on this planet...

[The future is] not going to be paradise, immediately. I think that the standard of living of the western cultures...civilised countries...is going to have to take pause.

I think we are going to have to live more economically than we do.

And we can do that and, I believe we will do it more happily, not less happily.

And that the excesses the capitalist system has brought us, have got to be curbed somehow.

That doesn't mean to say that capitalism is dead and I'm not an economist and I don't know.

But I believe the nations of the world, ordinary people worldwide, are beginning to realise that greed does not actually lead to joy.

These comments seem to indicate Attenborough had moved quickly beyond the simple goal of mitigating rising CO2 levels, although such utopian ideas about the future have so far not appeared in any of his documentaries.

In other words, agreeing to collaborate with Netflix to narrate the *Our Planet* series in 2018 was a pivotal moment for Attenborough. It really launched him into orbit in his new role as a passionate climate change activist.

He had said he'd chosen to partner with Neflix because it would get his hard-hitting climate change message out to many more people than BBC-produced television films.

Not only had this strategy worked but the public outcry over the falling walrus sequence kept Attenborough and his climate change message in the news for weeks. A series of hard-hitting, but factually dubious documentaries soon followed that kept up the pressure on the public and on policymakers.

Hot on the heels of all the Netflix publicity and in the midst of the ensuing walrus controversy, on 18 April 2019 another Attenborough BBC special documentary *Climate Change – The Facts* debuted on television in the UK. Less than two weeks after *Our Planet* had hit the screens, the timing of this release cannot have been an accident: it would have been part of the strategic plan.

However, one reviewer at The Guardian (UK) was taken in by the ruse:[253]

You sense that *Our Planet* was unfortunately timed for the BBC. In *Climate Change: The Facts*, the gloves are now not so much off as thrown to the floor in a certain rage.

Another reviewer conveniently described the foundation of Attenborough's marketing plan – the fact that he was a trusted figurehead:[254]

> At a time when public debate seems to be getting ever more hysterical, it's good to be presented with something you can trust.
>
> And we all trust Attenborough.

*Climate Change – The Facts* was dubbed by the media as a 'rousing call to arms' because of its focus on 'irreversible damage to the natural world.' In the hour-long diatribe of apocalyptic disasters, tipping points, and calls for urgent action, there was nothing about Arctic sea ice, polar bears, or walrus – and therefore, not much of particular interest to me.[255]

However, it kicked up quite a bit of controversy because not everyone was happy with the result.

Some were concerned that the program had offered few solutions to the problems that were featured: that it was too little, too late.[256]

In contrast, the GWPF issued a strongly worded and detailed press release in which they accused Attenborough and the BBC of serious errors and misleading statements that were not supported by the scientific facts presented in the latest report of the Intergovernmental Panel on Climate Change (IPCC).

For example, while the film suggested that storms, floods, heatwaves and sea level rise were all rapidly getting worse as a result of climate change, the IPCC stated categorically that no trends in these events had been documented.[257]

Journalist David Rose for The Mail on Sunday (UK) concurred:[258]

> No one has done more to convey the marvels of the natural world than Attenborough, and his long career has rightly earned him public acclaim.

Sadly, on this occasion, I believe he has presented an alarmist argument derived from a questionable use of evidence, whose nuances he has ignored...

Watching it did fill me with horror, but not at the threat from global warming.

It was at the way Sir David and the BBC presented a picture of the near future which was so much more frightening than is justified....

In both critiques, the onus for these errors and misleading statements were laid at Attenborough's feet, as I had done for the *Our Planet* walrus sequence. This was fair.

Ultimately, as the narrator, he was responsible for the veracity of the words that came out of his mouth: if he wasn't prepared to own them, he should not have said them. He had to take the blame for any errors or misinformation in the film, even if some people thought he was a saint and therefore above reproach.[259]

However, the criticisms of both films didn't slow Attenborough down: he was on a roll and thereafter in high demand for interviews and appearances.[260]

In July 2019, he addressed the UK parliamentary committee on Business, Energy and Industrial Strategy and had some harsh words to say when asked if the UK should bring forward its new target of reducing greenhouse gas emissions to net zero by 2050, as some campaigners had called for. He insisted: 'we cannot be radical enough in dealing with these issues'.[261]

At the same event, he was also supportive of the efforts of Swedish teenager Greta Thunberg and the generation she claimed to represent, which not only boosted her profile but undoubtedly generated loyalty to Attenborough from a tranche of young people that might not have been possible before.

Although apparently they did not meet at the time, sixteen year old Greta had made a rousing speech at the same 2019 WEF meeting in

Davos where Attenborough and *Our Planet* had featured so prominently, where she famously declared:[262]

> I don't want your hope. I don't want you to be hopeful. I want you to panic...and act as if your house is on fire. Because it is.

That summer, the nominations for the 2019 Emmys were revealed, as discussed in Chapter 6, which generated more publicity and interviews, as did the actual win of the award for Attenborough and the 'Frozen Worlds' episode from *Our Planet* containing the falling walrus sequence a few months later.

The campaign was going better than expected (or maybe not – perhaps the producers had accurately judged the mood of those in high places in the television world who wanted more from Attenborough on climate change and anticipated they would be more than happy to reward him with an Emmy for the falling walrus sequence).

The next climate change themed film was the BBC's *Seven Worlds* extravaganza that aired in early November, which I've already discussed in detail (Chapter 7).

It was the third major documentary series in six months for Attenborough. However, yet another WWF/Netflix collaboration, Attenborough's life story, called *A Life On Our Planet,* was set for release within months. A *Life On Our Planet* had been scheduled for release in early April 2020, exactly one year after *Our Planet*, but was postponed to early October due to the pandemic.[263]

This had to have been a strategic plan to break Attenborough out of his cocoon of climate reticence.

Some might argue that he was just a naïve participant going along with a WWF/BBC game plan, but I am convinced he had to have been one of the architects – being, if nothing else, his own man – and that the iconic falling walrus scene was the pinnacle event around which his butterfly-emergence on climate change was built, with his explicit consent and active input.

With these four documentaries and the attending publicity coming in rapid succession, Attenborough used his position of trust to sway public opinion and convince the most politically powerful people in the world to accept his view about the effects of climate change on the natural world – which also happened to be the view taken by the WWF.

Ultimately, it didn't matter to him that the walrus facts in the Netflix film were exposed as false in April. In part, this was likely because he and the others knew the truth would come out anyway in November when the BBC film was aired.

However, I surmise he guessed correctly that the horrifying *Our Planet* walrus-death footage – along with his earnest message – would motivate the world's most powerful movers-and-shakers to sit up and pay attention as they had never done before. It was critical to get as much mileage out of that footage as possible while it was still hot news, even if it was later revealed as false and taken out of context.

The WWF did not get to be the richest conservation organisation in the world by backing popular moral causes. The organisation was founded by businessmen, not conservationists, and later amassed its incredible wealth by learning one critical lesson: horrifying images of animals dying or in apparent peril made people feel overwhelmingly guilty, which they assuaged by donating money.

The bigger the emotional hit, the bigger the donation. Attenborough, after a lifetime of accepting the word of the WWF on all issues of conservation science, finally learned that lesson. Once he saw that falling walrus footage, he must have realised it was animal tragedy porn he could not pass up: it was just too powerful to waste.

Of course, the WWF already knew what the falling walrus footage would do for them, which almost certainly explains why it was part of the plan for the series all along: the spike in donations and visits to the WWF website that had been reported after the publicity surrounding the 'Frozen Worlds' walrus episode was not a happy accident.[264]

It seems likely the WWF were able to sell it to Attenborough as the key to his own success. We see this happening again in Attenborough's life story project – *A Life On Our Planet: My Witness Statement and a Vision for the Future* – in which he used the same 'witness statement' phrase coined by the WWF in its climate change campaign back in 2004 (Chapter 1).

Having first adopted the brutal animal tragedy porn approach with the falling walrus, this was Attenborough taking on WWF strategies yet again, perhaps encouraged by Colin Butfield who was WWF's executive producer for his life story film.[265] Furthermore, this documentary clearly marked Attenborough's climate action campaign as a legacy issue: the thing he wanted to be remembered for after he was dead.[266]

In what was slated to be the fifth production after *Our Planet* (but ended up being the fourth released, in part because pandemic protocols wouldn't allow the premier events for *A Life On Our Planet* to be held), the BBC special *Extinction: The Facts* narrated by Attenborough got inserted into the mix in mid-September 2020.

It featured the so-called Sixth Mass Extinction that had been a WWF hobbyhorse since 2016 and one Attenborough had eagerly climbed aboard from the beginning. However, this concept has few supporters and many critics: it is not something serious scientists espouse.[267]

Presumably to help promote the new film, Attenborough uncharacteristically signed up to the social media site Instagram at this point, amassed more than 6 million followers and then promptly signed off six weeks later.[268]

The film got well-deserved criticism as well as the usual, almost automatic, raves.[269] However, *Extinction: The Facts* was different from the others in one important respect: it was the first time the Covid-19 pandemic entered Attenborough's narrative, which included:[270]

> 'Scientists have even linked the destructive relationship with nature to the emergence of Covid-19.
>
> If we carry on like this we will see more epidemics....We've seen an increasing rate of pandemic emergencies.

Blaming the emergence of Covid-19 on declining biodiversity turned out to be the companion to a bizarre notion that climate change itself had been largely responsible for the Covid-19 epidemic, which Attenborough and the BBC now seemed to be actively promoting.

This unsubstantiated claim provided the foundation for increasing pressure on nations and their citizens to ensure that a global agreement to deal with climate change was reached in 2020.

# Chapter 11

# The COP26 End Game

Opportunities for climate activists to make their 'crisis' seem real to the disinterested public are always few and far between, and campaigners routinely have to resort to repeating the same messages.

The problem for those pressing for action on climate change in 2020 was that the campaign had been going on for a long time and there was a real risk the public had tuned out – there had been a huge climate-crisis messaging push before the last big UN climate meeting (COP25) in 2015 (the so-called Paris Agreement) but public attention had quickly turned elsewhere after the meeting closed.[271]

The next big meeting was coming up in 2020 and Attenborough became central to the PR push ahead of it.

Attenborough's high-profile voice gave the movement a huge boost. Because his remarks on the topic had formerly been so nuanced, his new passion and stridency that emerged in 2018 was newsworthy.

When Attenborough said there was a climate emergency, newspapers around the world reported it – and each time he released a new documentary purporting to show the effects of a climate emergency, they reported that too.

He kept the 'crisis' message in the public eye and gave the climate change action agenda new life, all built on the momentum created by the *Our Planet* falling walrus deception in early 2019.

However, a totally unexpected disaster threw a spanner in the works of the climate change PR plan.

Between the release of *Seven Worlds* (BBC) in November 2019 and the scheduled release of *A Life On Our Planet* (WWF/Netflix), the emergence of SARS-CoV-2 (the virus that causes Covid-19) in early 2020 not only scuttled Attenborough's plans for a high-profile premiere for his life-story documentary but threatened to derail his entire climate awareness agenda.

He told journalist Lucy Siegle and filmmaker Tom Mustill during a late May 2020 podcast for So Hot Right Now:[272]

> The trouble is that right now the climate issue is also seen as being rather in the distant future because we've got the virus to think about.
>
> And so what are the papers full of? The virus. Quite right, that's what I want to know about, too.
>
> But we have to make sure that this issue, which was coming to the boil with the next COP meeting in Glasgow, has suddenly been swept off the front pages.
>
> And we've got to get it back there.

With virtually everyone in the world suddenly ordered to stay at home week after week in early 2020, Netflix was sitting pretty: their subscribers (and profits) were increasing.

However, Attenborough and his colleagues at the WWF and the BBC had a big problem on their hands. All their work milking the dividends of dying Russian walrus was potentially down the toilet.

Citizens and governments around the world, in a panic, were struggling to cope with unprecedented fear and economic survival: climate change was the furthest from anyone's mind.

Worse yet, the UN climate meeting in Glasgow Scotland (COP26), originally scheduled for November 2020, had to be postponed to November 2021 because of the pandemic.

This had to have been a time of panic for climate activists everywhere, which led to different ways of leveraging the pandemic to benefit the cause.

Some tried to keep their issue at the front of public consciousness by blaming climate change and loss of biodiversity for the emergence of the virus. Although it may seem implausible that anyone would say something so outlandish, Attenborough's statement in *Extinction: The Facts* in September 2020 is proof that it happened.

Such claims make no sense when examined carefully and rationally.

Although we have been warned for years that we could expect a rise in some infectious diseases in a future warming world, that is a far cry from blaming one particular epidemic on climate change, well before any so-called 'dangerous' warming has even occurred.[273]

Moreover, as Ross Clark pointed out in his biting critique of *Extinction: The Facts,* while novel diseases are indeed becoming more common (in part because we are getting so much better at isolating and identifying them), fewer people are actually being affected:[274]

> A study by Brown university in 2014, published in the Journal of the Royal Society, found that there has been a rise in the number of outbreaks of novel infectious diseases since 1980, but also that there has been a decline in the numbers of people being affected by them.
>
> We have become much better at identifying diseases, and much better at controlling them.

Other activists were more subtle in linking Covid-19 and the climate agenda, simply using the pandemic response as an example of how to press harder for climate action.

Here is how billionaire Bill Gates put it in a short video produced for the WEF in August 2020:[275]

> Finding and deploying green solutions [to climate change] could take decades.
>
> We need to act with the same urgency as we have for Covid-19.
>
> ...
>
> The world didn't listen to the warnings about a pandemic.

But we have the chance to deal with climate change differently.

Similarly, Prince Charles – heir to the British throne – was on board with any plan to deal with climate change that might create a more sustainable and equitable world after seeing what the response to Covid-19 had done:[276]

> We have a golden opportunity to seize something good from this [COVID-19] crisis.
>
> Its unprecedented shock waves may well make people more receptive to big visions of change.
>
> ...
>
> Unless we take the action necessary, and build in a greener and more inclusive and sustainable way, then we will have more and more pandemics.

Clearly, Attenborough wasn't alone in his concern that too much light was shining on the Covid-19 crisis and not enough on climate change. However, in contrast to the others, he wasn't afraid to say so explicitly.

For example, at a virtual wildlife film festival in late October 2020, he told Greta Thunberg:[277]

> I am worried that people will take their eyes off the environmental issue because of the immediate problems they have on [sic] Covid-19.

Of course, Attenborough himself was barely inconvenienced by the Covid-19 lockdowns and he wasn't alone in that: few elites of his caliber around the world were seriously impacted.

While millions were thrown out of work, lost their businesses, and descended into madness, he was comfortable at home in his detached house in the UK with its large garden and a devoted daughter to take care of him.[278] Easy for him to suggest that people's legitimate, desperate concerns for day-to-day survival should not get in the way of dealing with climate change.

However, the fact of the postponement of COP26 meeting could not be avoided. It meant that activists had no choice but to try to keep the public on edge about climate change for another entire year by keeping climate change issues in the public eye as much as possible.

This appears to be why Attenborough ramped up his output in late 2020 and early 2021.

There was plenty of material available: September 2020 saw the planned release of the BBC special *Extinction: The Facts*, and the Netflix/WWF Attenborough docudrama *A Life On Our Planet* release followed in early October (postponed from April), as discussed in Chapter 7. Both films gave Attenborough numerous chances to make strong statements that generated a lot of public attention worldwide.

For example, his life story documentary generated a televised, high profile interview with American journalist Anderson Cooper, in which he told the reporter:[279]

> I would say that the time has come to put aside national ambitions and look for an international ambition of survival.

In addition, just days after the release of *A Life On Our Planet* in October, Attenborough teamed up with fellow WEF supporter Prince William to announce a new 'environmental' endeavour: the Earthshot Prize.

It was later explained that the five winners of £1 million each (about US$1.4 million, to be announced on 17 October 2021 in London) would be decided by an extremely elite council that included Attenborough, Prince William, and the head of the IPCC.

The goals were lofty:[280]

> ...to incentivise change, inspire collective action, and help repair our planet over the next ten years.

> At the heart of The Prize are five Earthshots – simple but ambitious goals for our planet, which if achieved by 2030 will improve life for us all, for generations to come.

Together, they form a unique set of challenges rooted in science, which aim to generate new ways of thinking, as well as new technologies, systems, policies and solutions.

On Christmas Day, 2020 the New York Times published an interview with Attenborough that was billed as a 'filled with hope' message but which was actually part of the pre-release promotion of yet another documentary series produced by the BBC/Silverback Films partnership: *A Perfect Planet*, which had been in the works since 2016.[281]

In other words, *A Perfect Planet* was part of the long-term climate change messaging agenda that appeared to have been mapped out in 2015 and which involved both the BBC and Netflix.

Released in early January 2021, filming on *A Perfect Planet* had been completed before Covid-19 lockdowns restricted travel. Production was barely impacted, although precautions were taken to protect Attenborough, who apparently had to do his narrations at his dining room table after the room had been retrofitted with wall-hangings of duvets to buffer the sound.

The five-part series was a look at the wonders of the world but also a diatribe of the unsubstantiated evils that the wanton burning of fossil fuels by humanity was said to have inflicted on the planet (wildfires! hurricanes! dead coral reefs!), which would otherwise be 'perfect'.[282]

As Silverback Films producer Alastair Fothergill stated in a promotional radio interview regarding natural disasters like 'regular hurricanes along the East Coast' [of North America]:[283]

> You have to question whether these are small blips or there is a genuine concern that we have upset the perfect planet.
>
> And that is what we wanted to address in the series.

As if North Atlantic hurricanes, including very strong ones, have not been a regular phenomenon for thousands of years![284]

In the same interview, Attenborough insisted that people simply must deal with the issue of climate change at the COP26 meeting in Glasgow.

He indicated he believed – with little evidence to suggest he was correct – that citizens of the world had given politicians a mandate to act at a global level on their behalf [my emphasis]:

> I think the COP meeting...is of crucial importance for the future of humanity.
>
> It's our last chance to get it right.
>
> *We've been saying this is the last chance again and again, but this time it really is our last chance.*
>
> If we don't fix it this time, we are going to be in real trouble.
>
> We know how to fix it.
>
> All we have to do is to sort out amongst ourselves what we're going to deal with and to get onto looking at things internationally and globally instead of nationally and parochially.
>
> *My feeling is that people of the world are willing politicians, are urging politicians, to get together and sort this out as a team, a united team.*
>
> We're all on the same side; we're trying to help the natural world.
>
> Rationalizing is over – or should be.

However, there is little proof Attenborough's 'feeling' that most people in the world support his convictions is actually true.

In fact, strong evidence points to the contrary: even though most people say they consider climate change a critical concern they nevertheless rank it well below other issues they also considered important (such as health care and the economy).

For example, a recent IPSO poll in the UK showed only 18% of responders mentioned climate change and pollution as 'the most important issue facing Britain today' in April 2021, up from 9% (for 'pollution and environment') in October 2020 and 15% (for 'pollution and environment') in September 2019.

In addition, most people also said they were unwilling to cut their travel 'carbon footprint' if it cost them more or was less convenient, according to an Ipso Global Advisor study in September 2019:[285]

> Only one in seven people in the UK (13%) said they would use a form of transportation with a lower carbon footprint than air travel if it were less convenient or more expensive, which aligns with the world average (14% across 27 countries).
>
> Interest in using travel modes with a lower carbon footprint than airplanes varies widely across countries; in China, nearly 38% would do so even if it were less convenient or more expensive, compared to just 7% in Canada and 4% in Japan.

Other studies show comparable results.[286]

Regardless, Attenborough pushed on. He was doing a decent job of keeping the climate change agenda from falling completely off the radar during the pandemic.

From his safe haven in Britain, at every opportunity he hammered home his message of climate apocalypse on the horizon.

After the release of *A Perfect Planet* in January he barely took a breath. He went on to make a virtual address to the UN Security Council in February 2021, at which he said climate change was the biggest security threat that modern humans had ever faced:[287]

> There is no going back – no matter what we do now, it's too late to avoid climate change and the poorest, the most vulnerable, those with the least security, are now certain to suffer...

> If we continue on our current path, we will face the collapse of everything that gives us our security: food production, access to fresh water, habitable ambient temperature and ocean food chains.
>
> And if the natural world can no longer support the most basic of our needs, then much of the rest of civilization will quickly break down.

However, representatives from Russia, India and China were not impressed with Attenborough's address or similar pleas from others.

The subsequent call for the creation of a UN 'special envoy for climate and security' and annual reports to the Security Council by UN Secretary General António Guterres did not pass because Russia used its veto: it warned 'against any move to recognise warming as a threat to global security'.[288]

It was a nice try, but as Attenborough himself intoned sadly in *Seven Worlds* (describing a polar bear's attempt to catch a walrus by its rear flipper, see Chapter 7): 'He's failed.'

Still, he continued.

Not visibly discouraged, Attenborough and his BBC team next produced a Covid-19 nature documentary called *The Year Earth Changed* in time for release on 16 April 2021, just prior to Earth Day that year (22 April). Again, timing was everything.

Earth Day needed the boost: for more than 50 years, its largely unjustified accusations that humans were destroying the planet had been strenuously promoted but had had little real impact.[289]

This time, instead of partnering with Netflix, Attenborough and the BBC had teamed up with AppleTV+ to ensure the documentary reached international viewers immediately.

*The Year Earth Changed* featured some incidents of wild animals invading human spaces devoid of people that occurred in some areas during the severe lockdowns of 2020, such as leopards wandering empty streets and turtle eggs hatching on empty beaches. How they got the footage of these events is a bit of a mystery, given the travel restrictions in place at the time: none of the descriptions of the film explained, although it is likely there was a heavy use of local photographers.[290]

But it presented a message dear to Attenborough's heart: what a world without humans might look like. In the film, Attenborough concluded 'the natural world would do better if we weren't there at all'.[291]

Such a brutal sentiment was hardly unexpected, given that it came from the man who only a few years previously had stated publicly that humans were 'a plague on the Earth' (Chapter 1). Attenborough had long ago accepted the long-discredited Malthusian notion there were simply too many people for the planet to support.[292]

Never off-message for even a moment, Attenborough presented the relaxation of wild/urban boundaries as further irrefutable evidence that humans were destroying the planet.

Never mind that crop yields and other commodities were up and natural catastrophes down in 2020, as they had been in 2019:[293] Attenborough remained a glass-half-empty kind of guy.

There still wasn't an Attenborough documentary that offered solutions to all these supposed problems but viewers didn't have much longer to wait: the third Netflix/Silverback Films collaboration for Attenborough, released 4 June 2021, was called *Breaking Boundaries – The Science of Our Planet*. This one looked like it might be the finale of Attenborough's full-court-press 'climate action' on-screen messaging ahead of the COP26 meeting in November (spoiler alert: it wasn't).

In the video preview, he is quoted as saying, 'we have no time to lose' and in the official Netflix description, he added:[294]

> With major global decisions on biodiversity and climate change taking place this year there has never been a more

important time to communicate the science of what is happening to our planet.

The research featured in Breaking Boundaries is one of the clearest explanations I've seen of the threats we face and how we might tackle them.

I hope that after watching this film many more people will see the urgency of our current situation and be inspired by the possibility of creating a stable healthy future for ourselves and the rest of the natural world.

However, there is a real problem with this message: this film is focused completely on a dated theoretical concept and outmoded language. It presents as fact that there are so-called 'planetary thresholds' we must not exceed because they might be 'tipping points' that generate irreversible changes.

These theoretical thresholds were defined years ago by 'sustainability' specialist Johan Rockström, who has had the ear of Attenborough, the WWF, and other high-profile movers and shakers at the WEF since 2009.[295] He had a message these people wanted to hear: that climate change could potentially pass a critical point of no return if nothing was done to stop the rise of CO2 emissions.

The concept assumes that before we realize what has happened, it will be too late: an unavoidable global catastrophe will be generated.

The Arctic is presumed to be closest to such a tipping point. For example, a 2019 UN Environment Program report on Global Linkages claimed that the Arctic was already locked in to experience by 2050 a rise in winter temperatures over the ocean of 3-5$^0$C above 1986-2005 levels (even if Paris Agreement emissions cuts were attained) and that this could lead to a devastating tipping point of melting permafrost and Greenland ice sheets.[296]

However, the so-called locked in winter temperatures in the Arctic have not yet been observed and the anticipated tipping points are just model outputs.[297]

Both are still very much predicted effects that depend on a number of unproven assumptions and known uncertainties: they are not facts.[298]

Simply put, all of the tipping point talk is prophesy, not reality. Moreover, the focus on tipping points (which had also been raised in another Attenborough-narrated documentary, *Climate Change – The Facts*) reveals where these documentary script-writers were getting their information.

Rockström and collaborator Will Steffen produced two papers in prestigious science journals – one in 2009 and another in 2015 – which garnered a lot of media attention at the time. Yet, it's unlikely you've heard of him (I haven't).

His name and his notion of planetary thresholds and tipping points are not household terms in 2021 because his sustainability theories are not being talked about by anyone except his close colleagues, the WWF and WEF supporters (including radical environmental journalist George Monbiot): most serious scientists consider the concept of human-induced climate 'tipping points' to be exaggerated rhetoric.[299]

Why Attenborough's supporters would devote an entire documentary to promoting one man's obscure theory as if he were a new-age Darwin seems an odd move, until you realise this film is part of an elaborate plan hatched many years ago that put the WWF in charge of supplying scientific information.[300]

Therefore not surprisingly, Rockström is said to be a sustainability advisor to Netflix and that he 'will continue in this capacity as a part of the company's independent advisory group of experts.'[301]

Oh dear.

In addition to the dubious validity of the tipping point concept, the approach taken in the film (as well as by Attenborough in his remarks over the past few years) is apt to backfire.

A number of critics have noted that 'last chance to save the world' messages really put people off. Not only does it seem to be an ultimatum but when there are few real changes (as happened after the 2009 and 2015 COP meetings) and the world doesn't fall apart, the entire climate change movement loses more credibility.[302]

*Breaking Boundaries* was another significant act in Attenborough's desperate ploy to help change the world. He really has nothing to lose. If he wins (i.e. big changes do come out of the 2021 UN climate meeting), he's a hero forever to some segment of the population: he's earned his legacy.

If he loses and no big changes occur, he'll soon be dead and won't have to see people who once supported him shrug their shoulders and walk away – or refuse to pay money to watch his movies.

As a consequence, Attenborough kept up the pressure, with help from his supporters in the media and other high places.

In the second week of May, 2021, it was announced that Attenborough had been chosen by the British government as the 'Peoples Advocate' for the upcoming COP26 climate meeting:[303]

> 'David Attenborough has already inspired millions of people in the UK and around the world with his passion and knowledge to act on climate change and protect the planet for future generations.
>
> There is no better person to build momentum for further change as we approach the COP26 climate summit in November,' said Prime Minister Boris Johnson.
>
> Johnson, who is keen to burnish his environmental credentials, has said he will push leaders at the G7 summit he will chair to make firm climate commitments.
>
> Attenborough said COP26 had to succeed.
>
> 'There could not be a more important moment that we should have international agreement.

The epidemic has shown us how crucial it is to find agreement among nations if we are to solve such worldwide problems,' he said.

And there it is: the acknowledgement from the British Prime Minister that Attenborough's hard sell on climate change succeeded in convincing many government leaders that immediate action this year was essential.

However, this message could only have been as successful as it was because Attenborough began his three year campaign with fraudulent animal tragedy porn to deliberately shock viewers into action – including some of those government leaders.

And while Attenborough may indeed have 'inspired millions' around the world, that is hardly the endorsement it appears. The fact that Attenborough has presented a false view of the world in these recent documentaries means any support he believes he has from viewers is a sham and he has no authority to speak on their behalf.

However, Attenborough certainly *can* speak for the WWF and the powerful supporters of the WEF – although if Johnson had called this licence-to-grandstand appointment 'the WWF Advocate' or 'the WEF Advocate', it might not have been received as cheerfully.

Nevertheless, the appointment meant Attenborough would have a chance to get in a 'famous last word' to world leaders, as the 'Peoples Advocate' role provided him a speaking slot at the climate change summit.

Soon after the appointment, Attenborough was asked by the British government to use his Peoples Advocate position in June 2021 to lecture the leaders of G7 countries (Canada, France, Germany, Italy, Japan, the United Kingdom, the United States and the European Union), at a pre-COP26 meeting in the UK, regarding the need to commit to a date to phase out all coal-fired energy.

Not surprisingly, as at the UN Security Council meeting a few months before, he failed at influencing the decision: the USA refused and so did Japan.[304]

You may think I must finally be at the end of my litany of Attenborough's activist film performances but you'd be wrong. There were not one but two additional documentaries!

It's true: the Netflix/BBC/Attenborough-inspired film extravaganza did not end with *Breaking Boundaries*. As if eight documentaries and television series were not enough, there was a ninth film released before COP26 and another which premiered at the meeting itself (for general release in 2022.

It appears that as part of the promotion of the Earthshot Prize announced in October 2020 mentioned earlier in this chapter, there was a five-part 'climate crisis' television series produced by the BBC and Silverback Films called *The Earthshot Prize: Repairing Our Planet*.

The five one-hour promotional films aired from 2 October 2021, building up to the gala event announcing the winners of the Earthshot Prize on 17 October in London

For a double hit of propaganda, a companion book to the film ('Earthshot: How to Save Our Planet') was released in the UK and Europe on Thursday 30 September 2021 (and in North America on 5 October). And surprise, surprise: the 'Earthshot' book is co-authored by none other than Colin Butfield of the WWF, who played such a large role in *Our Planet* and *A Life On This Planet*. The book, like the companion film, is said to contain 'inspirational case studies of the incredible solutions happening globally to repair our planet'.[305]

The WWF were not the only ones to have benefitted from the association with Attenborough's campaign. Silverback Films (which was bought out by All3Media in December 2020 for an undisclosed amount – thank you, *Our Planet* Emmy awards!) launched a new production arm called 'Studio Silverback'.

Its mission statement sounds like something straight out of a WWF propaganda leaflet, which is not surprising since Colin Butfield is now one of its directors:[306]

> ...to use the power of film-making and story-telling to reveal the urgent truth of our changing planet to a global audience.

This is the most important decade in human history. Humanity must change now.

As Sir David Attenborough has said — achieving the right outcome is no longer a technological problem, it is a communications problem. If enough people can see the path to a sustainable future, we may just start down it in time.

The Studio is purpose-built to deliver this story and this vision, by joining with partners to create World-class environmental content for theatrical release, television, social media, major events and projects — anything and everything necessary to succeed.

The Directors of Studio Silverback are Colin Butfield, Jonnie Hughes, Keith Scholey and Alastair Fothergill.

That's right: Silverback Films and the WWF now have a formal business relationship to produce documentary films with a conservation message. This means we must be prepared for a continued onslaught of high-definition WWF propaganda, which could well contain statements from Attenborough until he is no longer able to appear on camera.

And finally, we get to the last Attenborough documentary in this short campaign.

The decisive film onslaught from Attenborough was saved for an exclusive audience of COP26 attendees: a BBC documentary series about the plant world narrated by Sir David called *The Green Planet.*

It apparently 'investigates the crucial role plants play in controlling our climate and maintaining our ecosystems.' The film was announced in 2019 as a five part series to be released in 2021 but a special episode was added for a premiere event screening on the eve of the climate meetings in Glasgow (31 October 2021), with general release of the original five parts in January 2022. [307]

The opening address of the pre-COP26 IMAX screening was given by Attenborough's fellow WWF Global Ambassador, Maisie Williams, and Attenborough was of course in attendance and told the BBC:[308]

> It is quite fitting that The Green Planet will receive its premiere at COP26, and I'm pleased that I could be in Glasgow to see it with an audience.
>
> For years plant life has been largely ignored when talking about climate change, but as viewers will see from watching the series, the green ecosystem is at the heart of all life on earth and thus it's vital that we tackle biodiversity and climate change together.

The same BBC review of the event also revealed:

> The giant 80x60ft IMAX screen also played a provocative animation ahead of the premiere featuring an electrocardiogram heartbeat that turns into a green plant stem and flatlines, perilously voiced by David Attenborough.
>
> As the audience exited the screening, they were confronted with a living plant installation that was abundant at the start of the screening but now appeared decaying and withered bearing the message: 'Let's not make Fossil Forests be our Future.'

The Green Planet premiere event was the closing act of Attenborough's aggressive climate change messaging accomplished through documentary film.[309]

Just like the exclusive preview of the first film series (Our Planet), with its emotionally wrenching falling walrus sequence created for an audience of powerful WEF attendees in Davos, this exclusive episode of The Green Planet series was likewise reserved for influential people at COP26.

Ultimately, however, it didn't make any difference at all.

# Chapter 12

# The Icon Falls

COP26 ended up a bitter result for Attenborough and his supporters. Given what they'd hoped to accomplish, it was a failure, as even staunch British environmentalist George Monbiot has admitted.[310]

Three years of hard-hitting public statements and ten propaganda-filled documentaries that misrepresented science had gotten Sir David nowhere.

Although even a few months beforehand, Attenborough's position appeared to have massive support,[311] it turned out that securing agreements for the ambitious climate action plans he was after was more difficult than he had anticipated.

Third world nations were still demanding billions from developed countries for adaption to climate change but now western governments were cash-strapped from dealing with their responses to the pandemic.[312] Most critically, there still wasn't the international support needed: China and India both rejected severe restrictions.[313]

Attenborough seemed particularly reticent to speak after news of the weak COP26 final agreement was made public. I could find only one interview with him after the meeting ended and in it, he made a vague statement that could perhaps be taken as a reference to the COP26 outcome:[314]

Sir David feels glad to have helped raise climate awareness through his documentaries and thinks there is hope for a healthier world.

"I believe TV is really very important from that point of view," he says.

"It is essential. We're only going to get out of this mess if nations get together and say 'We're facing a crisis'.

"Yes, I do think that the world is coming to its senses.

Whether it comes quickly enough and clearly enough is of course the problem."

However, his most dedicated supporters seemed not to have blamed Attenborough for the failure of COP26 to generate an earth-shattering international agreement: a poll taken by an eco-energy company just after the meeting ended found Attenborough topped the UK public's list of inspirational 'green' celebrities, beating out Greta Thunberg (second place), Leonardo DiCaprio (seventh place), Prince William and Prince Charles ('in the top ten').[315]

Obviously, for some the UK's 'national treasure' could *still* do no wrong.

However, others like me could see that Attenborough had not only failed to secure his legacy but had demeaned himself in the process.

He wasn't the only one in history who has succumbed to this inevitable fate of noble cause corruption – and certainly won't be the last – but he has been the most high-profile example in recent years. I knew another example from my work with polar bears and the similarities are striking.

I had shown in other work that the 2007 USGS forecast for future polar bear survival had failed spectacularly. Before the ink was dry on the prediction report, September ice extent dropped suddenly to levels not anticipated until 2050 – and remained there for a decade – yet global polar bear numbers may actually have risen.[316]

Through that analysis, I learned that the scientist who played the largest role in getting the polar bear classified as 'threatened' on the US Endangered Species List – former USGS biologist Steven Amstrup (now at Polar Bears International) – was not only intensely proud of this achievement but was fêted with awards. One came with a substantial amount of cash ($100,000 for the Indianapolis Prize in 2012) and another elevated him to rock-star status (for a BAMBI award, also in 2012).[317]

Amstrup's accomplishment depended upon a computer model that was fed his (and *only his*) assumptions and personal opinions regarding what polar bears would do in response to markedly reduced summer sea ice – treated by the model as facts – which in turn depended on untested model predictions of future Arctic summer sea ice coverage. Despite the high probability of the interconnected models being false due to their inherent uncertainty, the final output was accepted as a scientific result.[318]

Opinions and assumptions *had to* stand in for facts in the polar bear model because dramatically low sea ice coverage had not yet occurred while the bears were under study: no one knew for sure what effects such reduced ice would have. In other words, in the face of uncertainty due to lack of data, it was considered scientifically acceptable for opinions and assumptions to masquerade as facts.

Modelling of this nature is an increasingly common approach that is very worrying for conventional scientists and the public alike, a topic I'll return to later in this chapter.[319]

However, having polar bears declared 'threatened' on the basis of this model result was not enough for Amstrup.

What he appears to desire is a career legacy that gives him credit for spear-heading greenhouse gas emissions legislation being pushed through in the United States (something which has still not happened). He has become so focused on attaining that political goal – and defending it fiercely – that nothing else matters.[320]

I saw the same Amstrup legacy-building syndrome in Attenborough, except that Sir David was not only richer but far more influential. He also had a much grander goal: it seemed that nothing less than changing the way that society operated would be quite good enough.

He wasn't a scientist like Amstrup but Attenborough thought he had science behind him because he believed what the WWF told him was true.

Both men wanted to be remembered for saving the world with what they considered to be a science-based argument – or at least, for playing a big part in that salvation.

I've come to conclude that for men like Amstrup and Attenborough, the closer to the end of their careers they get – Amstrup is now 71 and Attenborough is 95 but both are still professionally active – the more desperate they become to accomplish their legacy goals, regardless of what is required – including discarding the public trust they had previously cultivated with care.

Ultimately, it seems hard to attribute such behaviour to anything other than vanity.

When viewed from afar, the agenda-driven narratives Attenborough has been spinning over the last few years certainly seem characteristic of legacy-seeking. Since 2018, he has taken on a distinctly pessimistic view of the world with unexpected fervour and promoted it aggressively.

I was truly shocked to see the raw brutality of the falling walrus footage in *Our Planet*, so uncharacteristic of an Attenborough film, be used to kick-start a hard-line political climate change mitigation campaign. It was a bomb used to get the worlds' attention.

I can only conclude that using the footage in this way was deliberate because it required such strategic planning and timing to attain. Moreover, the sequence had a distinct WWF-style flavour to it because the WWF had been given so much control in its production.

We know that the WWF had knowledge of the recurring phenomenon of polar bears driving walrus over the cliff at Cape Schmidt as early as 2011 because they had paid informants on the ground nearby. It was therefore highly likely that this information was one of the critical assets this organization brought to the *Our Planet* project.

It seems highly likely the WWF were the ones to approach Netflix about a film that included this phenomenon, although perhaps they approached SilverBack Films first and together the pair pitched the idea to Netflix.

However, by 2015 the *Our Planet* series, with all collaborators except Attenborough and the BBC acknowledged, was announced. Coincidentally or not, this was the same year Attenborough signed on to the WWF as an official 'Ambassador'.

As I pointed out in Chapter 1, WWF not only provided the funding for the series, it was also instrumental in getting film crews to a number of remote, restricted-access locations (including the Russian walrus haulouts) and was allowed to apply their unique brand of conservation 'science' to the entire project. This gave them a huge amount of control over the final product. In fact, one could argue they held the upper hand.

It was obvious that Attenborough trusted the WWF absolutely and Attenborough's high opinion of the organization seemed to have rubbed off on the rest of the partners.

The two owners of Silverback Films, Keith Scholey and Alastair Fothergill, had produced documentaries for the BBC with Attenborough for years before they branched off on their own. Attenborough seemed to have had as much trust in them as he had for the WWF.

This tight circle of collegial experience, with Attenborough at its centre, made possible the historic deal between Netflix, the WWF, Silverback Films, and the BBC to share footage of the critical walrus incident, filmed by a joint crew, between the *Our Planet* series (produced by WWF and Netflix) and *Seven Worlds* series (produced by the BBC).

*Seven Worlds* showed polar bears driving hundreds of walrus over the cliff edge at Cape Schmidt but *Our Planet,* released six months earlier, showed walrus falling off the cliff to their deaths without the impetus of predators, instead laying the blame squarely on climate change.

It is therefore inconceivable to me that the WWF, Silverback Films, and Netflix did not have Attenborough in mind as narrator for *Our Planet* as soon as the project was conceived prior to 2015.

Which means it's also highly likely that both Attenborough and the BBC were included in discussions about the walrus episode even before the series was announced to the public in 2015, although we cannot be sure.

That said, the presence of a BBC director/producer and two BBC cameramen on the Silverback Films expedition to Russia in 2017 strongly suggests there had been a plan in place from at least the time of the series announcement in 2015 to split the final walrus footage between the *Our Planet* and *Seven Worlds* projects. This conclusion is based on comments made by Sophie Lanfear regarding the two and a half years it had taken to plan the expedition to Russia.

Significantly, as I mentioned in Chapter 2, Silverback Films producer Keith Scholey was quoted as saying that they 'knew' as soon as they saw it that the falling walrus scene 'was going to be the footage that would become most associated with the climate change horror that's happening to Arctic species.'[321] It retrospect, it appears that they didn't so much 'know' this would happen but rather, they developed a calculated plan to make sure it did.

However, I have shown in this volume that most of what was said and implied about walrus in the *Our Planet* sequence was misleading or inaccurate. This is not surprising given that years before the film aired both the WWF and scientific advisor Anatoli Kochnev were pushing a decidedly pessimistic and largely false version of Pacific walrus conservation biology.[322]

Unfortunately, Attenborough, Silverback Films and BBC script writers assumed that the WWF science provided to them was up-to-date, accurate, and unbiased – but it was not.

For example, it was misleading to say that walrus would not have been on land if not for lack of sea ice due to human-caused climate change or to imply that land haulouts are somehow new or 'unnatural' for walrus.

We know that historically Pacific walrus herds of females and calves have used ice-free beaches as haulouts even when sea ice over shallow water has been available – and that most walrus males leave the ice after mating in the spring to use ice-free beaches in the Bering Sea until the following winter. Walrus can and do feed just as easily and successfully from shore as they do from sea ice and this has always been true.

It was also dishonest to claim that walrus were forced by lack of space to crowd close together on the single enormous haulout at Serdtse-Kamen shown in the film: walrus prefer very close contact wherever they haul out, even if there is room to spread out.

Moreover, the small herd of approximately 5,000 walrus did not choose the cliff haulout at Cape Schmidt in 2017 because they there was no space for them at Cape Serdtse-Kamen, as Attenborough implied in his narration. Not only was there ample space available at Serdtse-Kamen (which is a beach complex 20 kilometres long) but movement of the animals along this coast in the fall is the other way around, from Cape Schmidt to Serdtse-Kamen. Accordingly, the Netflix/BBC crew were at Serdtse-Kamen in October *after* finishing their filming at Cape Schmidt in September.

Lastly, hundreds of walrus did not die at Cape Schmidt because they wanted to join the herd in the water and had no other way to get down, as Attenborough claimed in *Our Planet*: that was outright dishonesty. At most perhaps a dozen or so died this way and rest of the several hundred dead walrus shown in the film died days earlier when polar bears frightened them over the cliff, as was shown in the *Seven Worlds* BBC documentary six months later and described in the 2017 Siberian Times article discussed in Chapter 4.

Unfortunately, Attenborough, Netflix and the BBC assumed (as National Geographic had done before them with the starving polar bear video described in Chapter 8) that the public would not be turned off by inaccuracies and obvious falsehoods about animal victims of climate change. However, it seems they were wrong on this score.

In addition, Attenborough, the WWF, Netflix and the BBC all assumed that they could make people care more about climate change by using horrifying images and relentless messages of doom. But they were incorrect on that as well.

How many people thought the *Our Planet* statement that hundreds of walrus fell to their deaths from a Siberian cliff because of climate change was absurd? How many others believed it must be true because it was uttered by Attenborough, a person they thought they could trust?

And how many people ultimately turned against Attenborough and the message he was trying to deliver because of the deception and emotional manipulation that was eventually revealed? I'd guess quite a few.

It doesn't really matter exactly when Attenborough realised that the WWF had a plan to use falling walrus deaths as a political cudgel in the climate change war but it does matter that he agreed to do the same.

Most people realise that a documentary filled with big-eyed babies and jaw-dropping scenery does not fully reflect the reality of the natural world, where accidents happen and predators kill and eat their prey. But the walrus-falling-to-their-deaths scene was something else: it was gratuitous animal tragedy porn.

There was no need to show a half dozen animals die an agonising death in slow motion – except for the political agenda.

This scene had WWF written all over it because that's how they do business. Their organization's primary goal has always been to generate donations and they have discovered over time that what works best is emotional blackmail.

So when Attenborough agreed to this strategy – something he had never resorted to before – he showed his hand. He showed us all what he was prepared to do to achieve what he wanted.

He was not trying to make a point that nature can be harsh: he was delivering a political message he wanted people to never forget.

The fact that Attenborough ultimately failed to achieve the legacy goal he appeared to have set for himself didn't mean the walrus ruse was not a success for everyone else involved. Within about a year of its release, the falling walrus film sequence and subsequent media attention had resulted in huge benefits.

Netflix got boosted subscribers and acquired a new 'sustainability' advisor (Johan Rockström, the climate 'tipping point' guy).

The WWF got boosted donations but more importantly, future deals that gave them executive control over similar climate change propaganda films marketed as entertainment. This was a *huge* win for them and clearly one of their primary goals: this fund-raising organization, as always run by savvy businessmen, is now firmly embedded in the documentary film industry.

Silverback Films got a lucrative buyout a mere seven years after Alastair Fothergill and Keith Scholey pulled out of the BBC.[323] The producers were still in charge but massive funds were injected into making similar climate change projects.

Producer/Director Sophie Lanfear became an Emmy-award winning director at an incredibly young age.

Kochnev almost certainly got more cash in foreign currency for his part in the filming than he ever believed possible for a Russian government scientist working in the remote Far East. I know from discussions with a Russian colleague in a similar situation that these employees take home a salary that is broadly equivalent to minimum wage – barely enough to keep them alive and certainly not enough to ever get ahead.

The BBC seems to have garnered the confidence boost and determination it needed to continue doing more hard-hitting climate change documentaries.

Even Attenborough, at least initially, seem to get everything he could have wanted: even more notoriety plus his second and third Emmys in two years (for *Our Planet* and *Seven Worlds*). In the end, he also got an appointment by the British government to speak at COP26.[324]

None of it would have happened without the shock value of the falling walrus sequence.

It was only Attenborough who didn't achieve the goal that was most important to him: seeing a ground-breaking result at COP26 that would change the world.

However, the unique alliance that was formed then between Netflix, the WWF, Silverback Films, David Attenborough and the BBC to produce *Our Planet* was not just an auspicious occasion: it was also the beginning of a new strategy to influence public opinion and 'nudge' political policy through message-laden documentaries passed off as entertainment.[325] This form of propaganda is not going to stop despite the poor showing at COP26 and Attenborough's failure to secure a legacy.

The ten documentaries that came out between 2019 and 2021 – all on the same theme, many with the same producers, but all narrated by Attenborough – were filmed over the same few years and released at calculated intervals with copious media attention, all aimed at securing an international climate deal at COP26 in 2020. The unexpected appearance of the Covid-19 pandemic threatened to derail the plan but ended up extending the agenda by another year, to 2021.

Once kick-started by the walrus sequence in *Our Planet*, these documentaries constituted Attenborough's aggressive agenda on climate change action. His many media interviews and public presentations were the primary means of promoting the films.

The following list shows just how tight the scheduling of release dates for the documentaries and special episodes were, even with an extra year added:

**29 January 2019.** Special premiere edition with falling walrus sequence, for WEF in Davos, *Our Planet* (Eight part series; Netflix/WWF/SilverbackFilms/BBC/Attenborough)

**5 April 2019.** *Our Planet* (Eight part series; Netflix/WWF/Silverback Films/BBC/Attenborough)

**18 April 2019.** *Climate Change – The Facts* (Two part series, BBC/Attenborough)

**4 November 2019.** *Seven Worlds, One Planet* (Seven part series; BBC/Netflix/WWF/Attenborough)

**13 September 2020.** *Extinction: The Facts* (One hour documentary, BBC/Attenborough)

**4 October 2020.** *A Life On Our Planet* (One hour documentary, Netflix/WWF/Silverback Films/Attenborough)

**4 January 2021.** *A Perfect Planet* (Five part series, BBC/Silverback Films/Attenborough)

**16 April 2021.** *The Year Earth Changed* (One hour documentary, BBC/Attenborough/AppleTV)

**4 June 2021**. *Breaking Boundaries – The Science of Our Planet* (One hour documentary, Netflix/Silverback Films/Rockström/ Attenborough)

**30 September 2021**. *The Earthshot Prize: Repairing Our Planet* (Five part series, BBC/Silverback Films/Attenborough/Colin Butfield from WWF)

**31 October 2021**. Special premiere edition, the night before COP26 in Glasgow, *The Green Planet* (Five part series, BBC/Attenborough), general release scheduled for January 2022

Critically, the ten films and associated publicity spearheaded by Attenborough kept climate change issues in the public eye for the three years leading up to COP26.

It's telling that the plan was initiated by a special premiere episode that featured the horrifying falling walrus scenes and concluded with a similar special premiere episode, both directed at powerful global influencers. This suggests political elites were critical targets for these documentaries and the films were not meant *only* for public consumption.

However, in his hard-hitting promotion of the invisible catastrophes that supposedly demonstrate the existence of a 'climate emergency' – not proposed for some point in the future, but occurring *right now* – Attenborough has been spreading misinformation, biased opinions, and bad science.

And I'm not the only one that thinks so.[326]

Conditions in the natural world are simply not as bad as Attenborough and the WWF insist. Polar bears and walrus are not currently starving to death in great numbers because of reduced summer sea ice, despite high-profile experts insisting this might happen in the future.[327]

There is no evidence of a great ongoing extinction of named, visible species, although the WWF continue to say there is.[328] In fact, a good many species formerly driven to the brink of extinction by overhunting have recovered in spectacular fashion, including the polar bear, walrus, sea otter, northern elephant seal, humpback whale, grey whale, and bowhead whale.[329]

Moreover, the scariest and most extreme climate predictions of the future (including the newest models used to forecast polar bear survival) are the ones that get the most media attention and yet these have been shown to be based on quite implausible 'business as usual' scenarios that massively exaggerate possible future conditions.[330]

And while it is true that recent sea ice changes have presented challenges for Arctic peoples who had come to depend on a particular coverage of ice to hunt and travel at a particular time of year, this is not a new phenomenon.[331]

The Arctic is one of the harshest environments on Earth for all forms of life, including humans. Change in local weather and sea ice conditions over short and long time frames have always occurred but fortunately, humans and Arctic animals have demonstrated that they are spectacularly good at adaptation.[332]

Similarly, when examined dispassionately, weather disasters have not increased in recent years, despite virtually every storm being blamed on climate change: even the IPCC says so.[333] Weather disasters have always happened and always will – but fossil fuels have not only enabled us to better protect ourselves from their effects but to recover quickly once they have occurred.[334]

Lastly, crop yields for many critical commodities – particularly rice, corn, wheat, and sugarcane – were at or near record levels in 2020/2021, despite (and perhaps partly *because of*) much higher amounts of human-produced carbon dioxide in the atmosphere than there had been in the 1980s and which had generated many predictions of drought- and/or flood-related crop disasters.[335]

How can climate change be blamed for a catastrophe that has not taken place? How can there be a climate emergency if one is not discernible?

Insisting a climate emergency exists doesn't make it so, no matter how often or loudly Attenborough says it does.

What is even more worrying is that when his hard-hitting climate change films made Attenborough a sought-after media guest, it encouraged him to express even stronger opinions he could not have included in his documentaries.

He used one such occasion to promote a revolutionary concept about how future societies should operate that involved curtailing what he called the 'excesses' of capitalism, a utopian vision that many people in the world simply don't share.[336]

These statements exposed a radical side to Attenborough that hadn't really been evident before: he seemed to have become a mouth-piece for a fringe political movement populated by wealthy revolutionaries espousing extremist ideologies.

Is Attenborough really one of those wealthy elites who think that other people (certainly not *them*) are causing the destruction of the environment with their excesses and that the lives of those people must be controlled for the common good?

Such radicals — many of whom are supporters of the World Economic Forum (WEF) *and whose company Attenborough routinely keeps* — apparently see a global government as the only way to save humanity and the natural world.[337]

At its most basic, this goal of a global government and curbing capitalism is not a crazy conspiracy theory, as some media 'fact-checkers' still insist.[338] It is a well-developed and strongly articulated concept supported by individuals with enormous political power including (among others) heir to the British throne Prince Charles (and his son Prince William), US President Joe Biden, Canadian prime minister Justin Trudeau, and billionaire Bill Gates, as well as many organizations with enormous wealth including (among many others), all major vaccine manufacturers and pharmaceutical companies, major banks and money lenders (including PayPal, Mastercard, and Visa), the Bill and Melinda Gates Foundation, internet and social media powerhouses (including Facebook, Google, and Microsoft).[339]

Aggressively addressing climate change has been a focus of the WEF and its supporters for decades and it's no secret that some of them saw the Covid-19 pandemic as an opportunity for advancement of their utopian agenda.[340] However, despite the power and money behind their fanciful scheme, it is unlikely that anything will come of it – for the same reasons that COP26 failed.

The way I see it, predictive computer modelling, including the tipping point nonsense promoted in Attenborough's films, has played a huge role in fueling such ideologies. Forecast modelling has muddled the critical distinction between scientific facts (i.e. observations) and assumptions (i.e. opinions).

Widespread use and acceptance of predictive modelling to forecast all kinds of future conditions has contributed heavily to the political corruption of science because it allows opinion (potentially skewed by political ideology) to stand in for scientific facts that are not yet known.[341] Uncertainty, which once provided the impetus to keep collecting data before conclusions were drawn, now provides an excuse to accept model results as scientific facts.

Oddly, it's as if those involved believe that developing and running a computer model that gives facts and opinions equal weight is the same as conducting an actual scientific experiment developed to test a hypothesis – and that the model output deserves the same amount of scientific trust and respect as an experimental observation that can be replicated.

Science is no longer seen as a method of dispassionate investigation of how the natural world works – where constant questioning refines and hones the answers – but a tool to be weaponized for attaining political ends. On that score, this investigation truly opened my eyes.

This politicization of science is evident in the routine use of the phrase 'the science says' in defending climate change policy positions. But more terrifying still have been the 'expert' scientific opinions that could not be questioned and the predictive models based on implausible worst-case scenarios that have been used, over and over since early 2020, to justify draconian government containment measures for Covid-19 under the guise of a 'human health emergency'.[342]

The public's trust in science and medicine now appears to be at an all-time low. People who had been blind to the abuse of science rampant in the climate change narrative have had their eyes opened by the pandemic response. These things cannot be unseen.[343]

In a worrying trend, traditional scientists struggle to be heard or have their concerns and criticisms published, both for climate change and Covid-19 related issues, while predictive modelling projects seem to gobble up grant funds and media attention.[344]

Is science as we used to know it already dead? If so, how much of a role has Attenborough played in this progression? Over the last three years, he has used weaponized science presented to a trusting public in a most egregious manner.

My ultimate goal in writing this book is not to denigrate Sir David but to correct the misinformation he has deliberately or unwittingly promoted in his documentaries and public statements.

I am a traditional scientist standing up for science as it is meant to be – without activism and without politicization – because its loss to society will be incalculable.

Over the years but especially since 2018, Attenborough has shown that he lets others do his serious thinking for him and has often placed his trust where it was ill-advised, as he has done with the WWF. By that I mean he has relied on others to present information to him in an easily digestible manner rather than delving into the literature himself.

And having spent a lifetime taking this easy way out, when he decided he wanted his legacy to be something more substantial than 'a good storyteller', he seemed to take on the role of spokesman for others with ideological political agendas.

It appears to me that when he agreed to present the gruesome falling walrus film footage in *Our Planet* as evidence of climate change,

Attenborough compromised his principles to achieve a specific end result. Such noble cause corruption is common in the conservation world but it was new for Attenborough.

I am convinced that what Attenborough has done with the falling walrus episode will be remembered long after he's dead but not for the reasons he intended. It will go down as another 'own goal' for the climate change movement and judged as the moment Attenborough fell from grace as a trusted British icon.

# Notes

[1] Barkham 2019

[2] https://en.wikipedia.org/wiki/David_Attenborough [accessed 20 March 2021]

[3] General Register Office. England and Wales Civil Registration Indexes. *London, Eng*land: General Register Office. *1954, Volu*me 5c, Page 354; Taylor 2020; https://www.babycenter.ca/a559006/popular-baby-names-from-the-past [Canada, 1954]; https://www.babymed.com/baby-names/top-100-baby-names-england-and-wales-1954

[4] Barkham 2019; https://www.celebritynetworth.com/richest-celebrities/david-attenborough-net-worth/ [no date, accessed 20 March 2021]

[5] Ling 2019a

[6] https://en.wikipedia.org/wiki/RRS_Sir_David_Attenborough [*RRS Sir David Attenborough* made its inaugural journey to Antarctica in November 2021]

[7] Barkham 2019

[8] Barkham 2019; Whitworth 2019c

[9] Barkham 2019

[10] Barkham 2019; Hickman 2018; Monbiot 2018

[11] Hickman 2018.

[12] Booker 2011

[13] Attenborough is a trustee of the Optimum Population Trust, which campaigns for population reductions.

[14] Nolan 2013; https://www.livescience.com/26473-david-attenborough-humanity-plague.html [22 January 2013; accessed 20 March 2021]; see also Lyons 2009 and https://populationmatters.org/news/2018/10/sir-david-attenborough-we-must-act-population

[15] The international organization now goes by the name 'World Wide Fund for Nature' (WWF) but is still known as World Wildlife fund in the US and Canada and its website address is www.worldwildlife.org

[16] Schwarzenbach, A. 2011:81

[17] Kay 2014; Farhoud and Lines 2021

[18] Schwarzenbach, A. 2011; WWF no date

[19] Laframboise 2012

[20] Glüsing and Klawitter 2012; Laframboise 2011a; Laframboise 2011c; WWF 2011; shortly after this time, WWF-International seems to have stopped producing a document that shows its entire holdings (each subsidiary country produces its own), which obscures the immense wealth of the parent company.

[21] WWF, no date

[22] Booker 2012

[23] Laframboise 2011a; Laframboise 2011b; Laframboise 2011c
https://wwf.panda.org/?117540/Climate-Witness-Fact-Sheets [2009]

[24] Laframboise 2014

[25] Given 1993; Horton et al. 2016; Noss 1999; Westcott 2016; WWF 2016a; WWF 2018; WWF 2020b

[26] https://www.worldwildlife.org/publications

[27] Crockford 2019c; Wilder et al. 2017

[28] https://arcticwwf.org/newsroom/stories/tatyana-minenko-the-polar-bear-patrol-chief/ [Ryrkaipiy, 25 March 2020; https://www.worldwildlife.org/stories/one-arctic-town-s-very-busy-polar-bear-patrol [East Greenland, 26 Feb 2018]

[29] Zerehi 2016

[30] WWF 2016a; WWF 2018; https://wwf.panda.org/wwf_news/?345490/Our-Planet-highlights-need-for-global-action-to-protect-nature

[31] Booker 2017

[32] WWF 2016a

[33] BBC 2019c; Westcott 2016; WWF 2016b;
https://www.inverse.com/article/39394-david-attenborough-sixth-mass-extinction

[34] Hopton 2020; https://www.wildlife-film.com/-/Silverback-Films.htm

[35] McFarland 2015

[36] WWF 2015b, WWF 2020a; Whitworth 2019b

[37] Whitworth 2019a; WWF 2015b

[38] Hopton 2019

[39] Jones 2018

[40] Kamp 2018; Netflix 2018

[41] Whitworth 2019a

[42] Whitworth 2019a

[43] Moody 2020; https://financesonline.com/number-of-netflix-subscribers/ [accessed 24 March 2021]

[44] https://en.wikipedia.org/wiki/List_of_most_watched_television_broadcasts_in_the_United_Kingdom [accessed 24 March 2021]

[45] Fothergill was head of BBC Natural History Unit (NHU) 1992-1998 and Scholey was head from 1998-2003; Silverback Films has headquarters in Bristol, UK, where the BBC NHU is also located; https://en.wikipedia.org/wiki/BBC_Natural_History_Unit [accessed 26 March 2021]; Silverback Films was bought out by All3Media in December 2020 (Kanter 2020a).

[46] 'Our Planet – Frozen Worlds' (44:30):
https://www.netflix.com/watch/80094031

168

[47] 'Our Planet – Frozen Worlds' (44:30):
https://www.netflix.com/watch/80094031

[48] Whitworth 2019b

[49] Hopton 2019

[50] 'Our Planet|Walrus|Behind the Scenes|Netflix' [9 April 2019]
https://www.youtube.com/watch?v=qVJzQc9ELTE; see also
https://www.ourplanet.com/en/video/behind-the-scenes-walrus/

[51] Abbott 2019; Bender 2019; Ling 2019b; Letzter 2019; Macdonald 2019;
McPhee 2019; New Zealand Herald 2019; Pakalolo 2019; Slaughter 2019; Travers
2019; but see Midgley 2019; Kahn 2019 for not-so-glowing reviews

[52] Yong 2019

[53] Vineyard 2019

[54] Whitworth 2019b; a week later, WWF-UK tweeted a short video of the huge
haulout and stated: 'Walruses, the new symbol of climate change. They'd be on
ice if they could' https://twitter.com/wwf_uk/status/1116804504089968640 [12
April 2019]

[55] 'Behind the Scenes' video on the *Our Planet website*
https://www.ourplanet.com/en/video/behind-the-scenes-
walrus/?fbclid=IwAR0k2kRVMHPShwDxhyzcyt8iUmoo420Dyxptj5SjQpUEmM7M
etqWBCXnKBw [on or before 7 April 2019]; 'Behind the scenes of Our Planet's
walrus shoot' WWF International [10 April 2019] https://www.youtube.com/
watch?v=WNkJX2DgH9M

[56] Macdonald 2019; McPhee 2019; Slaughter 2019

[57] Hopton 2019

[58] CBC Radio 2019

[59] McPhee 2019

[60] CBC Radio 2019; https://twitter.com/netflix/status/1116024755356749824
[10 April 2019]

[61] Crockford 2014a; MacCracken et al. 2017

[62] Lindqvist et al. 2009

[63] Fay 1982:200-203

[64] Fay 1982

[65] Fay 1982; Lowry 2015;MacCracken et al. 2017

[66] Beatty et al. 2016; Fay 1982; Freitas et al. 2009

[67] Fay 1982; Fischbach et al. 2016

[68] Fay 1982; Lowry 2015; MacCracken et al. 2017; USFWS 2011

[69] Fay and Kelly 1980; Fay et al. 1984; Fischbach et al. 2016, Table 1; Garlich-
Miller et al. 2011

[70] Bockstoce and Botkin 1982; Fay et al. 1989

[71] Lowry 1985; Fay et al. 1989; Fay et al. 1997; Fay and Kelly 1980; Larsen Tempel and Atkinson 2020; Steele 2013; Taylor and Udevitz 2015; Taylor et al. 2018

[72] Beatty et al. 2019:4; MacCracken et al. 2017:25; Speckman et al. 2011: 516; USFWS 2017a; USFWS 2017b

[73] Brown et al. 2011; Coupel et al. 2019; Crockford 2021; Frey et al. 2020; Lewis et al. 2020; NSIDC 2020

[74] Fay 1982; NAMMCO 2021

[75] Fay and Kelly 1980; Steele 2013

[76] MacCracken et al. 2017; USFWS 2017a; USFWS 2017b

[77] http://polarbearscience.com/2019/04/07/attenboroughs-tragedy-porn-of-walruses-plunging-to-their-deaths-because-of-climate-change-is-contrived-nonsense/

[78] Charles Rotter, who moderates the popular science blog Watts Up With That, alerted me to the *Our Planet* claims being reported in the news

[79] https://www.youtube.com/watch?v=4tM1NJ3a4G0 ['Zoologist in trouble for refuting polar bear groupthink' – Tucker Carlson, 5 April 2019]; see also https://www.dailywire.com/news/45465/tucker-carlson-beats-cnns-entire-prime-time-line-ryan-saavedra

[80] Mclaughlin 2017; http://siberiantimes.com/ecology/others/news/village-besieged-by-polar-bears-as-hundreds-of-terrorised-walruses-fall-38-metres-to-their-deaths [19 October 2017, accessed 6 April 2019]; see also Stone 2017

[81] Basov 2017 [photo 23, taken 22 September 2017]; Montford 2019a

[82] https://basov-chukotka.livejournal.com/319273.html

[83] Associated Press 2007; Basov 2017; Fischbach et al. 2016; also the estimate of 3,000 dead walrus at Cape Schmidt in 2007 came from Anatoly Kochnev in a conversation with reporters that year but Fischbach and colleagues in their 2016 summary report say an 'unknown number' died in 2007, which sounds like they didn't believe him even though he was a co-author of the report; also https://wwf.ru/en/resources/news/arkhiv/na-mys-kozhevnikova-prishli-morzhi/ [2008]

[84] Fischbach et al. 2016 [for 2011]

[85] http://programmes.putin.kremlin.ru/en/bear/news/25203 [2015]

[86] Basov 2017

[87] https://www.youtube.com/watch?v=IA-_QsCEZ0U&feature=youtu.be

[88] Rode et al. 2014; Rode et al. 2018

[89] Berseneva 2013; Hanson 2019; Kearney 1989; RT News 2013; Stirling et al. 1977

[90] Berseneva 2013; Kavry et al. 2006; https://wwf.panda.org/wwf_news/?78640/Polar-bear-groups-on-patrol-in-Russias-northeast and

http://wwf.panda.org/knowledge_hub/where_we_work/arctic/what_we_do/cli
mate/climatewitness2/expedition_diary.cfm [undated WWF account but clearly
from 2007 based on historical references in the text]

[91] Mclaughlin 2017; http://siberiantimes.com/ecology/others/news/village-
besieged-by-polar-bears-as-hundreds-of-terrorised-walruses-fall-38-metres-to-
their-deaths [19 October 2017, accessed 6 April 2019];
https://tass.com/society/1235879 [16 December 2020, accessed 17 December
2020]

[92] Crockford 2017; Crockford 2019a

[93] Dikov 1988; Kochneva 2007

[94] Kochnev 2002

[95] Pereverzev and Kochnev 2012

[96] Crockford 2014a; Lydersen 2018; Ray et al. 2016; Taylor et al. 2018; Udevitz et
al. 2013; USFWS 2011; USGS 2008; http://worldanimalnews.com/conservation-
groups-urge-trump-administration-protect-pacific-walrus-arctic-sea-ice-melts/
[23 August 2017]

[97] Crockford 2019a; Siegel 2018; MacCracken et al. 2017;
https://www.biologicaldiversity.org/about/story/ [accessed 26 July 2021]

[98] MacCracken et al. 2017; USFWS 2017a; USFWS 2017b

[99] By late 2019, the legal appeals to overturn the decision had been lost and
though the CBD blamed this result on 'the Trump administration', this was a
specious claim: the strong evidence that was required to make the case simply
wasn't there. See US District Court Alaska 2019; https://biologicaldiversity.org/
w/news/press-releases/trump-administration-denial-protection-pacific-
walruses-appealed-2019-11-21/

[100] https://www.thegwpf.com/public-are-being-misled-by-attenboroughs-new-
netflix-show/ [9 April 2019]

[101] Knapton 2019

[102] Yong 2019

[103] Dyer and Macdonald 2019

[104] Australian 2019; Delingpole 2019a; Jones 2019; Peiser 2019; Prance 2019;
Verity 2019; Whigham 2019; https://www.tmz.com/2019/04/09/netflix-
defends-walrus-fall-scene-our-planet-docuseries-climate-change/;
https://fox5sandiego.com/2019/04/11/why-everyone-is-talking-about-a-walrus-
scene-on-netflix/

[105] McPherson tweets 14 Sept 2017 https://twitter.com/BooMcP/status/
908474217166860288 ['final leg to the north east...'] and 26 October 2017
https://twitter.com/BooMcP/status/923775808988110848 ['heading home after
one of the most amazing shoots I've ever been involved in...watch this space
(and BBC1 and Netflix 2019) to hear about it']

[106] Montford 2019a; https://helpdeskgeek.com/how-to/view-photo-exif-
metadata-on-iphone-mac-and-windows/

107 Basov 2017

108 Fischbach et al. 2016; Kochnev 2010

109 Kochnev 2010; Chalikev and Kochnev 2018; Chalikev and Kochnev 2019; Chakilev et al. 2015

110 https://www.usgs.gov/media/images/walruses-resting-shore-cape-serdtse-kamen-haulout-area

111 Chakilev and Kochnev 2018; Jay et al. 2012; Kochnev 2010

112 Chakilev and Kochnev 2018 [2015]; Fischbach et al. 2016; also https://www.usgs.gov/media/images/walruses-resting-shore-cape-serdtse-kamen-haulout-area [2009 and historical]

113 Montford 2019a; Burns 2013; New York Times 1996; Badger 1996

114 Garlich-Miller et al. 2011; https://www.fws.gov/refuge/Togiak/what_we_do/science/walrus.html

115 https://notalotofpeopleknowthat.wordpress.com/2019/04/14/why-attenboroughs-walrus-claims-are-fake/

116 USFWS 2018, USFWS 2019

117 Montford 2019b; Montford 2019c; Delingpole 2019b

118 Basov 2017

119 Homewood 2019; Montford 2019c; Moore [with Crockford] 2019

120 Arie 2019; Bastasch 2019; Foster 2019; Massey 2019; Miller 2019; Pochin 2019; Richardson 2019; Sarah D. 2019; https://en.wikipedia.org/wiki/Twitchy

121 Crockford 2019b; Mittermeier 2018; Crockford 2018a; Crockford 2018b; Crockford 2018c; Crockford 2019a; http://polarbearscience.com/2018/08/29/white-lie-polar-bear-starvation-is-virtually-never-caused-by-sea-ice-loss/

122 Dyer and Macdonald 2019

123 Bender 2019

124 TMZ 2019

125 Dyer and Macdonald 2019; Furdyk 2019; Jones 2019; National Post 2019; Stolworthy 2019; Toone 2019; https://www.complex.com/pop-culture/2019/04/netflix-stands-behind-graphic-walrus-death-scene-in-new-our-planet-documentary [9 April 2019]; https://www.stuff.co.nz/entertainment/tv-radio/111921431/debate-over-netflixs-shocking-wildlife-documentary-showing-climate-change-or-contrived-nonsense [10 April 2019]; https://www.oversixty.com.au/entertainment/movies/why-netflix-is-under-fire-for-this-tragic-walrus-scene-in-david-attenborough-s-our-planet [April 2019]; https://www.theedge.co.nz/home/scandal/2019/04/netflix-defends-graphic-scene-in--our-planet-.html [April 2019]

126 Ward 2019a; https://www.lse.ac.uk/granthaminstitute/profile/bob-ward/

127 Homewood 2020; Ridley 2019; Ward 2021

128 Fischbach et al. 2016; the 1994-1996 deaths of walruses at the cliffs at Cape Peirce in the Bering Sea

129 Crockford 2014a; Crockford 2014b; Appendix A

130 Harvey et al. 2018; see also Corcoran 2017; Crockford 2017; Crockford and Geist 2018; Laframboise and Crockford 2020; Rajan and Tol 2018; http://polarbearscience.com/2018/04/10/climate-mauling-polar-bears-and-the-self-inflicted-wounds-of-the-self-righteous/ [10 April 2018]

131 https://www.dailykos.com/stories/2019/4/16/1850695/-Deniers-Attack-Walrus-Deaths-Story-Showing-Who-s-The-Real-Threat-to-Our-Planet [16 April 2021]; https://thelogicofscience.com/2019/05/09/climate-change-denier-vs-attenborough-why-did-those-walruses-die/ [9 May 2019]

132 Pond 2019; https://www.silverbackfilms.tv/3782-2/ [no date]

133 https://www.emmys.com/bios/sir-david-attenborough

134 WWF 2015b, WWF 2020a; Whitworth 2019b; Holthaus 2016; Vineyard 2019

135 https://www.youtube.com/watch?v=jS4ASw1xFPw [Scholey and Lanfear at the Emmys, 11 October 2019]; https://www.silverbackfilms.tv/our-planet-wins-two-emmy-awards/; https://www.ourplanet.com/en/news-articles/our-planet-wins-two-emmy-awards/; https://www.worldwildlife.org/pages/our-planet

136 Pond 2019

137 Hale 2020

138 Kasper 2019; see also Leyfield 2019

139 Edwards 2019; Hoare 2019; MacAree 2019; Shelley 2019

140 Deguara 2019

141 BBC 2019d; https://www.dailymotion.com/video/x7w4rao [viewed 11 April 2021]

142 BBC 2019e; https://www.dailymotion.com/video/x7w4rao [viewed 11 April 2021]

143 BBC 2019e

144 BBC 2019e; https://www.dailymotion.com/video/x7w4rao [viewed 11 April 2021]; https://www.imdb.com/title/tt10340164/

145 McKinlay 2019; Hale 2020

146 https://www.emmys.com/bios/sir-david-attenborough

147 Collins 2017; Gibbons 2017; Robinson 2018; Vincent 2018; Watts 2017; https://www.youtube.com/watch?v=_JhaVNJb3ag [the original short video with captions (1:23), posted 11 December 2017 with 2.7 billion views at 8 May 2021]

148 Mittermeier 2018

149 As far as I can determine, Nicklen studied marine biology at the University of Victoria (BC, Canada) for an unspecified time but there is no claim he finished a 4 year bachelor of science program or has any other scientific credentials

150 CBC Radio 2017a; see Truett 1993 for a list of polar bear attractants

[151] Crockford 2019d

[152] https://www.instagram.com/p/BcU-6PsAoIp/?hl=en [5 December 2017]

[153] Gibbens 2017; https://www.nationalgeographic.com/magazine/2018/08/explore-through-the-lens-starving-polar-bear-photo/

[154] CBC Radio 2017a; Collins 2017; Gibbons 2017; Pappas 2017; Rosenberg 2017; Watts 2017

[155] https://polarbearscience.com/2017/12/09/one-starving-bear-is-not-evidence-of-climate-change-despite-gruesome-photos/ [published 9 December 2017 at 12:03 AM]

[156] Nuccitelli 2017; PBI 2017a; Popkin 2017; Weber 2017

[157] Harvey et al. 2018; but see also Corcoran 2017; Crockford 2019a; LaFrambroise and Crockford 2020; Rajan and Tol 2018; Moore 2021; http://polarbearscience.com/2018/04/10/climate-mauling-polar-bears-and-the-self-inflicted-wounds-of-the-self-righteous/ [10 April 2018]

[158] BBC 2017; CBC Radio 2017b; CBC Radio 2017c; Delingpole 2017; Hopper 2017; Leafe 2017; Wente 2017

[159] PBI 2017b [published 9 December 2017 at 9:29 PM]

[160] https://twitter.com/jeffwhigdon/status/939578081811009536 [9 December 2017 at 12:30 PM and the thread following]

[161] Stevens 2017

[162] Hopper 2017

[163] CBC Radio 2017b; CBC Radio 2017c

[164] Watts 2017

[165] Castro de la Guardia et al. 2017; Cherry et al. 2013; Crockford 2020b; Crockford 2021; Elliot 1875; Klein and Sowls 2011; Ovsyanikov 2010; Ovsyanikov and Menyushina 2015; Ramsay and Stirling 1988; Robbins et al. 2012; Rozel 2010; Stirling and Lunn 1997; Stirling et al. 1977

[166] Rosenberg 2019

[167] Aars et al. 2006; Crockford 2021; Regehr et al. 2016; Wiig et al. 2015

[168] Vincent 2018

[169] See also Wright 2018

[170] Mittermeier 2018

[171] https://www.youtube.com/watch?v=_JhaVNJb3ag [the original short video with captions (1:23), posted 11 December 2017; 2.7 billion views at 8 May 2021]

[172] Gibbens 2017; https://www.nationalgeographic.com/magazine/2018/08/explore-through-the-lens-starving-polar-bear-photo/

[173] Ferreras 2018; Hodge 2018; Richards 2018; Robinson 2018

[174] Bastasch 2018b; Blake 2018; Huff 2018; La Framboise 2018; Wright 2018

[175] http://polarbearscience.com/2018/07/26/the-truth-behind-the-baffin-bay-starving-polar-bear-video-is-worse-than-we-thought/

[176] Crockford 2018a; see also Crockford 2018b; Crockford 2018c

[177] Blake 2018

[178] Jones 2018

[179] e.g. https://www.ispot.tv/ad/qCWT/world-wildlife-fund-home-polar-bears [22 November 2021]

[180] WWF 2015a; https://arcticwwf.org/newsroom/the-circle/walruses-going-with-the-floes/ [Feb 2017]

[181] Pond 2019

[182] McLachlan 2019

[183] Amanpour 2019

[184] The film crew arrived in Chukotka in the middle of September 2019 and the announcement of the Netflix/WWF *Our Planet* deal was made on 15 April 2015

[185] Vineyard 2019

[186] Burns 2013

[187] WWF 2015a

[188] WWF 2020a [the role of Paul Harvey stated as: 'Paul heads the insight team at WWF who evaluated the impact of the Our Planet series on viewers...The aim of the series was to have a lasting impact on those who engaged with it, and his involvement was to support on behaviour change, identifying key audiences and evaluation.']

[189] https://www.researchgate.net/profile/Anatoly-Kochnev

[190] Kochnev 2010; Kochnev 2012a; Kochnev 2012b; Kochnev 2018; Chakilev and Kochnev 2018; Chakilev et al. 2015

[191] Kochnev 2002; Kochnev 2004

[192] Kochnev 2017; see also the entire WWF 'The Circle' magazine issue 2017 (2): https://arcticwwf.org/newsroom/the-circle/walruses-going-with-the-floes/

[193] MacCracken 2012; MacCracken et al. 2017; Lowry 2015; Taylor et al. 2018

[194] Garlick-Miller et al. 2011

[195] NAMMCO 2021

[196] MacCracken et al. 2017:25; Speckman et al. 2011: 516

[197] Garlich-Miller et al. 2011; see Chapter 3 for a discussion of the most recent walrus population estimates, i.e. Beatty et al. 2019

[198] Chakilev and Kochnev 2018; Chakilev and Kochnev 2019; Kochnev 2010

[199] Chakilev and Kochnev 2019; Kochnev 2010

[200] Chakilev et al. 2015

[201] https://arcticbiodiversity.is/winners [CAFF, 2014; accessed 30 March 2021]

[202] This cabin makes a fleeting appearance in the portion of the WWF 'Behind the Scenes' video that was shot at the Cape Serdtse-Kamen haulout but is not seen in the Netflix film; see 'Behind the scenes of Our Planet's walrus shoot' WWF International [10 April 2019] at

https://www.youtube.com/watch?v=WNkJX2DgH9M; the same cabin appears on the USGS website here: https://www.usgs.gov/media/images/walruses-resting-shore-cape-serdtse-kamen-haulout-area

203 https://arcticbiodiversity.is/winners [CAFF, 2014; accessed 30 March 2021]

204 BBC 2019d

205 Bender 2019

206 Kochnev 2018

207 Burgess et al. 2021; Christy 2019; Hausfather and Peters 2020; Lomborg 2001; Lomborg 2020a; Lomborg 2020b; O'Neil et al. 2020; Ridley 2010; Ridley 2014; Ridley 2015; Spencer 2021

208 Moore 2021

209 BBC 2019f; https://nationalpost.com/news/canada/were-going-to-die-toronto-mother-says-young-daughter-terrified-by-school-presentation-on-climate-change; see also https://judithcurry.com/2021/05/06/eco-anxiety/

210 Aars 2018; Boveng 2016; Crockford 2017; Crockford 2018c; Crockford 2019a; Crockford 2019b; Crockford 2021; Kovacs 2016; Lowry 2015; MacCracken et al. 2017; Obbard et al. 2016; Rode et al. 2014; Rode et al. 2018

211 Crockford 2020a; https://www.thegwpf.com/david-attenborough-blamed-for-epidemic-of-eco-anxiety-among-young-people/ [press release]

212 Derocher and Stirling 1992: Fig. 2 which includes the 1960s data (see also Derocher and Stirling 1995a; Derocher and Stirling 1995b; Derocher and Stirling 1996) vs. Stirling et al. 1999 which does not

213 Regehr et al. 2007; Stirling and Parkinson 2006

214 Obbard et al. 2010; Crockford 2020b; Crockford 2021

215 Wiig et al. 2015, including supplement

216 https://www.bbc.co.uk/programmes/p0342d1x [2015: 'The Hunt']

217 https://www.nydailynews.com/entertainment/tv/mom-baby-walrus-break-heart-article-1.3762006 and https://www.radiotimes.com/news/tv/2018-01-26/blue-planet-2-walrus/

218 Wiig et al. 2015

219 Ahearn 2020; Carr 2019; Williams 2020

220 https://www.bbc.co.uk/programmes/p07w41ll ['Seven Worlds, One Planet: North America']; Smith and Sjare 1990

221 Elliot 2017; Williams 2020

222 Elliot 2017; https://www.youtube.com/watch?v=C-kDbS_-OBo&feature=youtu.be ['The Wild Canadian Year: Summer', at 36:50; 8 December 2018]; see also https://www.cbc.ca/wildcanadianyear/episodes/series-preview/summer; in contrast, see Rolling Stone 2019 and https://www.youtube.com/watch?v=edHWwHE0kVA&feature=youtu.be [National Geographic, 11 April 2019, 'Hostile Planet']

223 BBC 2019f (video); Harvey 2019; Watts 2019

[224] https://www.bbc.co.uk/programmes/articles/270DpZjTRtdscc0qbQbmDH7/
10-things-we-learned-when-greta-thunberg-met-david-attenborough;
https://www.youtube.com/watch?v=tmrFUVOOR14 [Greta Thunberg talks to
David Attenborough, 30 December 2019]

[225] Crockford 2018a; Crockford 2018b; Crockford 2019a;
http://polarbearscience.com/2018/08/29/white-lie-polar-bear-starvation-is-
virtually-never-caused-by-sea-ice-loss/ (and references therein)

[226] e.g. Borenstein et al. 2021; Stirling and Parkinson 2006

[227] [2009 cannibalism]; http://www.naturalexposures.com/corkboard/polar-
bear-caught-in-act-of-infanticide-and-cannibalism/;
http://www.dailymail.co.uk/sciencetech/article-1234066/Is-global-warming-
causing-hungry-polar-bears-resort-cannibalism.html;
https://www.reuters.com/news/picture/polar-bear-turns-cannibal-
idUSRTXRLWU; rebutted in this story
http://www.nationalpost.com/Climate+change+blame+polar+bear+cannibalism/
2322656/story.htm; [2013 emaciated carcass]
http://www.theguardian.com/environment/picture/2013/aug/06/polar-bear-
climate-change-sea-ice; rebutted in this video Crockford 2018b; [2015 injured
emaciated bear] http://www.huffingtonpost.ca/2015/09/08/thin-polar-bear-
kerstin-langenberger_n_8106620.html rebutted in these two stories,
https://www.cbc.ca/news/trending/thin-bear-photo-kerstin-1.3232725 [17
September 2015]; http://www.side3.no/vitenskap/--virkeligheten-er-ikke-sa-
enkel-som-dette-bildet/3423136367.html; [2017 National Geographic starving
bear] Crockford 2018a; Crockford 2018b;
https://globalnews.ca/news/4361868/polar-bear-climate-change-national-
geographic/; https://www.dailymail.co.uk/news/article-6018447/National-
Geographic-admits-no-evidence-polar-bear-video-dying-climate-change.html;

[228] Thunberg 2019; Workman 2019; Rozsa 2020;
https://www.youtube.com/watch?v=M7dVF9xylaw ['Greta Thunberg: Our
House Is On Fire!', 25 January 2019] ;
https://www.weforum.org/agenda/2021/01/greta-thunberg-message-to-the-
davos-agenda/ [25 January 2021]

[229] Crockford 2017; Crockford 2019a

[230] Ryan 2019 [Belushya Guba polar bear story in Nilsen 2019 and Stewart 2019]

[231] Shields 2019

[232] https://www.telegraph.co.uk/science/2017/08/24/sir-david-attenborough-
optimistic-ever-aboutthe-future-planet/ [24 August 2017]

[233] BBC Sounds 2020; but see Beck 2022; Corcoran 2021b; Foster 2021; Morano
2021

[234] Whitworth 2019a

[235] Whitworth 2019c

[236] Ling 2019a

[237] Hopton 2019

[238] Hopton 2019; see also Dennis 2019 about the DC presentation

[239] According to WEF literature on the Global Risk Landscape, the two highest risk categories in terms of 'likelihood' and 'impact' are 'climate action failure' and 'extreme weather'. See Schwab and Malleret 2020:25; WEF 2020; see also https://www.weforum.org/reports/the-global-risks-report-2020

[240] Corcoran 2021b; see also www.weforum.org/about/world-economic-forum/

[241] https://www.weforum.org/agenda/2019/01/everything-you-need-to-know-about-davos-2019/ ['Who's coming to Davos 2019? 15 January 2019]; see also https://www.weforum.org/partners#search for 'Strategic Partners'

[242] Whitworth 2019a; https://www.youtube.com/watch?v=-oam6Ca-mkg ['Davos 2019: A conversation with Sir David Attenborough and HRH the Duke of Cambridge', 31 January 2019]

[243] Kochnev 2019

[244] https://www.ourplanet.com/en/video/behind-the-scenes-walrus/?fbclid=IwAR0k2kRVMHPShwDxhyzcyt8iUmoo420Dyxptj5SjQpUEmM7MetqWBCXnKBw

[245] BBC 2019a; Duboff 2019; WWF 2019; https://www.youtube.com/watch?v=-oam6Ca-mkg ['Davos 2019: A conversation with Sir David Attenborough and HRH the Duke of Cambridge', 31 January 2019]

[246] Hopton 2019

[247] https://www.weforum.org/agenda/2019/01/everything-you-need-to-know-about-davos-2019/

[248] Watts 2018 (November) vs. Carrington 2018 (December)

[249] Carrington 2018; McGrath 2018; https://www.youtube.com/watch?v=c_X4UkKI0Vk ['Poland: 'Continuation of civilization is in your hands' – Attenborough tells world leaders at COP24', 3 December 2018]

[250] https://www.weforum.org/agenda/2019/01/the-environment-was-high-on-the-agenda-in-davos-but-what-actually-happened/ [25 January 2019]

[251] Nicholson 2019

[252] BBC Sounds 2020

[253] Nicholson 2019

[254] O'Donovan 2019

[255] BBC 2019b; McGrath 2019; https://www.bbc.co.uk/programmes/m00049b1; https://www.youtube.com/watch?v=EOctIuyVfnA [12 May 2019]

[256] Stafford and Jones 2019; Vaughan 2019a

[257] IPCC 2014; https://www.thegwpf.org/bbc-accused-of-serious-errors-and-misleading-statements-in-david-attenboroughs-climate-show/

[258] Rose 2019; https://www.thegwpf.com/bbc-presents-climate-change-the-facts/

[259] Ward 2019b

[260] Barkham 2019

[261] Vaughan 2019b

[262] Thunberg 2019; Workman 2019; https://www.youtube.com/watch?v=M7dVF9xylaw ['Greta Thunberg: Our House Is On Fire!', 25 January 2019] ; Thunberg and Attenborough claim to have met for the first time during an interview aired on TV by the BBC in December 2019, see https://www.bbc.com/news/av/science-environment-50904881 and Ma 2019

[263] Attenborough 2020; Glynn 2019; Hale 2020; Shute 2019; Winkleman 2020; https://www.wwf.org.uk/updates/david-attenborough-life-our-planet [5 December 2019]

[264] Hopton 2019; https://www.worldwildlife.org/pages/financials [accessed 16 April 2021]; https://www.civilsociety.co.uk/news/wwf-increases-regular-givers-for-first-time-in-a-few-years.html [6 December 2019]

[265] https://www.wwf.org.uk/updates/david-attenborough-life-our-planet

[266] Cooper 2020; de Ferrer 2020; Imbler 2020; MacEachern 2020

[267] Book 2020; Lomborg 2001; Lomborg 2020a; Steele 2013; WWF 2016a; WWF 2016b

[268] Guy 2020

[269] Clark 2020; Doyle 2021; DTE Staff 2018; Jones 2020; Rowlatt 2020; Westcott 2016

[270] Clark 2020; for a summary of the almost word-for-word arguments used see DW News 2020

[271] Morano 2021

[272] Telegraph Reporters 2020; see also Fillon 2021

[273] Ogden and Gachon 2019; DW News 2020

[274] Clark 2020; Smith et al. 2014

[275] https://www.weforum.org/videos/this-is-what-the-fight-against-covid-19-can-teach-us-about-stopping-climate-change-according-to-bill-gates [WEF, 14 August 2020]

[276] https://www.youtube.com/watch?v=PzNbNblFJbE [Great Reset, 3 June 2020: HRH Prince of Wales, 'We have no alternative'], see also https://www.weforum.org/agenda/2020/06/covid19-great-reset-gita-gopinath-jennifer-morgan-sharan-burrow-climate/ and https://hedearnell.medium.com/the-great-reset-a-green-veneer-for-fake-climate-and-environmental-action-8ec190d15d43

[277] BBC 2020; Blum 2020; https://www.youtube.com/watch?v=fRFY4ss2W2A ['David and Greta in Conversation: The Planetary Crisis', 21 October 2020]

[278] Shute 2020

[279] Cooper 2020; see also Ehrlich 2020; de Ferrer 2020; Winkelman 2020; https://en.wikipedia.org/wiki/David_Attenborough:_A_Life_on_Our_Planet [accessed 10 April 2021]

[280] Kanter 2020a; https://www.youtube.com/watch?v=mFbwTRMwBAc [8 October 2020: 'Introducing The Earthshot Prize with Prince William and Sir David Attenborough']; https://earthshotprize.org/the-earthshot-prize-collaborates-with-count-us-in/ [31 December 2020]; https://earthshotprize.org/bbc-to-be-broadcast-partner-of-the-earthshot-prize/ [9 October 2020]

[281] Kanter 2020b; see also Shute 2020; Smallman 2020

[282] Alexander 2021; Bastasch 2018a; Christy 2019; Carter and Spooner 2013; Curry 2019; IPCC 2014; Lomborg 2001; Lomborg 2020a; Marohasy 2020; Moore 2021; but see Milman 2018; Thompson 2015

[283] Mosely and Raphelson 2021

[284] Lomborg 2020a; see also Irish et al. 2014; Young 2007

[285] https://www.ipsos.com/ipsos-mori/en-uk/flight-shame-are-we-willing-reduce-our-emissions [25 Sept 2019]; see also IPSO 2021, IPSO 2020; IPSO 2019

[286] Brenan 2021; Crawley et al. 2020; Crawley 2021

[287] Jenkins 2021; Le Masurier 2021; Waterman 2021

[288] Mathiesen 2021

[289] https://www.earthday.org/earth-day-2020/ and https://www.earthday.org/earth-day-2021/

[290] Andreeva 2021; Beard 2021; Brady-Brown 2021; Collins 2021; Croot 2021; https://www.youtube.com/watch?v=XswV_yqPq28 [The Year Earth Changed, Official Trailer, Apple TV+, 29 March 2021]

[291] Sommerlad 2021; see also Shukman 2021a

[292] Desrocher and Szurmak 2019; Ginzberg 2021; Lomborg 2001; Lomborg 2020a; Lyons 2009; Worstall 2018

[293] Alexander 2021; Crockford 2021; Curry 2019; Pooley and Tupy 2021; Lomborg 2020a; Lomborg 2021; Rosenthal 2021; Shellenberger 2020; Spencer 2021; see also Ocampo 2021; Vecchi et al. 2021

[294] https://about.netflix.com/en/news/breaking-boundaries-the-science-of-our-planet

[295] WWF 2016b

[296] Schoolmeester et al. 2019; see also https://www.unep.org/news-and-stories/press-release/temperature-rise-locked-coming-decades-arctic and https://oceantoday.noaa.gov/firstsignofclimatechange/ [a WWF video from 2008]

[297] Bates 2021; IPCC 2021

[298] Bush and Lemmen 2019; Curry 2017; Curry and Webster 2011; Irfan 2021; Palmer and Stevens 2019

[299] Rockström et al. 2009; Steffen et al. 2015; O'Neill et al. 2018; see also Dyke 2019 on the planetary boundaries concept (and who also claims capitalism is to blame for climate change) and of course, George Monbiot https://www.doubledown.news/watch/2022/january/11/the-tipping-point-that-will-destroy-the-world-george-monbiot [11 January 2022]

[300] Berry 2021

[301] https://www.thefancarpet.com/movie_news/netflix-announces-breaking-boundaries-the-science-of-our-planet-narrated-by-sir-david-attenborough-and-produced-by-silverback-films/ [22 April 2021]

[302] Rudgard 2021; Bannister 2021 (in which actor Arnold Schwarzenegger told fellow 'climate warriors' at the Austrian World Summit in Vienna that 'no one is going to invest huge sums of money in a movie where there is no hope'

[303] Reuters 2021

[304] Grylls 2021; Lawson 2021

[305] https://earthshotprize.org/earthshot-book-landing-later-this-year/ [21 July 2021]; https://www.silverbackfilms.tv/earthshots/ [20 October 2020]

[306] Kanter 2020a; https://www.silverbackfilms.tv/studio-silverback/ [28 January 2021]

[307] BBC 2021; see also Shersby 2021

[308] BBC 2021

[309] Armstrong 2021

[310] Adams 2021; Black 2021; Monbiot 2021; Masood and Tollefson 2021

[311] Griffin 2021; Rushton 2021; Shukman 2021b; Variety 2021; see also https://www.youtube.com/watch?v=GJ8usPRVlSE [29 October 2021: *Sir David Attenborough says Cop26 leaders must 'listen to the science'*]

[312] e.g. Berensen 2021:151-155 [US]; Snowdon 2020 [UK]

[313] Bloomberg News 2021; Crawley 2021; Hales and Mackey 2021; Homewood 2021; Rose 2021; Rowling 2021; see also IEA 2021 [report on global coal use]

[314] McCaffrey 2021

[315] Winter 2021

[316] In fact, by 2021 sea ice had remained stable at the predicted 2050 level for 15 years – despite assertions that the average Arctic temperature is now *4 times* the global average – and polar bear numbers by 2020 were possibly higher still. See Bates 2021; Crockford 2021; NSIDC 2019; NSIDC 2021; Swart et al. 2015; Rantanen et al. 2021; Voosen 2021b

[317] http://www.indianapolisprize.org/sites/prize/the-heroes/2012/; http://www.polarbearsinternational.org/news-room/news/pbi-scientist-receives-bambi-award

[318] Amstrup et al. 2007; Amstrup et al. 2008; Courtland 2008; Hassol 2004; Holland et al. 2006; Stroeve et al. 2007; Wang and Overland 2009

[319] Corcoran 2021a; Curry 2017; Gupta 2001; Nelson 2021; Ridley 2021; Scholz and Wellmer 2021; Varadarajan 2021

[320] Crockford 2019a; see also Amstrup et al. 2007; Amstrup et al. 2008; Amstrup et al. 2010; Borenstein et al. 2021; Crockford 2017; Crockford 2021; LaFramboise and Crockford 2020

[321] Hopton 2019

[322] Kochnev 2017 and the entire WWF 'The Circle' magazine issue 2017 (2): https://arcticwwf.org/newsroom/the-circle/walruses-going-with-the-floes/

[323] Kanter 2020a

[324] Grylls 2021; https://www.emmys.com/bios/sir-david-attenborough

[325] e.g. Dodsworth 2021

[326] Koonan 2021a; Lomborg 2020a; Lomborg 2020b; Wrightstone 2017

[327] Crockford 2019a; Crockford 2021; MacCracken et al. 2017; NAMMCO 2021

[328] Book 2020; Lomborg 2020a; Steele 2013

[329] Baker et al. 1993; Bockstoce and Botkin 1982; Clapham et al. 1999; Brend 2021; George et al. 2020; Sea Otter Recovery Team 2007; Thomas 2016; Weber et al. 2000

[330] Amstrup et al. 2008; Burgess et al. 2021; Christy 2019; Hausfather and Peters 2020; Molnár et al. 2010; Molnár et al. 2020; O'Neil et al. 2020; Ridley 2014; Spencer 2021; Voosen 2021a; See also https://www.science.org/content/article/un-climate-panel-confronts-implausibly-hot-forecasts-future-warming [27 July 2021]

[331] Aaris-Sørensen 2009; Crockford and Frederick 2007; Johnson 2021; Limoges et al. 2020; Polyak et al. 2010; Vibe 1967; Weber 2019

[332] e.g. Crockford 2008; Crockford and Frederick 2007; Crockford and Frederick 2011; Cronin and Cronin 2015; Desjardins 2018; Grønnow et al. 2011; Pitulko et al. 2015; Vibe 1967

[333] IPCC 2021: Chapter 11; see also Alexander 2021; Bastasch 2018a; Curry 2019; Koonan 2021b; Lomborg 2020a, 2020b; Pielke, Jr. 2018; Spencer 2021; Vecchi et al. 2021

[334] Epstein 2014

[335] Grain Brokers Australia 2021 [South Africa]; Nandy 2021 [India]; Ocampo 2021 [Philippines]; Pooley and Tupy 2021; Lomborg 2020a; Lomborg 2021; Shellenberger 2020; https://gml.noaa.gov/ccgg/trends/ ['Trends in Atmospheric Carbon Dioxide', showing 415.01 ppm at November 2021 vs. 413.12 ppm at November 2020 (updated 6 December 2021)]

[336] BBC Sounds 2020; but see Beck 2022; Corcoran 2021b; Foster 2021; Morano 2021

[337] WEF 2020; www.weforum.org/about/world-economic-forum/; https://www.weforum.org/agenda/2019/01/everything-you-need-to-know-about-davos-2019/ ['Who's coming to Davos 2019? 15 January 2019]

[338] BBC Monitoring and BBC Reality Check 2021; Corcoran 2020; Wells 2020; Spring 2021

[339] See also Chapter 10 and https://www.weforum.org/partners#search for a full list of so-called 'Strategic Partners'

[340] Schwab and Malleret 2020; https://www.weforum.org/agenda/archive/covid-19/

[341] Corcoran 2021a; Crockford 2019a; Curry 2019; Ridley 2014; Ridley 2015; Ridley 2021; Scholz and Wellmer 2021

[342] Berensen 2021; Dodsworth 2021; Harnett 2021; Hitchens 2021; Nelson 2021; PHAC 2021; Ridley 2021; Sumption 2020; Tasker 2021

[343] e.g. Ridley 2015

[344] Baker 2016; Horton 2015; Ioannidis 2005; Ridd 2020; but see Fanelli 2018

# References

Aaris-Sørensen, K. 2009. Diversity and dynamics of the mammalian fauna in Denmark throughout the last glacial-interglacial cycle, 115-0 kry BP. *Fossils and Strata* 57, Copenhagen, Denmark.

Aars, J. 2018. Population changes in polar bears: protected, but quickly losing habitat. *Fram Forum Newsletter 2018*. Fram Centre, Tromso.

Aars, J., Lunn, N. J. and Derocher, A.E. (eds.) 2006. Polar Bears: Proceedings of the 14th Working Meeting of the IUCN/SSC Polar Bear Specialist Group, 20-24 June 2005, Seattle, Washington, USA. Occasional Paper of the IUCN Species Survival Commission 32. IUCN, Gland (Switzerland) and Cambridge (UK).

Abbott, K. 2019. ''I never knew walruses climbed that high': Our Planet's scariest moments'. *The Guardian* (UK), 11 April. https://www.theguardian.com/tv-and-radio/2019/apr/11/i-got-bitten-by-sharks-every-night-our-planet-most-terrifying-moments-david-attenborough-netflix

Adams, P. 2021 China's Energy Dream. *Global Warming Policy Foundation* Briefing Paper 58. https://www.thegwpf.org/publications/fossil-fuels-for-china-decarbonisation-for-everyone-else/

Ahearn, V. 2020. 'Canadian polar bears' 'ingenious' survival strategy seen in BBC Earth series'. *Winnipeg Free Press/Canadian Press*, 15 January. https://www.winnipegfreepress.com/arts-and-life/entertainment/TV/canadian-polar-bears-ingenious-survival-strategy-seen-in-bbc-earth-series--567008782.html

Alexander, R. 2021. Extreme Weather 2020. *Global Warming Policy Foundation Report* 49. London.

Amanpour, C. 2019. 'Keith Scholey & Sophie Lanfear on Our Planet'. *PBS Amanpour and Company*, 15 April [television interview, transcript included]. https://www.pbs.org/wnet/amanpour-and-company/video/keith-scholey-sophie-lanfear-on-our-planet/

Amstrup, S.C., Marcot, B.G. and Douglas, D.C. 2007. Forecasting the rangewide status of polar bears at selected times in the 21st century. Reston, Virginia, Administrative Report, US Geological Survey.

Amstrup, S.C.,Marcot, B.G. and Douglas, D.C. 2008. A Bayesian network modeling approach to forecasting the 21st century worldwide status of polar bears. In: *Arctic Sea Ice Decline: Observations, Projections, Mechanisms, and Implications*, E.T. DeWeaver, et al. (eds.), American Geophysical Union, Washington, D.C., *Geophysical Monograph* 180:213-268. https://doi.org/10.1029/180GM14

Amstrup, S.C., DeWeaver, E.T., Douglas, D.C., et al. 2010. Greenhouse gas mitigation can reduce sea-ice loss and increase polar bear persistence. *Nature* 468:955–958. https://doi.org/10.1038/nature09653

Andreeva, N. 2021. 'David Attenborough's 'The Year Earth Changed' special tops Apple TV+'s unscripted viewership charts in debut'. *Deadline,* 21 April. https://deadline.com/2021/04/david-attenborough-the-year-earth-changed-special-apple-tv-viewership-1234741278/

Arie, B. 2019. 'Zoologist sets the record straight after Netflix tells kids climate change is killing walruses'. *Western Journal*, 15 April. https://www.westernjournal.com/ct/zoologist-sets-record-straight-netflix-tells-kids-climate-change-killing-walruses/

Armstrong, S. 2021. 'David Attenborough's Unending Mission to Save Our Planet'. *Wired Magazine*, 2 December. https://www.wired.com/story/david-attenborough-climate-crisis/

Attenborough, D., with Hughes, J. 2020. *A Life on Our Planet: My Witness Statement and a Vision for the Future.* Grand Central Publishing, Hachette Book Group, New York, NY.

Australian. 2019. 'Netflix series Our Planet accused of fake climate change claims'. *The Australian*, 9 April. https://www.theaustralian.com.au/world/netflix-series-our-planet-accused-of-fake-climate-change-claims/news-story/c6c4dfd006bdad17cb4ea7acd55a5aba?nk=52ed6d24a1df6f2b9732e62c4f445dd7-1554806019

Badger, T.A. 1996. 'Biologists puzzled by walruses' deadly falls from Alaska cliffs'. *Washington Post*, 31 August.

https://www.washingtonpost.com/archive/politics/1996/08/31/biologists-puzzled-by-walruses-deadly-falls-from-alaska-cliffs/2e6d8322-88b9-4036-a7a7-6771f2cae059/

Baker, C.S., Perry, A., Bannister, et al. 1993. Abundant mitochondrial DNA variation and world-wide population structure in humpback whales. *PNAS* 90:8239-8243.

Baker, M. 2016. 1,500 scientists lift the lid on reproducibility. *Nature* 533:452–454. https://doi.10.1038/533452a

Bannister, C. 2021. 'Schwarzenegger slams climate alarmism: No one's going to invest in a movie that has no hope'. *CNS News*, 2 July. https://www.cnsnews.com/blog/craig-bannister/schwarzenegger-slams-climate-alarmism-no-ones-going-invest-movie-has-no-hope

Barkham, P. 2019. 'The real David Attenborough.' *The Guardian* (UK), 22 October. https://www.theguardian.com/tv-and-radio/2019/oct/22/david-attenborough-climate-change-bbc

Bastasch, M. 2018a. 'UN's new report shows there's 'little basis' for a favorite claim of climate activists'. *Daily Caller*, 8 October. https://dailycaller.com/2018/10/08/un-climate-report-global-warming/

Bastasch, M. 2018b. 'It took National Geographic 7 months to admit it 'went too far' linking an iconic image of a dying polar bear to global warming'. *Daily Caller News*, 7 July. http://dailycaller.com/2018/07/27/national-geographic-polar-bear-global-warming-wrong/

Bastasch, M. 2019. 'Did 'Our Planet' lie to viewers when it claimed climate change drove walruses off a cliff?'. *Daily Caller*, 15 April. https://dailycaller.com/2019/04/15/netflix-our-planet-walruses/

Basov, Y. 2017. 'On Cape Schmidt'. *Live Journal*, 8 November. https://basov-chukotka.livejournal.com/319273.html [accessed 15 April 2019; Google Chrome to translate]

Bates, J.R. 2021. Polar Sea Ice and the Climate Catastrophe Narrative. *Global Warming Policy Foundation* Note 28. https://www.thegwpf.org/publications/polar-sea-ice-climate-catastrophe-narrative/

BBC. 2017. 'Polar bear video: Is it really the 'face of climate change'?'. *BBC News* (UK), 12 December. https://www.bbc.com/news/world-us-canada-42322346

BBC. 2019a. 'We could wreck natural world, David Attenborough tells Prince William'. *BBC News* (UK), 22 January. https://www.bbc.com/news/uk-46957085

BBC. 2019b. 'David Attenborough climate change TV show a 'call to arms''. *BBC News* (UK), 19 April. https://www.bbc.com/news/entertainment-arts-47988337

BBC. 2019c. 'David Attenborough to front BBC's Extinction: The Facts'. *BBC News* (UK), 22 August. https://www.bbc.com/news/entertainment-arts-49432824

BBC. 2019d. 'Team biographies'. *BBC Media Centre*, 22 October. https://www.bbc.co.uk/mediacentre/mediapacks/seven-worlds-one-planet/biographies

BBC. 2019e. 'Walrus on the Edge'. *BBC Programmes*, Articles, 3 November. https://www.bbc.co.uk/programmes/articles/4zh2Dd3JC8gprNZcGY6BbHB/walrus-on-the-edge

BBC. 2019f. 'Greta Thunberg: Teen activist says UK is 'irresponsible' on climate'. *BBC News* (UK) video, 23 April. https://www.bbc.com/news/uk-48017083

BBC. 2020. 'Sir David Attenborough says Covid-19 is 'threat to environment''. *BBC News* (UK), 21 October. https://www.bbc.com/news/uk-england-bristol-54624129

BBC. 2021. 'BBC curtain-raises COP26 in Glasgow with global premiere of new Attenborough BBC Studios Natural History Unit landmark The Green Planet.' *BBC News* (UK), 31 October. https://www.bbc.com/mediacentre/bbcstudios/2021/bbc-curtain-raises-cop26-glasgow-global-premiere-attenborough-bbc-studios-natural-history-unit-landmark-the-green-planet/

BBC Monitoring and BBC Reality Check. 2021. 'What is the Great Reset - and how did it get hijacked by conspiracy theories?' *BBC News*, 24 June. https://www.bbc.com/news/blogs-trending-57532368

BBC Sounds. 2020. 'David Attenborough - 'We have to believe it's possible'' [Sir David on the future, capitalism and tackling climate change since the pandemic]. *BBC Sounds Podcast 'What Planet Are We On,' with Liz Bonnin*, Episode 1, 7 October. https://www.bbc.co.uk/sounds/play/p08tmn3g

Beard, T. 2021. 'David Attenborough's 'The Year Earth Changed' shows the silver lining to a year of pandemic'. *The National News* (UK), 17 April. https://www.thenationalnews.com/arts-culture/film/david-attenborough-s-the-year-earth-changed-shows-the-silver-lining-to-a-year-of-pandemic-1.1205197

Beatty, W.S., Jay, C.V., Fischbach, A.S., Grebmeier, J.M., Taylor, R.L., Blanchard, A.L. and Jewett, S.C. 2016. Space use of a dominant Arctic vertebrate: effects of prey, sea ice, and land on Pacific walrus resource selection. *Biological Conservation* 203:25-32.

Beatty, W.S., Lemons, P.R., Sethi, S.A., et al. 2019. Estimating Pacific walrus abundance and demographic rates from genetic mark-recapture. US Department of the Interior, Bureau of Ocean Energy Management, Anchorage, Alaska. OCS Study BOEM 2019-059.

Beck, G. 2022. *The Great Reset: Joe Biden and the Rise of Twenty-First Century Fascism*. Forefront Books (Simon & Schuster).

Bender, K. 2019. 'Netflix producer on filming walruses falling to their deaths for Our Planet: It was traumatic'. *People Magazine*, 9 April 2019. https://people.com/pets/netflix-our-planet-walrus-death-scene-explained/

Berry, J. 2021. 'Breaking Boundaries: The Science of Our Planet release date – David Attenborough to narrate Netflix documentary'. *RadioTimes* (UK), 11 May. https://www.radiotimes.com/tv/documentaries/breaking-boundaries-the-science-of-our-planet-release-date-netflix/

Berensen, A. 2021. *Pandemia: How Coronavirus Hysteria Took Over Our Government, Rights, and Lives*. Regnery Publishing, Washington, DC.

Berseneva, A. 2013. 'Dozens of polar bears lay siege to village in Chukotka'. *RBTH News* (via a WWF report), 14 November. https://www.rbth.com/society/2013/11/14/dozens_of_polar_bears_lay_siege_to_village_in_chukotka_31713.html

Black, C. 2021. 'The ghastly charade in Glasgow and the West's self-flagellation over the climate'. *National Post* (Canada), 21 November. https://nationalpost.com/opinion/conrad-black-the-ghastly-charade-in-glasgow-and-the-wests-self-flagellation-over-the-climate

Blake, E. 2018. 'National Geographic says it 'went too far' with emaciated polar bear video'. *CBC News* (Canada), 17 August. https://www.cbc.ca/news/canada/north/emaciated-polar-bear-response-1.4788259

Bloomberg News 2021. 'With Time Ticking Down, Hope Is Waning for a Climate Deal'. *Bloomberg News*, 2 August. https://www.bloomberg.com/news/articles/2021-08-02/hope-is-waning-for-a-global-climate-deal-this-is-why

Blum, J. 2020. 'David Attenborough: Climate change must not be ignored even during a pandemic'. *The Huffington Post*, 22 October. https://www.huffpost.com/entry/david-attenborough-greta-thunberg-climate-change-covid-19_n_5f91abe2c5b66d4a0dbd12a4

Bockstoce, J.R. and Botkin, D.B. 1982. The harvest of Pacific walruses by the pelagic whaling industry, 1848 to 1914. *Arctic and Alpine Research* [now *Arctic, Antarctic and Alpine Research*] 14:183-188.

Book, J. 2020. 'The return of the dead: Countering extinction'. *Human Progress*, 22 July. https://humanprogress.org/article.php?p=2827

Booker, C. 2011. 'The BBC and climate change: A triple betrayal'. *Global Warming Policy Foundation* Report 5.

Booker, C. 2012. 'How climate change has got Worldwide Fund for Nature bamboozled.' *The Daily Telegraph*, 5 May. http://www.telegraph.co.uk/earth/environment/climatechange/9246853/How-climate-change-has-got-Worldwide-Fund-for-Nature-bamboozled.html

Booker, C. 2017. 'The time Prince Philip wrote to me in praise of my views on global warming - in marked contrast to his son'. *The Sunday Telegraph* (UK), 5 August. https://www.telegraph.co.uk/news/2017/08/05/time-prince-philip-wrote-praise-views-global-warming-marked/

Borenstein, S., Fassett, C. and Perry, K. 2021. 'Climate change diminishing Arctic sea ice and harming polar bears experts say'. *Global News (Canada)/Associated Press*, 6 November. https://globalnews.ca/news/8355396/climate-change-warming-arctic-sea-ice-polar-bears/

Boveng, P. 2016. *Pusa hispida ssp. hispida*. The IUCN Red List of Threatened Species 2016: e.T61382318A61382321.

Brady-Brown, A. 2021. 'David Attenborough documentary The Year Earth Changed suggests silver lining ahead of Earth Day 2021'. *ABC News*, 16 April. https://www.abc.net.au/news/2021-04-16/the-year-earth-changed-review-david-attenborough-documentary/100062704

Brenan, M. 2021. 'Water pollution remains top environmental concern in US'. *Gallup News*, 19 April. https://news.gallup.com/poll/347735/water-pollution-remains-top-environmental-concern.aspx

Brend, Y. 2021. 'Record 21 humpback calves spotted in Salish Sea over feeding season as whale numbers rebound'. *CBC News* (Canada), 22 October. https://www.cbc.ca/news/canada/british-columbia/humpback-whales-record-calves-salish-sea-1.6221049

Brown, Z.W., van Dijken, G.L. and Arrigo, K.R. 2011. A reassessment of primary production and environmental change in the Bering Sea. *Journal of Geophysical Research* 116:C08014.

Burgess, M.G., Ritchie, J., Shapland, J. and Pielke Jr., R. 2021. IPCC baseline scenarios have over-projected CO2 emissions and economic growth. *Environmental Research Letters* 16:014016.

Burns, G. 2013. *Walruses falling off Alaska cliffs* [News footage with US Fish & Wildlife Service interviews from Cape Pierce, Alaska 1996] https://www.dailymotion.com/video/x2m72ze

Bush, E. and Lemmen, D.S. (eds). 2019. *Canada's Changing Climate Report*. Government of Canada, Ottawa.

Carr, J. 2019. 'Incredible moment a starving polar bear kills a beluga whale in Canada as 'climate change' forces the predators to hunt new prey'. *The Daily Mail*, 30 November. https://www.dailymail.co.uk/news/article-7741099/Polar-bear-dives-pod-beluga-whales-David-Attenboroughs-Seven-Worlds-One-Planet.html

Carrington, D. 2018. 'David Attenborough: collapse of civilisation is on the horizon'. *The Guardian* (UK), 3 December. https://www.theguardian.com/environment/2018/dec/03/david-attenborough-collapse-civilisation-on-horizon-un-climate-summit

Carter, R. and Spooner, J. 2013. *Taxing Air: Facts & Fallacies about Climate Change*. Kelpie Press, Australia.

Castro de la Guardia, L., Myers, P.G., Derocher, A.E., et al. 2017. Sea ice cycle in western Hudson Bay, Canada, from a polar bear perspective. *Marine Ecology Progress Series* 564:225–233.

CBC Radio. 2017a. 'All of our team was in tears': Video shows polar bear starving in snowless North'. *CBC Radio/As It Happens* (Canada), 8 December. http://www.cbc.ca/radio/asithappens/as-it-happens-friday-edition-1.4439608/all-of-our-team-was-in-tears-video-shows-polar-bear-starving-in-snowless-north-1.4439616

CBC Radio. 2017b. 'Viral video of emaciated polar bear may not be what it seems, Nunavut bear monitor says'. *CBC Radio/As It Happens*, 11 December. http://www.cbc.ca/radio/asithappens/as-it-happens-monday-edition-1.4442887/viral-video-of-emaciated-polar-bear-may-not-be-what-it-seems-nunavut-bear-monitor-says-1.4442892

CBC Radio. 2017c. 'SeaLegacy's remarks about polar bear hunt 'racist and factually untrue,' says Iqaluit mayor'. *CBC Radio/As It Happens* (Canada), 14 December. https://www.cbc.ca/radio/asithappens/as-it-happens-thursday-edition-1.4448373/sealegacy-s-remarks-about-polar-bear-hunt-racist-and-factually-untrue-says-iqaluit-mayor-1.4448381

CBC Radio. 2019. 'After complaints from parents, Our Planet director defends footage of walruses plummeting to their death'. *CBC Radio/The Current* (Canada), 15 April. https://www.cbc.ca/radio/thecurrent/the-current-for-april-15-2019-1.5098114/after-complaints-from-parents-our-planet-director-defends-footage-of-walruses-plummeting-to-their-death-1.5098190

Chakilev, M.V., Bajderin, A.G. and Kochnev, A.A. 2015. The Pacific walrus (*Odobenus rosmarus divergens*) coastal haulout on Cape Serdtse-Kamen (Chukchi Sea) in 2013. In, *Marine Mammals of the Holarctic, Papers of The Eighth International Conference (22-27 September2014)*, Volume 2, pg. 270-274. Marine Mammal Council, Moscow. [Russian and English]

Chakilev, M.V. and Kochnev, A.A. 2018. Pacific walrus (*Odobenus rosmarus divergens*) coastal haulouts at Kolyuchin Island and Cape Serdtse-Kamen', Chukchi Sea, 2015. In, *Marine Mammals of the Holarctic, Papers of The Ninth International Conference (31 October-5 November 2016)*, Volume 2, pg. 242-247. Marine Mammal Council, Moscow. [Russian and English]

Chakilev, M.V. and Kochnev, A.A. 2019. Monitoring results of the Pacific walrus (*Odobenus rosmarus divergens*) haulout site at Cape Serdtse-Kamen (Chukchi Sea) in 2016-2017. In, *Marine Mammals of the Holarctic, Papers of the Tenth International Conference (29 October-2 November*

*2018)*, Volume 1, pg. 381-391. Marine Mammal Council, Moscow. [Russian and English]

Cherry, S.G., Derocher, A.E., Thiemann, G.W., Lunn, N.J. 2013. Migration phenology and seasonal fidelity of an Arctic marine predator in relation to sea ice dynamics. *Journal of Animal Ecology* 82:912-921.

Christy, J. 2019. The Tropical Skies: Falsifying Climate Alarm. *Global Warming Policy Foundation* Note 17.

Clapham, P. J., Young, S. B. and Brownell Jr., R. T. 1999. Baleen whales: conservation issues and the status of the most endangered populations. *Mammal Review* 29:35-60.

Clark, R. 2020. 'What David Attenborough's 'Extinction: The Facts' didn't tell you'. *The Spectator Magazine* (UK), 14 September. https://www.spectator.co.uk/article/what-david-attenborough-s-extinction-the-facts-didn-t-tell-you; see the video version here: https://www.cbsnews.com/video/david-attenborough-climate-change-a-life-on-our-planet-60-minutes-2020-09-27/

Collins, T. 2017. ''I filmed with tears rolling down my cheeks': Heart-breaking footage shows a starving polar bear on its deathbed struggling to walk on iceless land'. *The Daily Mail* (UK), 8 December. http://www.dailymail.co.uk/sciencetech/article-5160363/Soul-crushing-footage-starving-polar-iceless-land.html

Collins, T. 2021. 'Apple wins with The Year Earth Changed: Movie Review'. *Oakville News*, 24 April. https://oakvillenews.org/reviews/the-year-earth-changed-movie-review/

Cooper, A. 2020. 'Sir David Attenborough explains what he thinks needs to happen to save the planet'. *CBS News,* 27 September. https://www.cbsnews.com/news/david-attenborough-climate-change-a-life-on-our-planet-60-minutes-2020-09-27/

Corcoran, T. 2017. 'Canadian finds polar bears are doing fine — and gets climate-mauled *National Post/Financial Post* (Canada), 7 December. http://business.financialpost.com/opinion/terence-corcoran-canadian-finds-polar-bears-are-doing-fine-and-gets-climate-mauled

Corcoran, T. 2020. 'The Great Reset and the COVID pandemic'. *National Post/Financial Post* (Canada), 20 November. https://financialpost.com/opinion/terence-corcoran-the-great-reset-and-the-covid-pandemic

Corcoran, T. 2021a. 'Clubs of Doom and the Limits to Models'. *National Post/Financial Post* (Canada), 25 June. https://financialpost.com/opinion/terence-corcoran-clubs-of-doom-and-the-limits-to- models

Corcoran, T. 2021b. 'The murky rise of Klaus Schwab's stakeholder 'capitalism' and the WEF's Davos corporate plan'. *National Post/Financial Post* (Canada), 22 January. https://financialpost.com/opinion/terence-corcoran-the-murky-rise-of-stakeholder-capitalism

Coupel, P., Michel, C. and Devred, E. 2019. Case study: The Ocean in Bloom. In: *State of Canada's Arctic Seas*, Niemi, A., et al., Canadian Technical Report Fisheries and Aquatic Sciences 3344.

Courtland, R. 2008. Polar bear numbers set to fall. *Nature* 453:432–433. https://doi.org/10.1038/453432a

Crawley, S. 2021. 'Most people consider climate change a serious issue, but rank other problems as more important. That affects climate policy'. *The Conversation,* 18 May. https://theconversation.com/most-people-consider-climate-change-a-serious-issue-but-rank-other-problems-as-more-important-that-affects-climate-policy-161080

Crawley, S., Coffé, H. and Chapman, R. 2020. Public opinion on climate change: Belief and concern, issue salience and support for government action. *British Journal of Politics and International Relations* 22:102-121.

Crockford, S.J. 2008. Be careful what you ask for: Archaeozoological evidence of mid-Holocene climate change and implications for the origins of Arctic Thule. Pg. 113-131 in *Islands of Inquiry: Colonization, Seafaring, and the Archaeology of Marine Landscapes* (G. Clark et al., eds). ANU E Press, Terra Australis 29, Canberra.

Crockford, S. J. 2014a. On the Beach: Walrus Haulouts are Nothing New. *Global Warming Policy Foundation* Briefing Paper 11. http://www.thegwpf.org/susan-crockford-on-the-beach-2/

Crockford, S. J. 2014b.'The Walrus Fuss: Walrus Haulouts are Nothing New'. Video, *Global Warming Policy Foundation.* https://www.youtube.com/watch?v=cwaAwsS2OOY

Crockford, S. 2017. Testing the hypothesis that routine sea ice coverage of 3-5 mkm2 results in a greater than 30% decline in population size of polar bears (*Ursus maritimus*). *PeerJ Preprints* 2 March 2017. https://doi.10.7287/peerj.preprints.2737v3

Crockford, S.J. 2018a. 'The real story behind the famous starving polar bear video reveals more manipulation.' *National Post/Financial Post* (Canada), 29 August. https://business.financialpost.com/opinion/the-real-story-behind-the-famous-starving-polar-bear-video-reveals-more-manipulation

Crockford, S.J. 2018b. 'White Lie: The Cruel Abuse of a Starving Polar Bear.' Video, *Global Warming Policy Foundation*. https://www.youtube.com/watch?v=Z7KTfPlCrgY

Crockford, S.J. 2018c. State of the Polar Bear Report 2017. *Global Warming Policy Foundation Report* 29. London.

Crockford, S.J. 2019a. *The Polar Bear Catastrophe That Never Happened*. Global Warming Policy Foundation, London.

Crockford, S.J. 2019b. 'Netflix is lying about those falling walruses. It's another 'tragedy porn' climate hoax.' *National Post/Financial Post,* 24 April. https://business.financialpost.com/opinion/netflix-is-lying-about-those-falling-walruses-its-another-tragedy-porn-climate-hoax

Crockford, S.J. 2019c. Attenborough's Arctic Betrayal. Video, January. *Global Warming Policy Forum*, London. https://www.youtube.com/watch?v=-Rkv-ItznBE&t=77s [>174k views at 8 May 2021]

Crockford, S.J. 2019d. State of the Polar Bear Report 2018. *Global Warming Policy Foundation* Report 32, London.

Crockford, S.J. 2020a. 'How Attenborough's arctic claims cause eco angst and activism'. *Think Scotland*, 29 January. https://thinkscotland.org/2021/01/how-attenboroughs-arctic-claims-cause-eco-angst-and-activism/

Crockford, S.J. 2020b. State of the Polar Bear 2019. *Global Warming Policy Foundation* Report 39.

Crockford, S.J. 2021. State of the Polar Bear 2020. *Global Warming Policy Foundation* Report 48.

Crockford, S., and Frederick, G. 2007. Sea ice expansion in the Bering Sea during the Neoglacial: evidence from archaeozoology. *The Holocene* 17:699-706.

Crockford, S. J. and Frederick, G. 2011. Neoglacial sea ice and life history flexibility in ringed and fur seals. *pg. 65-90 In* T. Braje and R. Torrey (eds), *Human and Marine Ecosystems: Archaeology and Historical Ecology of*

*Northeastern Pacific Seals, Sea Lions, and Sea Otters.* University of California Press, LA.

Cronin, T. M. and Cronin, M.A. 2015. Biological response to climate change in the Arctic Ocean: the view from the past. *Arktos* 1:1-18.

Croot, J. 2021. 'The Year The Earth Changed: Apple's Attenborough doco delivers powerful message'. *Stuff* (NZ), 25 April. https://www.stuff.co.nz/entertainment/tv-radio/300282166/the-year-the-earth-changed-apples-attenborough-doco-delivers-powerful-message

Curry, J. 2017. Climate Models for the Layman. *Global Warming Policy Foundation Briefing* 24. London.

Curry, J. 2019. Recovery, Resilience, Readiness: Contending with natural disasters. *Global Warming Policy Foundation Report* 42. London.

Curry, J.A. and Webster, P.J. 2011. Climate science and the uncertainty monster. *Bulletin of the American Meteorological Society* 92(12):1667-1682.

de Ferrer, M. 2020. 'How did the internet react to David Attenborough's newest documentary?' *EuroNews*, 5 October. https://www.euronews.com/living/2020/10/05/how-did-the-internet-react-to-david-attenborough-s-newest-documentary

Deguara, B. 2019. ''Harrowing' and 'heartbreaking': Sir David Attenborough's new documentary shocks viewers'. *Stuff* (New Zealand), 5 November. https://www.stuff.co.nz/entertainment/tv-radio/117170122/harrowing-and-heartbreaking-sir-david-attenboroughs-new-documentary-shocks-viewers

Delingpole, J. 2017. 'The ugly truth about that dying polar bear'. *Breitbart News* (UK), 11 December. http://www.breitbart.com/big-government/2017/12/11/delingpole-ugly-truth-dying-polar-bear/

Delingpole, J. 2019a. 'Walrusgate – Attenborough nature doc accused of fake news 'tragedy porn'. *Breitbart* (UK), 10 April. https://www.breitbart.com/europe/2019/04/10/delingpole-walrusgate-attenborough-nature-doc-accused-fake-news-tragedy-porn/

Delingpole, J. 2019b. 'Walrusgate – Attenborough exposed in #fakeNews Netflix eco documentary scandal'. *Breitbart* (UK), 17 April. https://www.breitbart.com/europe/2019/04/17/walrusgate-the-netflix-attenborough-scandal-gets-worse/#

Dennis, B. 2019. 'David Attenborough gave the natural world a voice. Now he's talking about climate change like never before.' *The Washington Post*, 11 April. https://www.washingtonpost.com/climate-environment/2019/04/11/natural-world-is-under-attack-heres-why-david-attenborough-is-still-hopeful/

Derocher, A.E. and Stirling, I. 1992. The population dynamics of polar bears in western Hudson Bay. pg. 1150-1159 in D. R. McCullough and R. H. Barrett, eds. *Wildlife 2001: Populations.* Elsevier Sci. Publ., London, U.K.

Derocher, A.E., and Stirling, I. 1995a. Estimation of polar bear population size and survival in western Hudson Bay. *Journal of Wildlife Management* 59:215-221.

Derocher, A.E. and Stirling, I. 1995b. Temporal variation in reproduction and body mass of polar bears in western Hudson Bay. *Canadian Journal of Zoology* 73:1657-1665.

Derocher, A.E., and Stirling, I. 1996. Aspects of survival in juvenile polar bears. *Canadian Journal of Zoology* 74:1246-1252.

Desjardins, S.P.A. 2018. Neo-Inuit strategies for ensuring food security during the Little Ice Age climate change episode, Foxe Basin, Arctic Canada. *Quaternary International* 549:163-175. https://doi.org/10.1016/j.quaint.2017.12.026

Desrocher, P. and Szurmak, J. 2019. 'The long history of eco-pessimism'. *Spiked Online*, 25 October. https://www.spiked-online.com/2019/10/25/the-long-history-of-eco-pessimism/

Dikov, N.N. 1988. The earliest sea mammal hunters of Wrangell Island. *Arctic Anthropology* 25:80-93.

Dodsworth, L. 2021. *A State of Fear: How the UK Government Weaponized Fear During the Covid-19 Pandemic.* Pinter & Martin, London.

Doyle, J. 2021. 'Earth is doomed, probably, says David Attenborough in Extinction: The Facts'. *The Globe and Mail* (Canada), 30 March. https://www.theglobeandmail.com/arts/television/article-earth-is-doomed-probably-says-david-attenborough-in-extinction-the/

DTE Staff. 2018. 'Humans wiped out 60% of the world's wildlife in 44 years'. *Down To Earth*, 30 October. https://www.downtoearth.org.in/news/climate-change/-humans-wiped-out-60-of-the-world-s-wildlife-in-44-years--61980

DW News. 2020. 'Why are outbreaks of infectious diseases on the rise?'. *DW News Covid-19 Special Report* (Germany) video, 3 June. https://www.youtube.com/watch?v=4J1AqK0ayTE

Duboff, J. 2019. 'Prince William "turns the tables," interviews Sir David Attenborough in Davos'. *Vanity Fair* magazine, 22 January. https://www.vanityfair.com/style/2019/01/prince-william-sir-david-attenborough-davos

Dyer, C. and Macdonald, C. 2019. 'Netflix is accused of 'eco-tragedy porn' in new Attenborough documentary featuring walruses falling to their deaths 'because of climate change' after zoologist claims they were being CHASED by polar bears'. *Daily Mail* (UK), 8 April. https://www.dailymail.co.uk/news/article-6900011/Netflix-Walruses-fell-deaths-chased-polar-bears-NOT-climate-change.html

Dyke, J. 2019. 'Climate change: 'We've created a civilisation hell bent on destroying itself – I'm terrified', writes Earth scientist'. *The Conversation*, 24 May. https://theconversation.com/climate-change-weve-created-a-civilisation-hell-bent-on-destroying-itself-im-terrified-writes-earth-scientist-113055

Edwards, C. 2019. 'David Attenborough's Seven Worlds, One Planet viewers left "traumatised" by walrus scene'. *Digital Spy*, 3 November. https://www.digitalspy.com/tv/a29677980/david-attenborough-bbc-seven-worlds-one-planet-walrus-scene-reaction/

Ehrlich, D. 2020. ''David Attenborough: A Life on Our Planet' review: The legend gets personal with a plea for the future'. *IndieWire*, 2 October. https://www.indiewire.com/2020/10/david-attenborough-a-life-on-our-planet-review-netflix-1234590155/

Elliott, H.W. 1875 . Polar bears on St. Matthew Island. *Harper's Weekly Journal of Civilization,* May 1 issue. Harper and Brothers, New York.

Elliot, T. 2017. 'Polar bear triplets highlight summer at Seal River Heritage Lodge'. *Churchill Wild Polar Bear Blog*, 30 September. https://www.churchillwild.com/polar-bear-triplets-highlight-summer-at-seal-river-heritage-lodge/

Epstein, A. 2014. *The Moral Case for Fossil Fuels*. Portfolio/Penguin Books, London.

Fanelli 2018. Opinion: Is science really facing a reproducibility crisis, and do we need it to? *PNAS* 115(11):2628-2631.

Farhoud, N. and Lines, A. 2021. 'Royals' bloody trophy hunting past when Queen posed with tiger shot by Prince Philip'. *The Mirror* (UK), 29 January. https://www.mirror.co.uk/news/uk-news/royals-bloody-trophy-hunting-past-23410242

Fay, F.H. 1982. Ecology and biology of the Pacific walrus, *Odobenus rosmarus divergens*, Illiger. US Department of the Interior, Fish and Wildlife Service, North American Fauna, No. 74.

Fay, F.H., Eberhardt, L.L., Kelly, B.P., Burns, J.J. and Quakenbush, L.T. 1997. Status of the Pacific walrus population, 1950-1989. *Marine Mammal Science* 13:537-565.

Fay, F.H. and Kelly, B.P. 1980. Mass natural mortality of walruses (*Odobenus rosmarus*) at St. Lawrence Island, Bering Sea, autumn 1978. *Arctic* **33**:226-245.

Fay, F.H., Kelly, B.P., Gehnrich, P.H., et al. 1984. Modern populations, migrations, demography, trophics, and historical status of the Pacific walrus. US Department of Commerce, NOAA, *Outer Continental Shelf Environmental Assessment Program Final Report* 37:231-376.

Fay, F.H., Kelly, B.P. and Sease, J.L. 1989. Managing the exploitation of Pacific walruses: a tradegy of delayed response and poor communication. *Marine Mammal Science* 5:1-16.

Ferreras, J. 2018. 'This polar bear is starving, but it's not 'what climate change looks like': National Geographic'. *Global News* (Canada), 1 August. https://globalnews.ca/news/4361868/polar-bear-climate-change-national-geographic/

Fillon, L. 2021. 'Climate activists look to 2021 to rebound from pandemic'. *CTV News* (Canada), 16 April. https://www.ctvnews.ca/climate-and-environment/climate-activists-look-to-2021-to-rebound-from-pandemic-1.5389909

Fischbach, A.S., Kochnev, A.A., Garlich-Miller, J.L., and Jay, C.V. 2016. Pacific walrus coastal haulout database, 1852–2016—Background report. U.S. Geological Survey Open-File Report 2016–1108. http://dx.doi.org/10.3133/ofr20161108 and https://www.sciencebase.gov/catalog/item/57bf650ce4b0f2f0ceb75bdc

Foster, A. 2019. 'Allegations Netflix film crew lied about what caused mass walrus deaths'. *News* (Australia), 17 April. https://www.news.com.au/technology/environment/natural-wonders/allegations-netflix-film-crew-lied-about-what-caused-mass-walrus-deaths/news-story/15b405e0e6f4f3558168d7713fd379f1

Foster, P. 2021. 'Mark Carney, man of destiny, arises to revolutionize society. It won't be pleasant'. *National Post* (Canada), June 5. https://nationalpost.com/opinion/peter-foster-mark-carney-man-of-destiny-arises-to-revolutionize-society-it-wont-be-pleasant

Freitas, C., Kovacs, K.M., Ims, R.A. et al. 2009. Deep into the ice: overwintering and habitat selection in Atlantic walruses. *Marine Ecology Progress Series* 375:247-261.

Frey, K.E., Comiso, J.C., Cooper, L.W., et al. 2020. Arctic Ocean primary productivity: the response of marine algae to climate warming and sea ice decline. *2020 Arctic Report Card,* NOAA. https://doi.10.25923/vtdn-2198

Furdyk, B. 2019. 'Netflix defends brutal scene of walruses plummeting to their deaths in nature doc 'Our Planet''. *ET Canada*, 9 April. https://etcanada.com/news/439832/netflix-defends-brutal-scene-of-walruses-plummeting-to-their-deaths-in-nature-doc-our-planet/

Garlich-Miller, J.L., MacCracken, J.G., Snyder, J.A., et al. 2011. *Status review of the Pacific walrus (Odobenus rosmarus divergens).* US Fish and Wildlife Service, Anchorage, Alaska.

George, J.C., Moore, S.E. and Thewissen, J.G.M. 2020. Bowhead whales: recent insights into their biology, status, and resilience. *2020 Arctic Report Card*, NOAA. https://doi.10.25923/cppm-n265

Gibbens, S. 2017. 'Heart-wrenching video shows starving polar bear on iceless land'. *National Geographic News*, 7 December. https://news.nationalgeographic.com/2017/12/polar-bear-starving-arctic-sea-ice-melt-climate-change-spd/

Ginzberg, R. 2021. 'The anti-humanism of David Attenborough'. *Spiked Online*, 18 May. https://www.spiked-online.com/2021/05/18/the-anti-humanism-of-david-attenborough/

Given, D.R. 1993. What is conservation biology and why is it so important? *Journal of the Royal Society of New Zealand* 23:55-60.

Glüsing, J. and Klawitter, N. 2012. 'Green veneer WWF helps industry more than environment'. *Der Spiegel*, 19 May. https://www.spiegel.de/international/world/wwf-helps-industry-more-than-environment-a-835712.html

Glynn, P. 2019. 'Sir David Attenborough: 'People thought we were cranks". *BBC News*, 20 October. https://www.bbc.com/news/entertainment-arts-50066895

Grain Brokers Australia 2021. 'Bumper corn crop for South African farmers'. *Grain Central*, 1 June. https://www.graincentral.com/markets/bumper-corn-crop-for-south-african-farmers/

Griffin, L. 2021. 'Sir David Attenborough slams 'gross injustice' of poorest people facing climate crisis created by developed countries'. *The Metro* (UK), 14 October. https://metro.co.uk/2021/10/14/david-attenborough-slams-gross-injustice-of-climate-change-in-new-series-15408344/

Grønnow, B., Gulløv, H.C., Jakobsen, B.H., et al. 2011. At the edge: high Arctic walrus hunters during the little ice age. *Antiquity* 85:960-977.

Grylls, G. 2021. 'COP26: Sir David Attenborough will warn world leaders on climate change'. *The Times* (London), 10 May. https://www.thetimes.co.uk/article/cop26-david-attenborough-warn-world-leaders-climate-change-gcpndfd6f

Gupta, S. 2001. Avoiding ambiguity. *Nature* 412:589.

Guy, J. 2020. 'David Attenborough has left Instagram, just weeks after joining'. *CNN*, 25 November. https://www.cnn.com/2020/11/25/world/david-attenborough-leaves-instagram-scli-intl-gbr/index.html

Hale, M. 2020. 'Review: David Attenborough is back, and he brought the walruses. "*Seven Worlds, One Planet*," the latest nature documentary extravaganza'. *New York Times*, 15 January. https://www.nytimes.com/2020/01/15/arts/television/review-seven-worlds-one-planet.html

Hales, R. and Mackey, B. 2021. 'The ultimate guide to why the COP26 summit ended in failure and disappointment (despite a few bright spots)'. *The Conversation* (UK), 14 November. https://theconversation.com/the-ultimate-guide-to-why-the-cop26-summit-ended-in-failure-and-disappointment-despite-a-few-bright-spots-17172

Hanson, H. 2019. 'Polar bear threat 'becoming the norm' as 50+ assemble near Russian village'. *Huffington Post* (USA), 7 December. https://www.huffingtonpost.ca/entry/polar-bears-ryrkaypiy-climate-change_n_5dec1505e4b00563b85224d0?ri18n=true

Harnett, C. 2021. 'Worst-case Omicron scenario could see hospitals overwhelmed, new COVID modelling shows'. *Victoria Times-Colonist* (Canada), 15 December. https://www.timescolonist.com/local-news/worst-case-omicron-scenario-could-see-hospitals-overwhelmed-new-modelling-4865035

Harvey, J.A., van den Berg, D., Ellers, J., et al. 2018. Internet blogs, polar bears, and climate-change denial by proxy. *Bioscience* 68: 281-287. [online 29 November 2017] https://doi.org/10.1093/biosci/bix133

Harvey, O. 2019. 'Fears Greta Thunberg is being manipulated on climate change by pushy parents and energy giants'. *The Sun* (UK), 19 August. https://www.thesun.co.uk/news/9756307/greta-thunberg-climate-change-fears-parents/

Hassol, S.J. 2004. *Impacts of a Warming Arctic: Arctic Climate Impact Assessment Synthesis Report.* Cambridge University Press, Cambridge UK.

Hausfather, Z. and Peters, G.P. 2020. Emissions – the 'business as usual' story is misleading ['Stop using the worst-case scenario for climate warming as the most likely outcome — more-realistic baselines make for better policy']. *Nature* 577: 618-620.

Hoare, C. 2019. 'David Attenborough shocked as climate change forces 100,000 walruses to crowd Asian beach'. *The Express* (UK), 3 November. https://www.express.co.uk/showbiz/tv-radio/1198277/david-attenborough-climate-change-asia-arctic-circle-bbc-seven-worlds-one-planet-spt

Hodge, M. 2018. 'WHITE LIE: National Geographic admits 'no evidence' starving polar bear in viral video with 2.5 billion views was dying because of climate change'. *The Sun* (UK), 2 August. https://www.thesun.co.uk/news/6923730/starving-polar-bear-fake-national-geographic-arctic/

Holland, M.M., C.M. Bitz, and B. Tremblay. 2006. Future reductions in the summer Arctic sea ice. *Geophysical Research Letters* 33:L23503. https://doi.org/10.1029/2006GL028024

Homewood, P. 2019. 'How could Attenborough get it so wrong about the walruses?' *The Conservative Woman*, 16 April. https://www.conservativewoman.co.uk/how-could-attenborough-get-it-so-wrong-about-the-walruses/

Homewood, P. 2020. 'Bob Ward in bad mood—loses again. *Not A Lot of People Know That* blog, 6 November. https://notalotofpeopleknowthat.wordpress.com/2020/11/06/bob-ward-in-bad-mood-loses-again/

Homewood, P. 2021. 'COP26 ends in humiliating failure'. *Not A Lot of People Know That* blog, 14 November. https://notalotofpeopleknowthat.wordpress.com/2021/11/14/cop26-ends-in-humiliating-failure/#more-54019

Hopper, T. 2017. 'What everybody got wrong about that viral video of a starving polar bear'. *The National Post* (Canada), 11 December. http://nationalpost.com/news/canada/what-everybody-got-wrong-about-that-viral-video-of-a-starving-polar-bear

Hopton, A. 2019. How documentaries seek to bring climate change stories to life. *CBC News*, 21 June. https://www.cbc.ca/news/entertainment/our-planet-climate-change-documentary-david-attenborough-1.5178420

Horton, C.C., Peterson, T.R., Banerjee, P. and Peterson, M.J. 2016. Credibility and advocacy in conservation science. *Conservation Biology* 30:23-32.

Horton, R. 2015. Offline: What is medicine's 5 sigma? *The Lancet* 385:1380.

Hickman, L. 2018. 'The 2004 lecture that finally convinced David Attenborough about global warming'. *Carbon Brief*, 13 August. https://www.carbonbrief.org/the-2004-lecture-that-finally-convinced-david-attenborough-about-global-warming

Hitchens, P. 2021. 'We DID have a sensible Covid plan... but copied a police state instead'. *The Mail on Sunday* (UK), 13 February. https://hitchensblog.mailonsunday.co.uk/2021/02/supporters-of-strangling-the-country-always-demand-what-would-you-have-done-if-i-dare-to-criticise-the-governments.html

Holthaus, E. 2016. 'Hollywood Is Finally Taking on Climate Change. It Should Go Even Further.' *Slate*, 9 August. https://slate.com/technology/2016/08/leonardo-dicaprio-speech-is-the-most-influential-ever-on-climate-change.html

Huff, E. 2018. 'National Geographic finally comes clean: Super viral video of polar bear "starving from climate change" was totally fake news'. *Science News*, 3 August. https://www.science.news/2018-08-03-national-geographic-finally-comes-clean-video-of-polar-bear-starving-from-climate-change-fake-news.html

IEA. 2021. 'Coal power's sharp rebound is taking it to a new record in 2021, threatening net zero goals'. International Energy Agency press release, 17 December. https://www.iea.org/news/coal-power-s-sharp-rebound-is-taking-it-to-a-new-record-in-2021-threatening-net-zero-goals

Imbler, S. 2020. 'David Attenborough, why did it take you so long?'. *Sierra Club*, 17 October. https://www.sierraclub.org/sierra/david-attenborough-why-did-it-take-you-so-long

Ioannidis, J.P.A. 2005. Why most published research findings are false. *PLOS Medicine* 2(8):e124. https://doi.org/10.1371/journal.pmed.0020124

IPCC. 2014. *Climate Change 2014: Synthesis Report. Contribution of Working Groups I, II and III to the Fifth Assessment Report of the Intergovernmental Panel on Climate Change.* Geneva: IPCC.

IPCC. 2021. *Climate Change 2021: The Physical Science Basis. Contributions of Working Group I to the Sixth Assessment Report of the Intergovernmental Panel on Climate Change* (AR6 WG1), Cambridge University Press. Accepted version, 7 August. https://www.ipcc.ch/report/ar6/wg1/

IPSO. 2019. 'Ipso MORI Issues Index: September 2019: Lack of faith in politics reaches new high'. *Ispo,* 30 October. https://www.ipsos.com/ipsos-mori/en-uk/ipsos-mori-issues-index-september-2019-lack-faith-politics-reaches-new-high

IPSO. 2020. 'Ipso MORI Issues Index: October 2020'. *Ispo,* 13 November. https://www.ipsos.com/ipsos-mori/en-uk/ipsos-mori-issues-index-october-2020

IPSO. 2021. 'Ipso MORI Issues Index: April 2021'. *Ispo,* 17 May. https://www.ipsos.com/ipsos-mori/en-uk/ipsos-mori-issues-index-april-2021

Irfan, U. 2021. 'Scientists aren't sure what will happen to clouds as the planet warms'. *Vox,* 19 May. https://www.vox.com/22430792/cloud-science-mystery-unexplainable-podcast-climate-change

Irish, J.L., Sleath, A., Cialone, M.A., et al. 2014. Simulations of hurricane Katrina (2005) under sea level and climate conditions for 1900. *Climate Change* 122:635-649.

Jay, C.V., Fischbach, A.S. and Kochnev, A.A. 2012. Walrus areas of use in the Chukchi Sea during sparse sea ice cover. *Marine Ecology Progress Series* 468:1-13.

Jenkins, C. 2021. 'David Attenborough to UN: Climate change is biggest threat modern humans have ever faced'. *The Hill*, 23 February. https://thehill.com/homenews/news/540058-david-attenborough-warns-un-security-council-on-climate-change-i-dont-envy-you

Johnson, J. 2021. 'Alaska's northernmost town, made rich by oil, facing uncertain future as sea ice melts'. *The Daily Telegraph* (UK), 31 October. https://www.telegraph.co.uk/world-news/2021/10/31/thin-ice-thawing-freezers-whaling-threatened-inside-alaskan/

Jones, L. 2018. 'Sir David Attenborough blasts Bear Grylls for killing animals on TV after The Island contestants slaughterer a crocodile. *The Sun* (UK), 4 January. https://www.thesun.co.uk/tvandshowbiz/5271753/sir-david-attenborough-blasted-bear-grylls-crocodile-slaughter-the-island/

Jones, A. 2019. 'Netflix isn't backing down over Our Planet's disturbing walrus deaths'. *CinemaBlend*, 10 April. https://www.cinemablend.com/television/2470136/netflix-isnt-backing-down-over-our-planets-disturbing-walrus-deaths

Jones, J.P.G. 2020. ''Extinction: The Facts': Attenborough's new documentary is surprisingly radical'. *The Conversation*, 14 September. https://theconversation.com/extinction-the-facts-attenboroughs-new-documentary-is-surprisingly-radical-146127

Kahn, B. 2019. 'Netflix's Our Planet delivers trills, but something's missing'. *Earther Gizmodo*, 5 April. https://earther.gizmodo.com/netflix-s-our-planet-delivers-thrills-but-somethings-m-1833838340

Kamp, J. 2018. 'Netflix shares teaser for new documentary series Our Planet'. *Paste Magazine,* 8 November. https://www.pastemagazine.com/tv/our-planet/netflix-shares-teaser-for-new-doucmentary-series-o/

Kanter, J. 2020a. All3Media acquires 'Our Planet' producer Silverback Films. *Deadline*, 3 December. https://deadline.com/2020/12/all3media-acquires-silverback-films-1234637088/

Kanter, J. 2020b. 'David Attenborough says 2021 is "crucial moment" in climate crisis during New Year message'. *Deadline*, 31 December. https://deadline.com/2020/12/david-attenborough-new-year-message-climate-crisis-1234663334/

Kasper, J. 2019. David Attenborough's new BBC1 nature series sparks recycling row over use of old Netflix footage. *The Sun* (UK), 29 October. https://www.thesun.co.uk/tvandshowbiz/10238618/david-attenboroughs-bbc-netflix-footage-row/

Kavry, V.I., Kochnev, A.A., Nikiforov, V.V. and Boltunov, A.N. 2006. Cape Vankarem – nature-ethnic complex at the Arctic coast of Chukotka (northeastern Russia). In, *Marine Mammals of the Holarctic, Papers of the Fourth International Conference (10-14 September 2006, Saint Petersburg)*, Belkovich, V.M. (ed.), pg. 227-230. Marine Mammal Council, Moscow. [Russian and English]

Kay, R. 2014. 'Slaughter by Royal appointment: As Prince William campaigns to save endangered species, a rather embarrassing reminder that most of his relatives had a somewhat different approach'. *The Daily Mail, 17 December.* https://www.dailymail.co.uk/news/article-2878309/As-Prince-William-campaigns-save-endangered-species-relatives-different-approach.html

Kearney, S.R., 1989. The Polar Bear Alert Program at Churchill, Manitoba. In: Bromely, M. (Ed.), *Bear–People Conflict: Proceedings of a Symposium on Management Strategies,* Yellowknife, Northwest Territories Department of Renewable Resources, pp. 83–92.

Klein, D.R. and Sowls, A. 2011. History of polar bears as summer residents on the St. Matthew Islands, Bering Sea. *Arctic* 64:429-436.

Knapton, S. 2019. 'Netflix walruses were driven to death by polar bears not climate change, claims zoologist'. *The Daily Telegraph* (UK), 8 April (4:33 pm). https://www.telegraph.co.uk/science/2019/04/08/netflix-walruses-driven-death-polar-bears-not-climate-change/

Kochnev, A.A. 2002. Factors causing Pacific mortality on the coastal haulouts of Wrangel Island. In: *Marine Mammals (Results of Research conducted in 1995-1998)*, Collection of articles, A.A. Aristov et al. (eds.), pg. 191-215. [Translated from Russian into English by O. Romanenko, Anchorage, AK in 2009; uploaded to 'ResearchNet' by Kochnev on 24 April 2017]

Kochnev, A.A. 2004. Warming of eastern Arctic and present status of the Pacific walrus (*Odobenus rosmarus divergens*) population. In, *Marine Mammals of the Holarctic, Papers of The Third International Conference (11-17 October 2004)*, Belkovich, V.M. (ed.), pg. 284-288. Marine Mammal Council, Moscow. [Russian and English]

Kochnev, A.A. 2010. The haulout of Pacific walruses (*Odobenus rosmarus divergens*) on Cape Serdtse-Kamen, the Chukchi Sea. In, *Marine Mammals of the Holarctic, Papers of the Sixth International Conference (11-15 October 2010)*, pg. 281-285. Marine Mammal Council, Moscow. [Russian and English]

Kochnev, A.A. 2012a. Mortality levels at coastal haul-outs in Chukotka in fall 2007. In: *A Workshop on Assessing Pacific Walrus Population Attributes from Coastal Haul-outs, 19-22 March, 2012* (Anchorage, AK), USFWS Administrative Report R7/MMM 13-1, pp. 66-68.

Kochnev, A.A. 2012b. Present status of the Pacific walrus in the Russian Federation. In: *A Workshop on Assessing Pacific Walrus Population Attributes from Coastal Haul-outs, 19-22 March, 2012* (Anchorage, AK), USFWS Administrative Report R7/MMM 13-1, pp. 58-60.

Kochnev, A. 2017. 'Pacific walrus in Russia'. *The Circle* 2:18-20. WWF Arctic Program. https://arcticwwf.org/newsroom/the-circle/walruses-going-with-the-floes/

Kochnev, A.A. 2018. Autumnal observations of the polar bears on Cape Schmidt. *Biological Problems of the North Conference: The Romanticism of Working Routine* Vol III. http://www.ibpn.ru/en/online-journal-the-romanticism-of-working-routine/2018/volume-iii/165-autumnal-observations-of-the-polar-bears-on-cape-schmidt

Kochnev, A.A. 2019. 'Step towards death'. *Live Journal*, 7 April. https://panzer-bjorn.livejournal.com/55037.html [accessed 15 April 2019; Google Chrome to translate]

Kochnev, A.A., Fishbach, A.S. Jay, C.V. et al. 2008. Satellite radio-tracking of Pacific walruses (*Odobenus rosmarus divergens*) in the Chukchi Sea 2007. In, *Marine Mammals of the Holarctic, Papers of the Fifth International Conference (14-18 October 2008)*, Belkovich, V.M. (ed.), pg. 263-267. Marine Mammal Council, Moscow. [Russian and English]

Kochneva, S. 2007. Polar bear in material and spiritual culture of the native peoples of Chukotka: bibliographic information. Report prepared for the Association of Traditional Marine Mammal Hunters of Chukotka, Alaska Nanuuq Commission and Pacific Fisheries Research Center, Chukotka Branch, Anadyr. [translated by O. Romanenko, Anchorage, AK, 2008]

Koonan, S.E. 2021a. 'Obama administration scientist says climate 'emergency' is based on fallacy'. *New York Post*, 24 April. https://nypost.com/2021/04/24/obama-admin-scientist-says-climate-emergency-is-based-on-fallacy/

Koonan, S.E. 2021b. Unsettled: What Climate Science Tells Us, What It Doesn't, and Why It Matters. BenBella Books, Dallas, Texas

Kovacs, K.M. 2016. *Erignathus barbatus* . The IUCN Red List of Threatened Species 2016: e.T8010A45225428.

Laframboise, D. 2011a. 'How the WWF infiltrated the IPCC - Part 1'. *Nofrakkingconsensus* blog, 23 September. https://nofrakkingconsensus.com/2011/09/23/how-the-wwf-infiltrated-the-ipcc-%E2%80%93-part-1/

Laframboise, D. 2011b. 'How the WWF infiltrated the IPCC - Part 2'. *Nofrakkingconsensus* blog, 26 September. https://nofrakkingconsensus.com/2011/09/26/how-the-wwf-infiltrated-the-ipcc-part-2/

Laframboise, D. 2011c. *The Delinquent Teenager Who Was Mistaken for the World's Top Climate Expert*. CreateSpace Publishing.

Laframboise, D. 2012. 'The WWF's vast pool of oil money'. *Nofrakkingconsensus* blog, 11 April. https://nofrakkingconsensus.com/2012/04/11/the-wwfs-vast-pool-of-oil-money/

Laframboise, D. 2014. 'The WWF: Still donning the science costume'. *Nofrakkingconsensus* blog, 15 January. https://nofrakkingconsensus.com/2014/01/15/the-wwf-still-donning-the-science-costume/

Laframboise, D. and Crockford, S.J. 2020. Walruses, polar bears, and the fired professor. In: *Climate Change: The Facts 2020*, J. Marohasy (ed.), pp. 21-34. Institute of Public Affairs, Melbourne, Australia.

Larsen Tempel, J.T. and Atkinson, S. 2020. Pacific walrus (*Odobenus rosmarus divergens*) reproductive capacity changes in three time frames during 1975–2010. *Polar Biology* 43:861-875.

Lawson, D. 2021. 'An inconvenient truth: fossil fuels aren't going'. *The Sunday Times* (London), 20 June. https://www.thetimes.co.uk/article/an-inconvenient-truth-fossil-fuels-arent-going-2z3bbkgfb

Leafe, D. 2017. 'Are these photos REALLY proof that polar bears are being killed by climate change? Doubts raised over claims after it emerges that no post mortem was carried out'. *The Daily Mail* (UK), 29 December. http://www.dailymail.co.uk/news/article-5221939/Are-polar-bears-killed-climate-change.html

Le Masurier, J. 2021. ''Climate change biggest security threat,' David Attenborough tells UN'. *France 24* via *Thomson Reuters Foundation*, 23 February. https://www.france24.com/en/americas/20210223-climate-change-biggest-security-threat-david-attenborough-tells-un

Letzter, R. 2019. Is climate change really causing walruses to jump off cliffs? *LiveScience*, 13 April. https://www.livescience.com/65226-why-netflix-walruses-fall-off-cliffs.html

Lewis, K. M., van Dijken, G.L. and Arrigo, K.R. 2020. Changes in phytoplankton concentration now drive increased Arctic Ocean primary production. *Science* 369 (6500):198-202.

Leyfield, F. 2019. 'Seven Worlds, One Planet fans in tears as orangutan fights with a digger and walruses die in most traumatic scenes yet'. *The Sun* (UK), 4 November. https://www.thesun.co.uk/tvandshowbiz/10276726/seven-worlds-one-planet-tears-orangutan/

Limoges, A., Weckström, K., Ribeiro, S., et al. 2020. Learning from the past: impact of the Arctic Oscillation on sea ice and marine productivity off northwest Greenland over the last 9,000 years. *Global Change Biology* 26:6767-6786.

Lindqvist, C., Bachmann, L., Andersen, L.W., et al. 2009. The Laptev Sea walrus *Odobenus rosmarus laptevi*: an enigma revisited. *Zoologica Scripta* 38:113-127.

Ling, T. 2019a. 'Royals join David Attenborough for star-studded Our Planet Netflix premier'. *Radio Times,* 5 April. https://www.radiotimes.com/tv/documentaries/our-planet-netflix-david-attenborough-royalty-celebrities-premiere/

Ling, T. 2019b. 'Our Planet viewers are mourning walruses after the most "heart-breaking but crucial" natural history footage ever'. *Radio Times*, 8 April. https://www.radiotimes.com/tv/documentaries/our-planet-netflix-attenborough-walrus/

Lomborg, B. 2001. *The Skeptical Environmentalist: Measuring the Real State of the World*. Cambridge University Press, New York.

Lomborg, B. 2020a. *False Alarm*. Basic Books, New York.

Lomborg, B. 2020b. Welfare in the 21st century: Increasing development, reducing inequality, the impact of climate change, and the cost of climate policies. *Technological Forecasting & Social Change* 156:119981.

Lomborg, B. 2021. 'The truth about extreme weather events'. [graph update]. *Facebook*, 25 July. https://www.facebook.com/bjornlomborg/posts/374647437353599?mc_cid=e5aad1d13e&mc_eid=9b5429fe70

Lowry, L. 1985. 'Pacific Walrus – Boom or Bust?' *Alaska Fish & Game Magazine* July/August: 2-5.

Lowry, L. 2015. *Odobenus rosmarus ssp. divergens*. The IUCN Red List of Threatened Species 2015: e.T61963499A45228901

Lydersen, C. 2018. Walrus: *Odobenus rosmarus*. In: *Encyclopedia of Marine Mammals* (Third Edition), B. Würsig, J.G.M. Thewissen, and K.M. Kovacs (eds.), pg. 1045-1048. Academic Press/Elsevier, London.

Lyons, R. 2009. 'The sad decline of David Attenborough'. *Spiked Online*, 11 December. https://www.spiked-online.com/2009/12/11/the-sad-decline-of-david-attenborough/

Ma, A. 2019. 'Greta Thunberg and David Attenborough met for the first time, and the 2 climate icons fangirled over each other'. *Insider Magazine*, 30 December. https://www.insider.com/greta-thunberg-david-attenborough-interview-skype-call-2019-12

MacAree, G. 2019. 'Every animal face-off in the BBC's new nature documentary, rated: episode 2 Asia'. *SB Nation*, 7 November. https://www.sbnation.com/2019/11/7/20951323/seven-worlds-one-planet-episode-2-review

MacCracken, J.G. 2012._Pacific walrus and climate change: observations and predictions. *Ecology and Evolution* 2:2072-2090.

MacCracken, J.G., Beatty, W.S., Garlich-Miller, J.L., et al. 2017. Final Species *Status Assessment for the Pacific walrus (Odobenus rosmarus divergens).* US Fish and Wildlife Service, Anchorage, Alaska.

Macdonald, C. 2019. 'Shocking Our Planet footage shows how climate change is causing walruses to plunge to their deaths off cliffs 'they should never have scaled,' as retreating sea ice pushes them further onto shore' *Daily Mail* (UK), 5 April. https://www.dailymail.co.uk/sciencetech/article-6892449/Climate-change-caused-hundreds-walruses-plunge-deaths-offs-high-cliffs.html

MacEachern, R. 2020. 'David Attenborough to define his legacy in new book, A Life on Our Planet'. *Penguin Articles*, 28 May. https://www.penguin.co.uk/articles/2020/may/david-attenborough-life-on-our-planet.html

McCaffrey, J. 2021. 'David Attenborough lost for words at his face tattooed on girl's thigh in Borneo'. *The Mirror* (UK), 12 November. https://www.mirror.co.uk/tv/tv-news/david-attenborough-lost-words-face-25446268

McFarland, K. 2015. 'In 2015, Netflix became a TV network. Where does it go from here?'. *Wired*, 11 December. https://www.wired.com/2015/12/netflix-legit-tv-network/

McGrath, M. 2018. 'Sir David Attenborough: Climate change 'our greatest threat''. *BBC News*, 3 December. https://www.bbc.com/news/science-environment-46398057

McGrath, M. 2019. 'Climate change: Sir David Attenborough warns of 'catastrophe''. *BBC News*, 18 April. https://www.bbc.com/news/science-environment-47976184

McKinlay, R. 2019. 'Top of the Month: Attenborough and BBC's subtle change of tack might just change the world'. *PR Week*, 28 November. https://www.prweek.com/article/1667200/top-month-attenborough-bbcs-subtle-change-tack-just-change-world

McLachlan, M. 2019. 'Our Planet director Sophie Lanfear on that tragic walrus scene and documenting never-before-seen animal behaviors'. *Awards Daily*, 16 September. https://www.awardsdaily.com/2019/08/21/sophie-lanfear-our-planet-interview/

Mclaughlin, K. 2017. 'Sheep grazing on a hill? No... it's 200 POLAR BEARS scrambling down a mountain slope to feast on a bloated whale carcass in the Arctic'. *Daily Mail* (UK), 23 November. http://www.dailymail.co.uk/news/article-5110801/Polar-bears-scramble-mountain-feast-whale.html

McPhee, R. 2019. 'Netflix's Our Planet shows heartbreaking moment 'desperate' walruses fall to their deaths from cliff after their natural habitat is destroyed' *The Sun* (UK), 5 April. https://www.thesun.co.uk/tvandshowbiz/8800576/netflix-david-attenborough-our-planet-walrus-heartbreaking/

Marohasy, J. (ed.) 2020. *Climate Change: The Facts 2020.* Institute of Public Affairs, Melbourne.

Masood, E. and Tollefson, J. 2021. 'COP26 hasn't solved the problem': scientists react to UN climate deal. *Nature* 599:355-35614. https://doi.org/10.1038/d41586-021-03431-4

Massey, J. 2019. 'David Attenborough's Our Planet mass walrus death scene accused of being lie'. *Ladbible*, 19 April. http://www.ladbible.com/entertainment/film-and-tv-netflixs-our-planet-mass-walrus-death-scene-accused-of-being-lie-20190419

Mathiesen, K. 2021. 'UN Security Council hears of climate threat, does nothing'. *Politico*, 23 February. https://www.politico.eu/article/un-security-council-hears-of-climate-threat-does-nothing/

Midgley, C. 2019. Review: Our Planet, Netflix. *The Times* (UK), 2 April. https://www.thetimes.co.uk/article/review-our-planet-netflix-xd92hbv79

Miller, A. 2019. 'Sir David Attenborough's Our Planet accused of lying about the walrus massacre which shattered Netflix viewers'. *Metro* (UK), 19 April. https://metro.co.uk/2019/04/19/sir-david-attenboroughs-planet-accused-lying-walrus-massacre-shattered-netflix-viewers-9266354/

Milman, O. 2018. 'Climate change is making hurricanes even more destructive, research finds'. *The Guardian* (UK), 14 November. https://www.theguardian.com/environment/2018/nov/14/climate-change-hurricanes-study-global-warming

Mittermeier, C. 2018. 'Nothing prepared me for what I saw.' *National Geographic Magazine* August: 36–37. https://www.nationalgeographic.com/magazine/2018/08/explore-through-the-lens-starving-polar-bear-photo/

Molnár, P.K., Derocher, A.E., Thiemann, G.W., et al. 2010. Predicting survival, reproduction and abundance of polar bears under climate change. *Biological Conservation* 143:1612–1622.

Molnár, P.K., Bitz, C.M., Holland, M.M., et al. 2020. Fasting season length sets temporal limits for global polar bear persistence. *Nature Climate Change* 10:732-738. https://doi.org/10.1038/s41558-020-0818-9

Monbiot, G. 2018. 'David Attenborough has betrayed the living world he loves'. *The Guardian* (UK), 7 Novermber. https://www.theguardian.com/commentisfree/2018/nov/07/david-attenborough-world-environment-bbc-films

Monbiot, G. 2021. 'After the failure of Cop26, there's only one last hope for our survival'. *The Guardian* (UK), 14 November. https://www.theguardian.com/commentisfree/2021/nov/14/cop26-last-hope-survival-climate-civil-disobedience

Montford, A. 2019a. 'Has Netflix's Our Planet hidden the real cause of walrus deaths?' *The Spectator* (UK), 9 April. https://blogs.spectator.co.uk/2019/04/has-netflixs-our-planet-hidden-the-real-cause-of-walrus-deaths/

Montford, A. 2019b. 'Our Planet: Where was the camera?' *Global Warming Policy Foundation* Press Release, 15 April. https://www.thegwpf.com/camera/

Montford, A. 2019c. 'Another Attenborough tragedy porn exposé'. *Reaction Magazine*, 23 April. https://reaction.life/david-attenborough-dead-bats-radical-green-propaganda-relies-tragedy-porn/

Moody, R. 2020. Netflix subscribers and revenue by country. *Comparitech*, 20 July. https://www.comparitech.com/tv-streaming/netflix-subscribers/

Moore, P. 2021. *Fake Invisible Catastrophes and Threats of Doom.* Ecosense Environmental, Comox, B.C.

Moore, P. [with Crockford, S.J.]. 2019. 'What David Attenborough and Netflix's 'Our Planet' Get Wrong About Climate Change'. https://townhall.com/columnists/drpatrickmoore/2019/04/14/what-netflixs-our-planet-gets-wrong-about-climate-change-n2544726

Morono, M. 2021. *Green Fraud: Why The Green New Deal Is Even Worse Than You Think*. Regnery Publishing, Washington.

Mosley, T. and Raphelson, S. 2021. 'David Attenborough explains how humans jeopardize 'A Perfect Planet' for life 10:03'. *WBUR Radio* (Boston), 4 January. https://www.wbur.org/hereandnow/2021/01/04/a-perfect-planet-david-attenborough

NAMMCO. 2021. *Atlantic walrus*. North Atlantic Marine Mammal Commission Report for 2016, updated January 2021. Tromso, Norway. https://nammco.no/topics/atlantic-walrus/ [accessed 31 March 2021]

Nandy, S. 2021. 'India set to harvest record rice, wheat crops in 2020-21'. *SP Global*, 26 May. https://www.spglobal.com/platts/en/market-insights/latest-news/agriculture/052621-india-set-to-harvest-record-rice-wheat-crops-in-2020-21

National Post. 2019. 'A scene from Netflix's 'Our Planet' shows walruses jump off an 80-metre cliff to their deaths. It's as horrifying as it sounds'. *National Post* (Canada), 9 April. https://nationalpost.com/news/world/a-scene-from-netflixs-our-planet-shows-walruses-jump-off-a-60-metre-cliff-to-their-deaths-its-as-horrifying-as-it-sounds

NBC. News. 2007. '3,000 walruses die in stampedes tied to climate'. *NBC News/Associated Press*, 14 December. http://www.nbcnews.com/id/22260892/ns/us_news-environment/t/walruses-die-stampedes-tied-climate/

Nelson, F. 2021. 'I tackled a Sage Covid modeller on Twitter and it was quite the revelation'. *The Daily Telegraph* (UK), 19 December. https://www.telegraph.co.uk/opinion/2021/12/19/tackled-sage-covid-modeller-twitter-quite-revelation/

Netflix. 2018. 'Sir David Attenborough voices new Netflix serious Our Planet'. *Netflix*, 8 November. https://about.netflix.com/en/news/sir-david-attenborough-voices-new-netflix-series-our-planet-1

New York Times. 1996. 60 walruses plunge to their death, and Alaskans wonder why'. *New York Times*, 31 August.

https://www.nytimes.com/1996/08/31/us/60-walruses-plunge-to-their-death-and-alaskans-wonder-why.html

New Zealand Herald. 2019. 'Watch: Hundreds of walruses face plunging to death due to climate change'. *New Zealand Herald*, 7 April. https://www.nzherald.co.nz/world/watch-hundreds-of-walruses-face-plunging-to-death-due-to-climate-change/NE66JG6YELLUZZXCM7OWHM7MA4/

Nicholson, R. 2019. 'Climate Change: The Facts' review – our greatest threat, laid bare'. *The Guardian* (UK), 18 April. https://www.theguardian.com/tv-and-radio/2019/apr/18/climate-change-the-facts-review-our-greatest-threat-laid-bare-david-attenborough

Nilsen, T. 2019. 'Declares emergency: Polar bears invade military town.' *Barents Observer,* 9 February. https://thebarentsobserver.com/en/arctic/2019/02/declares-emergency-polar-bears-invades-military-town

Nolan, S. 2013. '... meanwhile, the man who's never OFF the telly says 'curb population or nature will do it for us': Wildlife legend Sir David warns that mankind is a 'plague on the Earth'. *Daily Mail* (UK), 21 January. https://www.dailymail.co.uk/news/article-2266237/David-Attenborough-warns-mankind-plague-Earth.html

Noss, R. 1999. Is there a special conservation biology? *Ecography* 22:113-122.

NSIDC. 2019. *Falling up. Arctic Sea Ice News,* National Snow and Ice Data Center, 3 October [accessed 3 October 2019], https://nsidc.org/arcticseaicenews/2019/10/falling-up/

NSIDC. 2020. 'Steep decline sputters out.' *Arctic Sea Ice News*, National Snow and Ice Data Center, 4 August [accessed 29 November 2021]. http://nsidc.org/arcticseaicenews/2020/08/steep-decline-sputters-out/

NSIDC. 2021. *September turning. Arctic Sea Ice News*, National Snow and Ice Data Center, 5 October [accessed 29 November 2021], http://nsidc.org/arcticseaicenews/2021/10/september-turning/

Nuccitelli, D. 2017. 'New study uncovers the 'keystone domino' strategy of climate denial'. *The Guardian* (UK), 29 November. https://www.theguardian.com/environment/climate-consensus-97-per-cent/2017/nov/29/new-study-uncovers-the-keystone-domino-strategy-of-climate-denial

Obbard, M.E., Cattet, M.R.I., Howe, E.J., Middel, K.R., Newton, E.J., Kolenosky, G.B., Abraham, K.F. and Greenwood, C.J. 2016. Trends in body condition in polar bears (*Ursus maritimus*) from the Southern Hudson Bay subpopulation in relation to changes in sea ice. *Arctic Science* 2:15-32. 10.1139/AS-2015-0027

Obbard, M.E., Theimann, G.W., Peacock, E. and DeBryn, T.D. (eds.) 2010. Polar Bears: Proceedings of the 15th meeting of the Polar Bear Specialists Group IUCN/SSC, 29 June-3 July, 2009, Copenhagen, Denmark. Gland, Switzerland and Cambridge UK, IUCN

Ocampo, K.R. 2021. 'Q1 palay harvest sets record'. *Business Inquirer*, 19 May 2021. https://business.inquirer.net/323144/q1-palay-harvest-sets-record

O'Donovan, G. 2019. 'Climate Change: the Facts review: David Attenborough's superb documentary offers hope for climate crisis'. *The Daily Telegraph* (UK), 18 April. https://www.telegraph.co.uk/tv/2019/04/18/climate-change-facts-review-david-attenboroughs-superb-documentary

Ogden, N.H. and Gachon P. 2019. Climate change and infectious diseases: What can we expect? *Canada Communicable Disease Report 2019* 45(4):76–80. https://doi.org/10.14745/ccdr.v45i04a01

O'Neil, B.C., Carter, T.R., Ebi, K., et al. 2020. Achievements and needs for the climate change scenario framework. *Nature Climate Change* 10:1074-1084.

O'Neill, D.W., Fanning, A.L., Lamb, W.F., et al. 2018. 'A good life for all within planetary boundaries'. *Nature Sustainability* 1:88-95.

Ovsyanikov, N. 2010. Polar bear research on Wrangel Island and in the central Arctic Basin. In, Proceedings of the 15th meeting of the Polar Bear Specialists Group IUCN/SSC, 29 June-3 July, 2009, Obbard, M.E., et al. (eds), pp. 171-178. Gland, Switzerland and Cambridge UK, IUCN.

Ovsyanikov, N.G. and Menyushina, I. E. 2015. Demographic processes in Chukchi-Alaskan polar bear population as observed in Wrangel Island region. pg. 37-55, In: *Marine Mammals of the Holarctic,* Collection of Scientific Papers. Vol. 2. Moscow.

Pakalolo, 2019. 'Lack of sea ice has forced hundreds of walrus to scale cliffs where they then plunge to their death'. *DailyKos*, 7 April. https://www.dailykos.com/stories/2019/4/7/1848381/-Lack-of-sea-ice-has-forced-hundreds-of-walrus-to-scale-cliffs-where-they-then-plunge-to-their-deaths

Palmer, T. and Stevens, B. 2019. The scientific challenge of understanding and estimating climate change. *Proceedings of the National Academy of Sciences of the United States of America* 116(49):24390-24395.

Pappas, S. 2017. 'Starving Polar Bear's Last Hours Captured in Heartbreaking Video'. *LiveScience*, 8 December. https://www.livescience.com/61151-starving-polar-bear-captured-on-video.html

PBI. 2017a. 'News Release: Polar Bears and the Climate-Change Denial Machine'. *Polar Bears International*, 29 November. https://polarbearsinternational.org/news/article-polar-bears/news-release-polar-bears-and-the-climate-change-denial-machine/

PBI. 2017b. 'Starving polar bear draws attention to climate change'. *Polar Bears International*, 9 December. https://polarbearsinternational.org/news/article-polar-bears/starving-polar-bear-draws-attention-to-climate-change/

Peiser, B. 2019. 'Attenborough and a shaggy walrus story'. *The Conservative Woman*, 10 April. https://www.conservativewoman.co.uk/attenborough-and-a-shaggy-walrus-story/

Pereverzev, A.A. and Kochnev, A.A. 2012. Marine mammals in the Cape Schmidt vicinity (Chukotka) in September-October 2011. In, *Marine Mammals of the Holarctic, Papers of the Sixth International Conference (11-15 October 2010)*, Vol. 2, pg. 176-181. Marine Mammal Council, Moscow. [Russian and English]

Pielke Jr., R. 2018. *The Rightful Place of Science: Disasters & Climate Change 2nd Edition.* Consortium for Science, Policy & Outcomes, Boulder, Colorado.

Pitulko, V. V., Ivanova, V. V., Kasparov, A., and Pavlova, E.Y. 2015. Reconstructing prey selection, hunting strategy and seasonality of the early Holocene frozen site in the Siberian High Arctic: A case study on the Zhokhov site faunal remains, De Long Islands. *Environmental Archaeology* 20:120-157. http://dx.doi.org/10.1179/1749631414Y.0000000040

Pochin, C. 2019. 'Tragic Our Planet scene showing mass walrus deaths accused of being a lie'. *The Mirror* (UK), 19 April. https://www.mirror.co.uk/tv/tv-news/tragic-planet-scene-showing-mass-14426615

Polyak, L., Alley, R.B., Andrews, J.T. et al. 2010. History of sea ice in the Arctic. *Quaternary Science Reviews* 29:1757-1778.

Pond, S. 2019. 'How 'Our Planet' became a surprise Emmy heavyweight – with more nominations than 'Veep''. *The Wrap*, 16 August. https://www.thewrap.com/our-planet-emmy-heavyweight/

Pooley, G. and Tupy, M.L. 2021. 'The Simon Abundance Index 2021'. *Human Progress*, 22 April. https://www.humanprogress.org/the-simon-abundance-index-2021/

Popkin, G. 2017. 'Revealing the methods of climate-doubting blogs'. *Inside Science*, 30 November. https://www.insidescience.org/news/revealing-methods-climate-doubting-blogs

Prance, S. 2019. 'Our Planet viewers are traumatised by the "horrific" walrus scene in the Netflix series'. *Pop Buzz,* 9 April. https://www.popbuzz.com/tv-film/news/our-planet-walrus-scene-netflix/

PHAC. 2020. *COVID-19 in Canada: Using data and modelling to inform public health action.* Public Health Agency of Canada, 9 April. https://www.canada.ca/en/public-health/services/diseases/coronavirus-disease-covid-19/epidemiological-economic-research-data/mathematical-modelling.html

Ramsay, M.A. and Stirling, I. 1988. Reproductive biology and ecology of female polar bears (*Ursus maritimus*). *Journal of Zoology London* 214:601–624.

Rantanen, M., Karpechko, A., Nordling, K. et al. 2021. The Arctic has warmed four times faster than the globe since 1980. *Research Square Preprints*, https://doi.org/10.21203/rs.3.rs-654081/v1

Ray, G.C., Hufford, G.L., Overland, J.E., et al. 2016. Decadal Bering Sea seascape change: consequences for Pacific walruses and indigenous hunters. *Ecological Applications* 26:24-41.

Regehr, E.V., Laidre, K.L, Akçakaya, H.R., et al. 2016. Conservation status of polar bears (*Ursus maritimus*) in relation to projected sea-ice declines. *Biology Letters* 12: 20160556.

Regehr, E.V., Lunn, N.J., Amstrup, S.C. and Stirling, I. 2007. Effects of earlier sea ice breakup on survival and population size of polar bears in Western Hudson Bay. *Journal of Wildlife Management* 71:2673-2683.

Reuters 2021. 'David Attenborough named COP26 People's Advocate ahead of key climate summit'. *Thomson Reuters Foundation*, 10 May. https://www.reuters.com/world/uk/david-attenborough-named-cop26-peoples-advocate-ahead-key-climate-summit-2021-05-09/

Richards, K. 2018. 'People did not see 'full story' behind iconic starving polar bear image, photographer says'. *The Independent* (UK), 6 August. https://www.independent.co.uk/news/world/americas/polar-bear-photo-starving-climate-change-nat-geo-cristina-g-mittermeier-a8479946.html

Richardson, V. 2019. 'Netflix series challenged on claim that climate change causes cliff-diving walruses'. *Washington Times*, 22 April. https://www.washingtontimes.com/news/2019/apr/22/netflix-our-planet-hit-climate-change-walrus-cliff/

Ridd, P. 2020. *Reef Heresy? Science, Research and the Great Barrier Reef.* Connor Court Publishing, Brisbane.

Ridley, M. 2010. *The Rational Optimist: How Prosperity Evolves*. Harper, New York.

Ridley, M. 2014. 'Even if you pile crazy assumption upon crazy assumption, you cannot even manage to make climate change cause minor damage'. *National Post/Financial Post* (Canada), 19 June. https://business.financialpost.com/opinion/ipcc-climate-change-warming

Ridley, M. 2015. The Climate Wars and the Damage to Science. *Global Warming Policy Foundation* Essay 3.

Ridley, M. 2019. The BBC, Bob Ward and the climate catastrophists' attack on dissent. *Reaction*, 30 December. https://reaction.life/the-bbc-bob-ward-and-the-climate-catastrophists-attack-on-dissent/

Ridley, M. 2021. 'Flawed modelling is condemning Britain to lockdown'. *The Daily Telegraph* (UK), 21 June. https://www.telegraph.co.uk/news/2021/06/21/flawed-modelling-condemning-britain-lockdown/

Robbins, C.T., Lopez-Alfaro, C., Rode, K.D., et al. 2012. Hibernation and seasonal fasting in bears: the energetic costs and consequences for polar bears. *Journal of Mammalogy* 93(6):1493-1503.

Robinson, J. 2018. ''We went too far': National Geographic admits there was no evidence starving polar bear in video watched by 2.5 billion was dying due to climate change'. *The Daily Mail* (UK), 2 August. http://www.dailymail.co.uk/news/article-6018447/National-Geographic-admits-no-evidence-polar-bear-video-dying-climate-change.html

Rockström, J., Steffen, W., Noone, K., et al. 2009. A safe operating space for humanity. *Nature* 461:472-475.

Rode, K.D., Regehr, E.V., Douglas, D., et al. 2014. Variation in the response of an Arctic top predator experiencing habitat loss: feeding and reproductive ecology of two polar bear populations. *Global Change Biology* 20(1):76-88. http://onlinelibrary.wiley.com/doi/10.1111/gcb.12339/abstract

Rode, K. D., Wilson, R.R., Douglas, D.C., et al. 2018. Spring fasting behavior in a marine apex predator provides an index of ecosystem productivity. *Global Change Biology* 24:410-423.

Rolling Stone. 2019. 'See a starving polar bear hunt for beluga whales in startling clip'. *Rolling Stone Magazine*, 6 May. https://www.rollingstone.com/culture/culture-news/nat-geo-hostile-planet-bear-grylls-starving-polar-bear-beluga-whales-831057

Rose, D. 2019. 'What David Attenborough told BBC viewers about this raging orangutan fighting a digger is only part of the truth... and that's just one of the flaws in the great naturalist's 'alarmist' new documentary, writes DAVID ROSE'. *The Mail on Sunday*, 20 April. https://www.dailymail.co.uk/news/article-6943475/What-Attenborough-told-BBC-viewers-orangutan-fighting-digger-truth.html

Rose, D. 2021. ''Useful idiots' who let China off the hook: Why is there such an apparent lack of concern over their determination to keep burning coal, asks DAVID ROSE'. *The Daily Mail* (UK), 14 November. https://www.dailymail.co.uk/debate/article-10201999/Why-lack-concern-burning-coal-asks-DAVID-ROSE.html

Rosenberg, E. 2017. ''We stood there crying': Emaciated polar bear seen in 'gut-wrenching' video and photos'. *The Washington Post*, 9 December. https://www.washingtonpost.com/news/animalia/wp/2017/12/09/we-stood-there-crying-the-story-behind-the-emotional-video-of-a-starving-polar-bear/

Rosenthal, Z. 2021. 'May snaps long-standing streak for strong tornadoes in US'. *AccuWeather,* 10 June. https://www.accuweather.com/en/severe-weather/may-snaps-long-standing-us-streak-for-ef3-tornadoes/955116

Rowlatt, J. 2020. 'Sir David Attenborough makes stark warning about species extinction'. *BBC News* (UK), 12 September. https://www.bbc.com/news/science-environment-54118769

Rowling, M. 2021. 'Pandemic delays leave many nations facing climate action catch-up in 2021'. *Thomson Reuters Foundation*, 8 January. https://news.trust.org/item/20210108060129-ksfio/

RT News. 2013. 'Bear scare: Crowds of polar predators 'besiege' Russian Far East town'. *RT News* (Russia), 11 November. http://rt.com/news/polar-bears-siege-chukotka-russia-539/

Rozel, N. 2010. 'The missing polar bears of St. Matthew Island'. *Alaska Science Forum*, 8 June (article #2015). http://www.gi.alaska.edu/AlaskaScienceForum/article/missing-polar-bears-st-matthew-island

Rozsa, M. 2020. 'Thunberg: "When your house is on fire, you don't wait a few more years to start putting it out"'. *Salon*, 5 March. https://www.salon.com/2020/03/04/thunberg-when-your-house-is-on-fire-you-dont-wait-a-few-more-years-to-start-putting-it-out/

Rushton, S. 2021. 'Sir David Attenborough has two reasons for hope at Cop26'. *The National News* (UK), 13 October. https://www.thenationalnews.com/world/uk-news/2021/10/13/sir-david-attenborough-has-two-reasons-for-hope-at-cop26/

Ryan, B. 2019. 'These days, it's not about the polar bears'. *The New York Times*, 12 May. https://www.nytimes.com/2019/05/12/climate/climate-solutions-polar-bears.html

Sarah, D. 2019. ''Serious ethical issues': Did climate change documentary misrepresent this disturbing footage to push 'propaganda'?'. *Twitchy*, 17 April. https://twitchy.com/sarahd-313035/2019/04/17/serious-ethical-issues-did-climate-change-documentary-misrepresent-this-disturbing-footage-to-push-propaganda/

Scholz, R.W. and Wellmer, R.W. 2021. Endangering the integrity of science by misusing unvalidated models and untested assumptions as facts: General considerations and the mineral and phosphorus scarcity fallacy. *Sustainability Science* 16:2069-2086. https://doi.org/10.1007/s11625-021-01006-w

Schoolmeester, T., Gjerdi, H.L., Crump, J., et al. 2019. *Global Linkages – A graphic look at the changing Arctic* (rev.1). UN Environment and GRID-Arendal, Nairobi and Arendal, Norway.

Schwab, K. and Malleret, T. 2020. *Covid-19: The Great Reset.* Forum Publishing, World Economic Forum, Geneva.

Schwarzenbach, A. 2011. *Saving the World's Wildlife: The WW's First Fifty Years*. Profile Books, London.

Sea Otter Recovery Team 2007. *Recovery strategy for the sea otter (Enhydra lutris) in Canada.* Species at Risk Act Recovery Strategy Series. Fisheries and Oceans Canada, Vancouver.

Shellenberger, M. 2020. *Apocalypse Never: Why Environmental Alarmism Hurst Us All.* Harper Collins, London.

Shelley, J. 2019. 'The most shocking, sickening, footage David Attenborough has EVER had? Mankind's treatment of orangutans was shameful in Seven Worlds, One Planet'. *The Daily Mail* (UK), 4 November. https://www.dailymail.co.uk/tvshowbiz/article-7646645/Mankinds-treatment-orang-utans-shameful-Seven-Worlds-One-Planet-Jim-Shelley.html

Shersby, M. 2021. '*The Green Planet* to premiere at COP26'. *Discover Wildlife*, 8 October. https://www.discoverwildlife.com/news/the-green-planet-to-premiere-at-cop26/

Shields, F. 2019. 'Why we're rethinking the images we use for our climate journalism'. *The Guardian* (UK), 18 October. https://www.theguardian.com/environment/2019/oct/18/guardian-climate-pledge-2019-images-pictures-guidelines

Shukman, D. 2021a. 'Sir David Attenborough's new doc: 'Humans are intruders''. *BBC News* (UK), 15 April (video). https://www.bbc.com/news/av/science-environment-56752541

Shukman, D. 2021b. 'Climate change: Sir David Attenborough in 'act now' warning'. *BBC News* (UK), 25 October. https://www.bbc.com/news/science-environment-59039485

Shute, J. 2019. 'Sir David Attenborough: 'I don't think people should fly just for the hell of it''. *The Daily Telegraph* (UK), 20 October. https://www.telegraph.co.uk/men/thinking-man/sir-david-attenborough-dont-think-people-should-fly-just/

Shute, J. 2020. 'Sir David Attenborough: 'At 94, I think I can jump the vaccine queue''. *The Daily Telegraph*, 19 December. https://www.telegraph.co.uk/men/thinking-man/sir-david-attenborough-94-think-can-jump-vaccine-queue/

Siegel, K. 2018. Keeping fossil fuels in the ground is the only way to save polar bears ravaged by climate change. *The Hill*, 26 May 2018. http://thehill.com/opinion/energy-environment/389493-keeping-fossil-fuels-in-the-ground-is-the-only-way-to-save-polar

Slaughter, G. 2019. ''Heartbreaking' scene shows walruses fall off cliff in Netflix's 'Our Planet' 9 April 2019. https://www.ctvnews.ca/entertainment/heartbreaking-scene-shows-walruses-fall-off-cliff-in-netflix-s-our-planet-1.4372461

Smallman, E. 2020. 'David Attenborough still has hope for our future'. *New York Times*, 25 December. https://www.nytimes.com/2020/12/25/arts/television/david-attenborough-perfect-planet.html

Smith, K.F., Goldberg, M., Rosenthal, S., Carlson, L., Chen, J., Chen, C. and Ramachandran, S. 2014. Global rise in human infectious disease outbreaks. *Journal of the Royal Society Interface* 11:20140950.

Smith, T.G. and Sjare, B. 1990. Predation of belugas and narwhals by polar bears in nearshore areas of the Canadian High Arctic. *Arctic* 43(2):99-102.

Snowdon, C. 2020. 'The true cost of coronavirus on our economy'. *The Spectator* (UK), 24 September. https://www.spectator.co.uk/article/the-true-cost-of-coronavirus-on-our-economy

Sommerlad, J. 2021. 'Climate crisis: 'Humans are intruders' and the natural world is better off without us, says Sir David Attenborough'. *The Independent* (UK), 14 April. https://www.independent.co.uk/climate-change/news/climate-change-david-attenborough-documentary-b1831791.html

Speckman, S. G., V. I. Chernook, D. M. Burn, M. S. Udevitz, A. A. Kochnev, et al. 2011. Results and evaluation of a survey to estimate Pacific walrus population size, 2006. *Marine Mammal Science* 27:514–553.

Spencer, R.W. 2021. 'An Earth Day reminder: 'Global Warming' is only ~50% of what models predict. *Dr. Roy Spencer* blog, 22 April. https://www.drroyspencer.com/2021/04/an-earth-day-reminder-global-warming-is-only-50-of-what-models-predict/

Spring, M. 2021. 'Covid denial to climate denial: How conspiracists are shifting focus'. *BBC News* (UK), 15 November. https://www.bbc.com/news/blogs-trending-59255165

Stafford, R. and Jones, P.S. J. 2019. ''Climate Change – The Facts': the BBC and David Attenborough should talk about solutions'. *The Conversation*, 17 April. http://theconversation.com/climate-change-the-facts-the-bbc-and-david-attenborough-should-talk-about-solutions-114544

Steele, J. 2013. *Landscapes and Cycles: An Environmentalist's Journey to Climate Scepticism*. CreateSpace Publishing.

Steffen, W., Richardson, K., Rockström, J., et al. 2015. Planetary boundaries: Guiding human development on a changing planet. *Science* 347(6223):736 and 1259855-1 to 1259855-10.

Stevens, M. 2017. 'Video of Starving Polar Bear 'Rips Your Heart Out of Your Chest''. *New York Times*, 11 December. https://www.nytimes.com/2017/12/11/world/canada/starving-polar-bear.html

Stewart, W. 2019. 'State of emergency is declared after more than 50 polar bears invade Russian town and 'chase terrified residents.'' *Daily Mail* (UK), 10 February. https://www.dailymail.co.uk/news/article-6687731/State-emergency-declared-50-polar-bears-invade-Russian-town.html

Stirling, I. and Parkinson, C.L. 2006. Possible effects of climate warming on selected populations of polar bears (*Ursus maritimus*) in the Canadian Arctic. *Arctic* 59:261-275.

Stirling I, Jonkel C, Smith P, et al. 1977. The ecology of the polar bear (*Ursus maritimus*) along the western coast of Hudson Bay. *Canadian Wildlife Service Occasional Paper* 33.

Stirling, I. and Lunn, N.J. 1997. Environmental fluctuations in arctic marine ecosystems as reflected by variability in reproduction of polar bears and ringed seals. In *Ecology of Arctic Environments,* Woodin, S.J. and Marquiss, M. (eds), pg. 167–181. Blackwell Science, UK.

Stirling, I., Lunn, N.J. and Iacozza, J. 1999. Long-term trends in the population ecology of polar bears in Western Hudson Bay in relation to climate change. *Arctic* 52:294-306.

Stolworthy, J. 2019. Our Planet: Netflix defends 'devastating' walrus scene in David Attenborough documentary. *The Independent* (UK), 10 April. https://www.independent.co.uk/arts-entertainment/tv/news/our-planet-netflix-walrus-death-watch-video-cliff-david-attenborough-a8862711.html

Stone, M. 2017. 'Polar bears drive hundreds of walruses off cliff in Siberian bloodbath'. *Earther Gizmodo*, 25 October. https://earther.gizmodo.com/a-freak-walrus-slaughter-in-siberia-reminds-us-how-clim-1819802967

Stroeve, J., Holland, M.M., Meier, W., et al. 2007. Arctic sea ice decline: Faster than forecast. *Geophysical Research Letters* 34:L09501. https://doi.org/10.1029/2007GL029703

Sumption, J. 2020. 'This is how freedom dies: The folly of Britain's coercive Covid strategy'. *The Spectator* (UK), 28 October. https://www.spectator.co.uk/article/-this-is-how-freedom-dies-the-folly-of-britain-s-coercive-covid-strategy

Swart, N.C., Fyfe, J.C., Hawkins, E., et al. 2015. Influence of internal variability on Arctic sea ice trends. *Nature Climate Change* 5:86-89. https://doi.org/10.1038/nclimate2483

Tasker, J. P. 2021. 'COVID-19 infections are on the rise and omicron could quadruple daily case counts, federal modelling says'. *CBC News* (Canada), 10 December. https://www.cbc.ca/news/politics/covid-infections-rising-federal-modelling-1.6281026

Taylor, E. 2020. 'A History of Queen Elizabeth's Lifelong Corgi Appreciation'. *Vogue Magazine*, 24 April. https://www.vogue.com/slideshow/history-queen-elizabeth-lifelong-corgi-appreciation

Taylor, R.L. and Udevitz, M.S. 2015. Demography of the Pacific walrus (*Odobenus rosmarus divergens*):1974–2006. *Marine Mammal Science* 31:231-254.

Taylor, R.L., Udevitz, M.S., Jay, C.V., et al. 2018. Demography of the Pacific walrus (*Odobenus rosmarus divergens*) in a changing Arctic. *Marine Mammal Science* 34:54-86.

Telegraph Reporters 2020. 'Sir David Attenborough: 'Coronavirus pandemic has swept climate change off the front pages''. *The Daily Telegraph*, 25 May. https://www.telegraph.co.uk/news/2020/05/24/sir-david-attenborough-coronavirus-pandemic-has-swept-climate/

Thomas, M. 2016. 'U.S. removes most humpback whales from endangered list'. *CBC News* (Canada), 8 September. http://www.cbc.ca/news/canada/british-columbia/humpback-populations-bc-coast-1.3753510

Thompson, A. 2015. 'Was there a link between climate change and Hurricane Katrina?'. *Grist*, 27 August. https://grist.org/climate-energy/was-there-a-link-between-climate-change-and-hurricane-katrina/

Thunberg, G. 2019. ''Our house is on fire': Greta Thunberg, 16, urges leaders to act on climate'. *The Guardian* (UK), 25 January. https://www.theguardian.com/environment/2019/jan/25/our-house-is-on-fire-greta-thunberg16-urges-leaders-to-act-on-climate

TMZ. 2019. 'Netflix defends graphic walrus scene in 'Our Planet''. *TMZ News*, 9 April. https://www.tmz.com/2019/04/09/netflix-defends-walrus-fall-scene-our-planet-docuseries-climate-change/

Toone, S. 2019. 'Netflix defends graphic walrus death scene in new documentary'. *Fox 23/The Atlanta Journal-Constitution*, 10 April. https://www.fox23.com/news/trending-now/netflix-defends-graphic-walrus-death-scene-in-new-documentary/938771494/

Travers, B. 2019. 'Our Planet review: Netflix's stunning nature doc is here to tell you we're screwed'. *IndieWire*, 5 April. https://www.indiewire.com/2019/04/our-planet-netflix-review-planet-earth-1202056165/

Truett, J. C. (ed.). 1993. Guidelines for Oil and Gas Operations in Polar Bear Habitats. Minerals Management Service Alaska, US Dept. of the Interior Report 93-0008.

Udevitz, M.S., Taylor, R.L., Garlich-Miller, J.L., et al. 2013. Potential population-level effects of increased haulout-related mortality of Pacific walrus calves. *Polar Biology* 36:291-298.

US District Court Alaska 2019. 'Order re Motions for Summary judgment: Center for Biological Diversity (plaintiff) vs. David Bernhardt in his official capacity as Secretary of the US Department of the Interior (defendants)'. Case No. 3:18-cv-00064-SLG, 26 September. Anchorage, Alaska.

USFWS. 2011. *Walrus Factsheet*. US Fish and Wildlife Service, Anchorage, Alaska. http://www.fws.gov/alaska/fisheries/mmm/walrus/esa.htm

USFWS. 2017a. 'After Comprehensive Review, Service Determines Pacific Walrus Does Not Require Endangered Species Act Protection'. Press Release, 4 October. US Fish and Wildlife Service.

USFWS. 2017b. 'Endangered and threatened wildlife and plants; 12-month findings on petitions to list 25 species as endangered or threatened species'. *Federal Register* 82(192):46618-46645.

USFWS. 2018. 'Regulations of drones, unmanned aircraft systems (UAS)'. [accessed 1 December 2019]. https://www.fws.gov/refuge/buenos_aires/visit/drone_rules.html [See also 50 CFR 27.34]

USFWS 2019. 'Notice to Public: Cinder River Critical Habitat Area', US Fish & Wildlife Service/Alaska Department of Fish & Game Special Notice, 17 July 2019 [accessed 1 December 2019]. http://www.adfg.alaska.gov/index.cfm?adfg=bristolbay.permits.

USGS. 2008. *Fact Sheet: Pacific walrus response to Arctic sea ice losses*. Compiled by C.V. Jay and A.S. Fischbach, US Geological Survey.

Varadarajan, T. 2021. 'How Science Lost the Public's Trust'. *Wall Street Journal*, 23 July. [interview with Matt Ridley]. https://www.wsj.com/articles/covid-china-media-lab-leak-climate-ridley-biden-censorship-coronavirus-11627049477 [also available at https://www.mattridley.co.uk/blog/how-science-lost-the-public-s-trust/]

Variety. 2021. 'BBC, Channel 4, ITV Among U.K.'s Biggest Broadcasters Committing to Climate Content Pledge at COP26'. *Variety* magazine (UK), 2 November, https://variety.com/2021/tv/news/climate-content-pledge-cop26-1235101792/

Vaughan, A. 2019a. 'David Attenborough finally talks climate change in prime time BBC slot'. *New Scientist*, 13 April. https://www.newscientist.com/article/2199490-david-attenborough-finally-talks-climate-change-in-prime-time-bbc-slot/

Vaughan, A. 2019b. 'David Attenborough on climate change: 'We cannot be radical enough''. *New Scientist*, 9 July. https://www.newscientist.com/article/2209126-david-attenborough-on-climate-change-we-cannot-be-radical-enough/

Vecchi, G.A., Landsea, C., Zhang, W., et al. 2021. Changes in Atlantic major hurricane frequency since the late-19th century, *Nature Communications* 12:4054. DOI: 10.1038/s41467-021-24268-5

Verity, S. 2019. 'Netflix's "Our Planet" and that walrus scene'. *Outdoor Journal,* 23 April. https://www.outdoorjournal.com/gear/video/netflixs-planet-walrus-scene/

Vibe, C. 1967. Arctic animals in relation to climatic fluctuations. *Meddelelser om Grønland* 107(5).

Vincent, E.M. 2018. 'Most popular climate change stories of 2017 reviewed by scientists'. *Climate Feedback*, 17 January. https://climatefeedback.org/most-popular-climate-change-stories-2017-reviewed-scientists/#1

Vineyard, J. 2019. 'A Netflix nature series says to viewers: Don't like what you see? Do something about it'. *New York Times*, 8 April. https://www.nytimes.com/2019/04/08/arts/television/netflix-our-planet-climate-change.html

Voosen, P. 2021a. Climate panel confronts implausibly hot models. *Science* 373(6554):474-475. https://doi.10.1126/science.373.6554.474

Voosen, P. 2021b. 'The Arctic is warming four times faster than the rest of the world.' *Science News*, 14 December. https://doi.10.1126/science.acz9830

Wang, M. and Overland, J.E. 2009. A sea ice free summer Arctic within 30 years? *Geophysical Research Letters* 36:L07502. https://doi.org/10.1029/2009GL037820

Ward, B. 2019a. 'Climate change deniers haul out a daft conspiracy theory about Attenborough's new programme'. *Grantham Research Institute on Climate Change and the Environment* (London School of Economics and Political Science), 10 April. https://www.lse.ac.uk/granthaminstitute/news/climate-change-deniers-haul-out-a-daft-conspiracy-theory-about-attenboroughs-new-programme/

Ward, B. 2019b. 'The 'Mail on Sunday' uses fake news to attack Sir David Attenborough'. *Grantham Research Institute on Climate Change and the Environment* (London School of Economics and Political Science), 26 April. https://www.lse.ac.uk/granthaminstitute/news/the-mail-on-sunday-uses-fake-news-to-attack-sir-david-attenborough/

Ward, B. 2021. The climate crisis cover-up. *Hacked Off*, 26 February. https://hackinginquiry.org/special-report-chapter-one-the-climate-crisis-cover-up/

Waterman, G. 2021. 'Sir David Attenborough tells UN 'It is too late to avoid climate change''. *Climate Action*, 26 February. https://www.climateaction.org/news/sir-david-attenborough-tells-un-it-is-too-late-to-avoid-climate-change

Watts, J. 2018. 'David Attenborough: too much alarmism on environment a turn-off'. *The Guardian* (UK), 4 November. https://www.theguardian.com/environment/2018/nov/04/attenborough-dynasties-ecological-campaign

Watts, J. 2019. 'Greta Thunberg, schoolgirl climate change warrior: 'Some people can let things go. I can't''. *The Guardian* (UK), 11 March. https://www.theguardian.com/world/2019/mar/11/greta-thunberg-schoolgirl-climate-change-warrior-some-people-can-let-things-go-i-cant

Watts, R. 2017. 'UVic alumnus records widely viewed video of starving polar bear'. *Victoria Times-Colonist* (Canada), 8 December. http://www.timescolonist.com/news/local/uvic-alumnus-records-widely-viewed-video-of-starving-polar-bear-1.23117832

Weber, B. 2017. ''Bit of an echo chamber:' Study finds climate denier blogs ignore science'. *National Post* (Canda), 29 November. http://nationalpost.com/pmn/news-pmn/canada-news-pmn/study-finds-climate-denier-blogs-ignore-polar-bear-sea-ice-science

Weber, B. 2019. ''Not what it used to be:' Warm Arctic autumn creates ice hazards for Inuit'. *Victoria Times-Colonist* (Canada), 24 November. https://www.timescolonist.com/not-what-it-used-to-be-warm-arctic-autumn-creates-ice-hazards-for-inuit-1.24017538

Weber, D. S., Stewart, B. S., Garza, J. C., and Lehman, N. 2000. An empirical genetic assessment of the severity of the northern elephant seal population bottleneck. *Current Biology* 10:1287-1290.

WEF. 2020. *The Global Risks Report 2020*, 15th edition. World Economic Forum, Geneva.

Wells, P. 2020. 'The Great Reset is mostly just Liberals blowing off steam. Mostly.' *Macleans Magazine* (Canada), 23 November. https://www.macleans.ca/politics/ottawa/the-great-reset-is-mostly-just-liberals-blowing-off-steam-mostly/

Wente, M. 2017. 'Is fake news okay if the cause is good?' *The Globe and Mail* (Canada), 11 December. https://www.theglobeandmail.com/opinion/is-fake-news-okay-if-the-cause-is-good/article37290997/

Westcott, B. 2016. 'Sixth mass extinction? Two-thirds of wildlife may be gone by 2020: WWF'. *CNN*, 28 October. https://www.cnn.com/2016/10/26/world/wild-animals-disappear-report-wwf/index.html

Whigham, N. 2019. ''WARNING GRAPHIC IMAGES: Netflix documentary scene shocks viewers'. *Fox News*, 9 April. https://www.foxnews.com/science/warning-graphic-images-netflix-documentary-scene-shocks-viewers

Whitworth, D. 2019a. 'Why David Attenborough has made Our Planet for Netflix'. *The Times* (London), 22 March. https://www.thetimes.co.uk/article/why-david-attenborough-has-made-our-planet-for-netflix-8w73nqjtw

Whitworth, D 2019b. 'David Attenborough's Our Planet: Walruses plunging to deaths become new symbol of climate change', *The Times* (London), 5 April. https://www.thetimes.co.uk/article/david-attenborough-s-our-planet-walruses-plunging-to-deaths-become-new-symbol-of-climate-change-23sbkwzlt

Whitworth, D. 2019c. 'David Attenborough on climate change, Greta Thunberg and becoming a 'fishetarian''. *The Times* (London), 19 November. https://www.thetimes.co.uk/article/david-attenborough-interview-on-chatham-house-prize-climate-change-greta-thunberg-and-becoming-a-fishetarian-ztgmdfz73

Wiig, Ø., Amstrup, S., Atwood, T., Laidre, K., Lunn, N., Obbard, M., et al. 2015. *Ursus maritimus. The IUCN Red List of Threatened Species 2015*: e.T22823A14871490. http://www.iucnredlist.org/details/22823/0 [be sure to see the 'supplement' as well]

Wilder, J.M., Vongraven, D., Atwood, T., et al. 2017. Polar bear attacks on humans: implications of a changing climate. *Wildlife Society Bulletin* 41:537-547.

Williams, G. 2020. 'Seal River polar bears appear in new BBC Earth series Seven Worlds, One Planet. New Arctic adventures on the horizon.' *Churchill Wild Polar Bear Blog*, 25 January. https://churchillwild.com/seal-river-polar-bears-hunting-belugas-appear-in-new-bbc-earth-series-seven-worlds-one-planet-new-arctic-adventures-on-the-horizon/

Winkleman, N. 2020. ''David Attenborough: A Life on Our Planet' Review: Ruin and Regrowth'. *New York Times*, 4 October. https://www.nytimes.com/2020/10/04/movies/david-attenborough-a-life-on-our-planet-review.html

Winter, M. 2021. 'David Attenborough tops list of nation's most inspirational 'green' celebrities'. *The Mirror* (UK), 11 November. https://www.mirror.co.uk/3am/celebrity-news/david-attenborough-inspirational-green-celebrities-25431357

Workman, J. 2019. ''Our house is on fire.' 16 year-old Greta Thunberg wants action.' *World Economic Forum*, 25 January. https://www.weforum.org/agenda/2019/01/our-house-is-on-fire-16-year-old-greta-thunberg-speaks-truth-to-power/

Worstall, T. 2018. 'David Attenborough goes way over-the-top on climate change'. *The Washington Examiner*, 3 December. https://www.washingtonexaminer.com/opinion/david-attenborough-goes-way-over-the-top-on-climate-change

Wright, R. 2018. 'National Geographic's polar bear problem'. *Robert Wright* blog, 27 July. https://robertwright.ca/crisis-what-crisis/2018/7/27/national-geographic-polar-bear and https://web.archive.org/web/20180903171842/https://robertwright.ca/crisis-what-crisis/2018/7/27/national-geographic-polar-bear

Wrightstone, G. 2017. *Inconvenient Facts: The Science That Al Gore Doesn't Want You to Know*. G. Wrightstone.

WWF. no date. *History*. Accessed 25 March 2021. https://www.worldwildlife.org/about/history

WWF. 2011. *Annual Review 2010*. WWF International, Gland, Switzerland.

WWF. 2015a. 'Walrus Calf Falls Off Rock'. *WWF*, 13 January.
https://www.youtube.com/watch?v=PAegOrGiDnA

WWF. 2015b. 'Netflix teams with Silverback Films and WWF to create
Our Planet'. *WWF*, 15 April.
https://www.wwf.org.au/news/news/2015/netflix-teams-with-
silverback-films-and-wwf-to-create-our-planet#gs.x29fmm

WWF. 2016a. *Living Planet Report 2016: Risk and Resilience in a New Era*.
WWF International, Gland, Switzerland.

WWF. 2016b. 'Sir David Attenborough and Professor Johan Rockstrom |
WWF Living Planet Lecture 2016'. *WWF-UK*, 22 November.
https://www.youtube.com/watch?v=V_gX0cTt10A

WWF. 2018. *Living Planet Report 2018: Aiming Higher*. Grooten, M. and
Almond, R.E.A. (eds). WWF International, Gland, Switzerland.

WWW. 2019. 'WWF welcomes call by Sir David Attenborough for global
environmental action'. *WWF International*, 22 January.
https://wwf.panda.org/?341770/WEF-2019-WWF-welcomes-call-by-Sir-
David-Attenborough-for-global-environmental-action

WWF. 2020a. 'Five things you need to know about 'Our Planet'. *WWF*, no
date. updated September 2020. https://www.wwf.org.uk/updates/five-
things-you-need-know-about-our-planet

WWF. 2020b. *Living Planet Report 2020: Bending the curve of biodiversity
loss*. Almond, R.E.A., et al. (eds). WWF International, Gland, Switzerland.

Yong, E. 2019. 'The disturbing walrus scene in Our Planet'. *The Atlantic*, 8
April. https://www.theatlantic.com/science/archive/2019/04/why-are-
walruses-walking-off-cliffs/586510

Young, E. 2007. 'Climate myths: Hurricane Katrina was caused by global
warming'. *New Scientist Magazine*, 16 May.
https://www.newscientist.com/article/dn11661-climate-myths-
hurricane-katrina-was-caused-by-global-warming/

Zerehi, S.S. 2016. 'Arviat polar bear patrols reduce bear deaths, says
WWF-Canada'. *CBC News*, 24 February. https://www.cbc.ca/news/
canada/north/polar-bear-patrol-arviat-1.3460947

# Appendix A Crockford Publications

Crockford, S. J. 1997a. *Osteometry of Makah and Coast Salish Dogs,* Archaeology Press #22, Simon Fraser University, Burnaby, B.C.

Crockford, S. J. 1997b. Archaeological evidence of large northern bluefin tuna, *Thunnus thynnus,* in coastal waters of British Columbia and northern Washington. *Fishery Bulletin* 95:11-24.

Crockford, S. J. 2000a. Dog evolution: a role for thyroid hormone physiology in domestication changes. pg. 11-20. *In:* S.J. Crockford (ed.) *Dogs Through Time: An Archaeological Perspective.* Oxford, U.K., Archaeopress S889.

Crockford, S. J. 2000b. A commentary on dog evolution: regional variation, breed development and hybridization with wolves. pg. 295-312. *In:* S.J. Crockford (ed.) *Dogs Through Time: An Archaeological Perspective.* Oxford, U.K., Archaeopress S889.

Crockford, S. J. 2002. Animal domestication and heterochronic speciation: the role of thyroid hormone. pg. 122-153. *In:* N. Minugh-Purvis and K. McNamara (eds.) *Human Evolution Through Developmental Change.* Baltimore, Johns Hopkins University Press.

Crockford, S. J. 2003a. Commentary: Thyroid hormones in Neandertal evolution: A natural or a pathological role? *Geographical Review* 92:73-88.

Crockford, S. J. 2003b. Thyroid hormone phenotypes and hominid evolution: a new paradigm implicates pulsatile thyroid hormone secretion in speciation and adaptation changes. *International Journal of Comparative Biochemistry and Physiology Part A* 135:105-129.

Crockford, S. J. 2004. Animal Domestication and Vertebrate Speciation: A Paradigm for the Origin of Species. Ph.D. dissertation. University of Victoria, Canada.

Crockford, S. J. 2006. *Rhythms of Life: Thyroid Hormone and the Origin of Species.* Trafford, Victoria.

Crockford, S. J. 2008a. Some Things We Know – and Don't Know – About Polar Bears. Science and Public Policy Institute (SPPI).

Crockford, S. J. 2008b. Be careful what you ask for: archaeozoological evidence of mid-Holocene climate change in the Bering Sea and implications for the origins of Arctic Thule. In *Islands of Inquiry: Colonisation, Seafaring and the Archaeology of Maritime Landscapes,* 113-131. G. Clark, et al. (eds.). Terra Australis 29 ANU EPress, Canberra.

Crockford, S. J. 2009. Evolutionary roots of iodine and thyroid hormones in cell-cell signaling. *Integrative and Comparative Biology* 49:155-166.

Crockford, S. J. 2012a. A History of Polar Bears, Ringed Seals, and other Arctic and North Pacific Marine Mammals over the Last 200,000 Years. A report Prepared for The State of Alaska Department of Commerce, Community and Economic Development and The University of Alaska Fairbanks. Pacific Identifications Inc., Victoria, British Columbia.

Crockford, S. J. 2012b. Annotated Map of Ancient Polar Bear Remains of the World. Spotted Cow Presentations Inc., Victoria, British Columbia. ISBN 978-0-9917966-0-1. Available at http://polarbearscience/references/

Crockford, S. J. 2014a. On the Beach: Walrus Haulouts are Nothing New. *Global Warming Policy Foundation* Briefing Paper 11. http://www.thegwpf.org/susan-crockford-on-the-beach-2/

Crockford, S. J. 2014b.The Walrus Fuss: Walrus Haulouts are Nothing New. Video, Global Warming Policy Foundation. https://www.youtube.com/watch?v=cwaAwsS2OOY

Crockford, S.J. 2014c. Healthy Polar Bears, Less than Healthy Science. Vido interview, Global Warming Policy Foundation. 17 June. https://www.youtube.com/watch?v=Eg7R2GYvQz8

Crockford, S.J. 2015a. The Arctic Fallacy: Sea Ice Stability and the Polar Bear. *Global Warming Policy Foundation* Briefing Paper 16. Available at http://www.thegwpf.org/susan-crockford-the-arctic-fallacy-2/

Crockford, S.J. 2015b. Unstable thinking about polar bear habitat. *The Arctic Journal.* 7 October. http://arcticjournal.com/opinion/1869/unstable-thinking-about-polar-bear-habitat

Crockford, S. 2015c. *EATEN: A novel.* CreateSpace Publishing. http://www.amazon.com/Eaten-novel-Susan-Crockford/dp/151930255X

Crockford, S. 2015d. A Harrowing Encounter: Polar Bear vs. Lawyer in Labrador. *Range Magazine* Spring 2015:42-43.

Crockford, S. 2016a. *Polar Bear Facts and Myths.* CreateSpace Publishing. https://www.amazon.com/dp/1541123336 [also available in French, German, Dutch, and Norwegian translations]

Crockford, S. 2017a. Testing the hypothesis that routine sea ice coverage of 3-5 mkm2 results in a greater than 30% decline in population size of polar bears (*Ursus maritimus*). *PeerJ Preprints* 2 March 2017. Doi: 10.7287/peerj.preprints.2737v3

Crockford, S. 2017b. Polar Bear Scare Unmasked: The Saga of a Toppled Global Warming Icon. Video, Global Warming Policy Foundation. https://www.youtube.com/watch?v=z6bcCTFnGZ0

Crockford, S. 2017c. The Death of a Climate Icon. Video, Global Warming Policy Foundation. https://www.youtube.com/watch?v=XCzwFall8OQ

Crockford 2017d. Twenty good reasons not to worry about polar bears: an update. *Global Warming Policy Foundation Briefing Paper 28.*

Crockford, S.J. 2017e. *Polar Bears: Outstanding Survivors of Climate Change.* CreateSpace Publishing. https://www.amazon.com/dp/1541139712/

Crockford, S.J. 2018a. State of the Polar Bear Report 2017. *Global Warming Policy Foundation Report* 29. London.

Crockford, S.J. 2018b. 'Polar bears keep thriving even as global warming alarmists keep pretending they're dying.' *National Post/Financial Post*, 27 February. http://business.financialpost.com/opinion/polar-bears-keep-thriving-even-as-global-warming-alarmists-keep-pretending-theyre-dying

Crockford, S.J. 2018c. 'The real story behind the famous starving polar bear video reveals more manipulation.' *National Post/Financial Post*, 29 August. https://business.financialpost.com/opinion/the-real-story-behind-the-famous-starving-polar-bear-video-reveals-more-manipulation

Crockford, S.J. 2018e. 'White Lie: The Cruel Abuse of a Starving Polar Bear.' Video, Global Warming Policy Foundation, London. https://www.youtube.com/watch?v=Z7KTfPlCrgY

Crockford, S. 2018e. Prehistoric mountain goat *Oreamnos americanus* mother lode near Prince Rupert, British Columbia and implications for the manufacture of high-status ceremonial goods. *Journal of Island and Coastal Archaeology* 13:319-340. https://doi.org/10.1080/15564894.2016.1256357

Crockford, S.J. 2019a. Attenborough's Arctic Betrayal. Video, January. Global Warming Policy Forum, London. https://www.youtube.com/watch?v=-Rkv-ltznBE&t=77s

Crockford, S.J. 2019b. State of the Polar Bear Report 2018. *Global Warming Policy Foundation* Report 32, London.

Crockford, S.J. 2019c. *The Polar Bear Catastrophe That Never Happened*. Global Warming Policy Foundation, London.

Crockford, S.J. 2019d. 'Netflix is lying about those falling walruses. It's another 'tragedy porn' climate hoax.' 24 April opinion, *National Post/Financial Post*. https://business.financialpost.com/opinion/netflix-is-lying-about-those-falling-walruses-its-another-tragedy-porn-climate-hoax

Crockford, S.J. 2019e. 'Netflix, Attenborough and cliff-falling walruses: the making of a false climate icon.' Video, May. Global Warming Policy Forum, London. https://www.youtube.com/watch?v=latVKZZcPG0

Crockford, S.J. 2019f. 'The truth about Attenborough's falling walruses' Video, September. *Global Warming Policy Foundation*, London. https://www.youtube.com/watch?v=tFcwAKZEnHY

Crockford, S.J. 2019g. 'No climate emergency for polar bears.' Video September. *Global Warming Policy Foundation*, London. https://www.youtube.com/watch?v=jQRle6pgBCY

Crockford, S.J. 2019h. 'Falling walrus: Attenborough tacitly admits Netflix deception.' Video December. *Global Warming Policy Foundation*, London. https://www.youtube.com/watch?v=U5Ji6ME3Vlo

Crockford, S.J. 2020a. 'New footage reveals Netflix faked walrus climate deaths.' Video, 19 November. *Global Warming Policy Forum*, London. https://www.youtube.com/watch?v=kV8d26oziVM

Crockford, S.J. 2020b. State of the Polar Bear 2019. *Global Warming Policy Foundation* Report 39, London.

Crockford, S.J. 2020c. 'How Attenborough's arctic claims cause eco angst and activism'. *Think Scotland*, 29 January. https://thinkscotland.org/2021/01/how-attenboroughs-arctic-claims-cause-eco-angst-and-activism/

Crockford, S.J. 2020d. *UPHEAVAL: a short novel*. S.J. Crockford, Printed by KDP.

Crockford, S.J. 2021. State of the Polar Bear 2020. *Global Warming Policy Foundation* Report 48.

Crockford, S., and Frederick, G. 2007. Sea Ice Expansion in the Bering Sea during the Neoglacial: Evidence from Archaeozoology. *The Holocene* 17: 699– 706.

Crockford, S.J. and Frederick, G. 2011. Neoglacial sea ice and life history flexibility in ringed and fur seals. pg. 65-91 In, T. Braje and R. Torrey, eds. *Human and Marine Ecosystems: Archaeology and Historical Ecology of Northeastern Pacific Seals, Sea Lions, and Sea Otters.* U. California Press.

Crockford, S.J. and C.J. Pye. 1997. Forensic reconstruction of prehistoric dogs from the Northwest coast. *Canadian Journal of Archaeology* 21:149-153.

Crockford, S.J., Frederick, G. and Wigen, R. 1997. A humerus story: albatross element distribution from two Northwest Coast sites, North America. *International Journal of Osteoarchaeology* 7:378.1-5.

Crockford, S.J. and Geist, V. 2018. Conservation Fiasco. *Range Magazine*, Winter 2017/2018:26-27. [Open access]

Crockford, S.J. and Kuzmin, Y. V. 2012. Comments on Germonpré et al., Journal of Archaeological Science 36, 2009 "Fossil dogs and wolves from Palaeolithic sites in Belgium, the Ukraine and Russia: osteometry, ancient DNA and stable isotopes", and Germonpré, Lázkičková-Galetová, and Sablin, Journal of Archaeological Science 39, 2012 "Palaeolithic dog skulls at the Gravettian Předmostí site, the Czech Republic." *Journal of Archaeological Science* 39:2797-2801.

Crockford, S.J., Moss, M.L., and Baichtal, J.F. 2011. Pre-contact dogs from the Prince of Wales archipelago, Alaska. *Alaska Journal of Anthropology* 9:49-64.

Hatfield, V., et al. [including Crockford]. 2016. At the foot of the Smoking Mountains: the 2014 scientific investigations in the Islands of the Four Mountains. *Arctic Anthropology* 53(2):141-159.

Leathlobhair, M.N., et al [including Crockford]. 2018. The evolutionary history of dogs in the Americas. *Science* 361:81-85.

McKechnie, I., Moss, M.L. and Crockford, S.J. 2020. Domestic dogs and wild canids on the Northwest Coast of North America: animal husbandry in a region without agriculture? *Journal of Anthropological Archaeology* 60:101209.

Martinsson-Wallin, H. and Crockford, S.J. Early settlement of Rapa Nui (Easter Island). *Asian Perspectives* 40(2):244-278.

Ovodov, N. D., Crockford, S.J., Kuzmin, Y. V., et al. 2011. A 33,000 year old incipient dog from Altai Mountains of Siberia: evidence for the earliest domestication disrupted by the Last Glacial Maximum. *PLoS One* 6(7):e22821.

Rolland, N. and Crockford, S.J. 2005. Late Pleistocene dwarf *Stegodon* from Flores, Indonesia? *Antiquity* 79 (June #304 Project Gallery). http://antiquity/ac.uk/projgall/rolland/

Tollit, D.J., Schulze, A., Trites, A.W., et al. [including Crockford]. 2009. Development and application of DNA techniques for validating and improving pinniped diet estimates. *Ecological Applications* 19:889-905.

Wilson, B, Crockford, S.J., Johnson, J.W., et al. 2011. Genetic and archaeological evidence of a breeding population of formerly endangered Aleutian cackling goose, *Branta hutchinsii leucopareia,* on Adak Island in the central Aleutians, Alaska. *Canadian Journal of Zoology* 89:732-743.

# Appendix B Walrus Haulouts

Table 1. Walrus haulouts at Cape Schmidt 2007-2021.

| Year | Dates | Number of walrus | Stampede deaths | Deaths from falls | Polar bears present | Notes |
|------|-------|------------------|-----------------|-------------------|---------------------|-------|
| 2007 | Sept- Oct | ~40,000 | ~800 | ? | ? | |
| 2008 | end Sept | ? | 108 | ? | ? | conflicting evidence |
| 2009 | Sept-Oct | 20,000-40,000 | some | yes | ? | |
| 2010 | none? | | | | | no report |
| 2011 | mid-Sept | ~5,000 | 123 | yes | yes (13) | mostly mothers with pups |
| 2012 | none? | | | | | no report |
| 2013 | Sept | ~1,000 | ? | ? | ? | |
| 2014 | Sept | ~10,000 | | 166 | | |
| 2015 | mid-Aug-mid-Oct | ~30,000 | >100 | ? | yes | mostly pups died |
| 2016 | none? | | | | | no report |
| 2017 | Sept | ~5,000 | 100s | 100s | yes (20) | 200-300 deaths total |
| 2018 | none? | | | | | no report |
| 2019 | Sept | thousands | ? | ? | ? | |
| 2020 | Sept | thousands | ? | ? | yes (9) | |
| 2021 | none? | | | | | no report; Chutotka beaches with ice |

## Citations (see main reference list for details)

Fischbach et al. 2016
Kochnev 2012a
MacCracken 2012
Kochnev et al. 2008 [for 2007, 2008, 2010, 2011];
NBC News 2007 [for 2007];
Kochnev 2012b [for 2009-2011];
Pereverzev and Kochnev 2012 [for 2011];
http://wwf.panda.org/knowledge_hub/where_we_work/arctic/what_we_do/cli mate/climatewitness2/expedition_diary.cfm [for 2007, based on historical references in the text];
http://programmes.putin.kremlin.ru/en/bear/news/25203 [for 2015];
https://wwf.panda.org/?uNewsID=164702 [for 2008];
https://www.rt.com/news/195252-walrus-fall-death-russia/ [for 2014];
https://www.youtube.com/watch?v=IA-_QsCEZ0U&feature=youtu.be [for 2009];
https://whistleblower.org/climate-research-and-assessment/global-climate-disruption-and-impacts/as-sea-ice-melts-in-a-warming-arctic-walruses-outpace-politicians/ [for 2013];
https://siberiantimes.com/other/others/news/polar-bear-chased-away-with-flares-after-wandering-close-to-a-secondary-school-at-chukotka/ [for 2020];
https://www.youtube.com/watch?v=8pehXXRUuNE [for 2019]
https://polarbearscience.com/2021/10/20/most-chukchi-sea-ice-in-20-years-means-no-walrus-feasts-for-polar-bears-at-famous-russian-cliffs/ [for 2021]